Scotland and Islandness

Studies in the History and Culture of Scotland

Volume 13

Valentina Bold, General Editor

PETER LANG
Oxford · Bern · Berlin · Bruxelles · New York · Wien

Scotland and Islandness

Explorations in Community, Economy and Culture

Kathryn A. Burnett, Ray Burnett,
Michael Danson (eds)

PETER LANG

Oxford · Bern · Berlin · Bruxelles · New York · Wien

Bibliographic information published by Die Deutsche Nationalbibliothek.
Die Deutsche Nationalbibliothek lists this publication in the Deutsche National-
bibliografie; detailed bibliographic data is available on the Internet at
http://dnb.d-nb.de.

A catalogue record for this book is available from the British Library.

Library of Congress Cataloging-in-Publication Data

Names: Burnett, Kathryn A., 1969- editor, author. | Burnett, Ray, 1946-
    editor, author. | Danson, Mike, editor, author.
Title: Scotland and islandness : explorations in community, economy and
    culture / Kathryn A. Burnett, Ray Burnett, Michael Danson.
Description: Oxford ; New York : Peter Lang, [2021] | Series: Studies in
    the history and culture of Scotland, 1661-6863 ; Vol. 13 | Includes
    bibliographical references and index.
Identifiers: LCCN 2020051790 (print) | LCCN 2020051791 (ebook) | ISBN
    9781789973778 (hardback) | ISBN 9781789974126 (ebook) | ISBN
    9781789974133 (epub) | ISBN 9781789974140 (mobi)
Subjects: LCSH: Islands--Scotland--History. | Islands--Scotland--Economic
    conditions. | Scotland--Social life and customs. | Sustainable
    development--Scotland. | Scotland--History, Local. | Scotland--Rural
    conditions. | National characteristics, Scottish.
Classification: LCC DA887 .S37 2021 (print) | LCC DA887 (ebook) | DDC
    941.1--dc23
LC record available at https://lccn.loc.gov/2020051790
LC ebook record available at https://lccn.loc.gov/2020051791

Cover design by Peter Lang Ltd.

ISSN 1661-6863
ISBN 978-1-78997-377-8 (print) • ISBN 978-1-78997-412-6 (ePDF)
ISBN 978-1-78997-413-3 (ePub) • ISBN 978-1-78997-414-0 (mobi)

© Peter Lang Group AG 2021

Published by Peter Lang Ltd, International Academic Publishers,
52 St Giles, Oxford, OX1 3LU, United Kingdom
oxford@peterlang.com, www.peterlang.com

This publication has been peer reviewed.

Magdalena Sagarzazu (1949–2020)

For Magda, who inspired and informed us in our research,
this work is dedicated with thanks and love.

Contents

Acknowledgements

This edited collection represents some of the network and research focus of the *Scottish Centre for Island Studies*. As editors we are most grateful to each of our contributors for their enthusiasm, commitment and patience throughout 2020 in bringing the collection together. We would like to thank the editorial team at Peter Lang, including Philip Dunshea for originally believing in the value of the collection, but most especially Lucy Melville who has championed this island studies focus, and been encouraging and accommodating throughout. Thank you to colleagues involved in the preparation for publication, most especially Ashita and Sasireka. We are grateful for the most helpful and supportive feedback and endorsement of this collection from scholars in island studies, Scottish and rural cultural economies, history and heritage but most especially Godfrey Baldacchino, Máiréad Nic Craith and Valentina Bold. We would like to say a very special thank you to Alasdair MacEachen, Chair of the Islands Book Trust for providing us with his foreword, and his own support and contributing expertise to aspects of the *Scottish Centre for Island Studies* activities and events over the years. References, in Alasdair's foreword, to the poetry of the South Uist (Peninerine) bard Donald John MacDonald have been included with the kind permission of Donald's John's daughter Margaret Campbell.

Lastly, this book is dedicated to Magdalena Sagarzazu.

Magdalena Sagarzazu, from the Basque Country, was a lifelong friend of the Campbells of Canna - John Lorne and Margaret Fay Shaw - supporting and championing their research work. She organised their papers into the Canna Archive for public access and earned the gratitude of countless visitors and scholars to the islands. Magda's family have agreed to this dedication and we thank especially Nerea Bello and Joaquin Gironza for their support.

In dedicating this book to Magda, we express our thanks and recognition of the often quietly unsung but critically important contribution and passions of those colleagues working and volunteering in archives, museums, local historical societies, and arts and cultural organisations across Scotland but most especially in its northern and western island communities. Their generosity of spirit, cultural and historical expertise and enduring community advocacy facilitates, emboldens and secures the future of Scotland's island studies scholarship and provides a legacy of riches for all.

Foreword

ALASDAIR MACEACHEN

'S ann mu thuath, fada tuath,	It is north, far to the north
Ri uchd-bualaidh muir-làin,	On the high tide's front line,
Tha eilean beag gorm a' chuain,	That little green isle in the ocean,
Tìr mo luaidh thar gach ceàirn.	Land I love above all others.
Ged tha mise fad' air falbh,	Though I am far away
'S mi sa Ghearmailt a' tàmh,	Confined in Germany,
Gum bi m'inntinn tric air chuairt	My mind often returns
Far 'n do ruaig mi nam phàist'.	To where I played as a child.

These opening words are taken from the Gaelic song Eilean Beag a' Chuain (Little Island in the Ocean) composed by the South Uist bard Donald John MacDonald (Dòmhnall Iain Dhonnachaidh) almost eighty years ago, while he was a Prisoner of War in Germany.

What image springs to mind when one hears mention of an island or islands? I think it is true to say that one pictures an area of land, probably a small area, surrounded by a greater vastness of sea or ocean. In the mind's eye, add a bit of colour to depict the lush green grass and the expanse of yellow, sandy beaches.

I often find that *bàrdachd* is a good starting point when one is looking for words of wisdom regarding island life – and death, for that matter. The bards give sound advice and express opinions on a wide range of subjects to do with island life, in good times and bad, thus playing an important role in island life, particularly where the Gaelic culture is strongest and rich in the oral tradition of tales and poetry.

As you read this collection of chapters, you will sample a number of topics, ranging from 'islands in the mind' as expressed by the island bard as he thought of his native island from where he was imprisoned in Germany, to the debates of the present day where terms such as *resilience* and *sustainability* are discussed alongside policies and legislation from Land Reform to 'island proofing' as described in the Islands (Scotland) Act 2018, through to statutory protection, and cultural policy, around our island food, heritage and craft products.

The chapters which follow highlight many of the challenges and issues which require particular attention in order to address the diverse situations that exist across such a wide, or rather long, range of Scottish island communities which extend from the island of Arran in the south west to the island of Unst in the north. A little over ten per cent of the nine hundred or so Scottish offshore islands, which are mainly off the western and northern coast of Scotland, are occupied by approximately 100,000 islanders.

As just one person in that statistic, my own upbringing was somewhat similar to that described by James Oliver (Seumas Chatriona Dhòmhnaill Aonghais Bhig) in the final chapter of this collection. My home is in Aird on the island of Benbecula, and I grew up as James describes 'in the north western corner of a north western island in the middle of an archipelago'. I can define my *islandness* in a similar way to that of the author, as being *on the ground* and *in the mind*.

In terms of *on the ground*, if I can borrow a few words from the reference to Martin Martin in the introductory chapter of this commentary on islandness and Scotland's inhabited islands, I would describe myself as a native islander, Gael and a member of a longstanding Hebridean family, able to give 'an inside view of the community' in which I have lived and worked and where I belong. Living and working in the community for over four decades has, therefore, brought me into contact with most of the issues and challenges which are met while driving forward key policies for the socio-economic well-being of viable island communities.

Returning again to the beginning, and the words of the bard Donald John MacDonald, supports the sentiment of Rosie Alexander's chapter on 'Young People and Out Migration', where she states that the 'homing desire is strong on the islands' and home is always in the mind, regardless of perceived challenges, peripherality or marginality. These may only be in the mind.

Key issues such as land, place, community and language inform much of the collection's explorations. On language, Andrew Jennings' chapter examines Shetlandic dialect, for example. Hugh Cheape's discussion of Gaelic perspectives on 'Island Cultural Heritage' underpins the continuing debate about the current use and the future of language as the vernacular in the remaining Gaelic communities, most notably the island communities of the Outer Hebrides. Similarly, alongside the conclusions on 'Community Land Ownership' in Calum MacLeod's chapter, the Land Reform debate continues, with requests for a closer look at bringing public interest to the fore and to the heart of a future programme of land reform, which better addresses many of the issues raised in this range of chapters and which include the reversal of depopulation, the creation of job opportunities, the building of affordable homes and the tackling of climate change.

The debates will continue beyond the views that bring each of these chapters to a conclusion. Reference is made to the current pandemic situation and its impact across the world although, fortunately, impacting less on our more isolated island communities.

I am pleased to say that the bard did make it home having survived five years in a German Prisoner of War camp and, in another of his compositions *Tighinn Dhachaigh* (Coming Home), he described the first sighting of his beloved island home.

> O chì mi bhuam far an d' fhuair mi m' àrach,
> 'S mi 'n seo air bòrd sa *Lochmor* air sàile;
> O chì mi bhuam e thar gual' a' bhàta
> 'S a cùrsa tuath gu tìr uain' a' chrà-gheòidh.

> Oh, I see yonder the land of my youth,
> From here on board the *Lochmor* at sea;
> I see it yonder over the ship's bow
> As she steers north to the green isle of the shelduck.

Having endured those five difficult years away from his island home, Donald John had no desire to leave the island again; and in 1986, his final wish was fulfilled when he was buried, among his own people, in the earth of his island home. The bard's sentiment is common to this day amongst island people who either choose to leave or must leave their island home but who cannot rest until they return there.

> 'S gum bi mi 'g iarraidh 's ag ùrnaigh
> Gum faigh mi ' chriochnachadh m' ùin' ann
> 'S gum bi mi tiodhlaict' an ùir mo luchd-eòlais.

> It is my wish and my prayer
> That I can end my days there
> And be buried in the earth of my kin.
>   (Moladh Uibhist (In Praise of Uist) Donald John MacDonald)

KATHRYN A. BURNETT, RAY BURNETT AND MIKE DANSON

1. Scotland and Islandness: Explorations in Community, Economy and Culture

Over almost two millennia, Scotland's western and northern isles have had complex and conflicting relationships both with the kingdom of Scotland and with the ensuing stateless nation that has its own issue with its neighbour on the 'fractured island' (Burnett 2013) that is the contested terrain of Britain. A feature of the global pursuit of 'island studies' in all diversity and unresolved complexities (*Shima* Editorial Board 2007; Baldacchino 2008, 2018; Grydehøj 2013a 2013b) is its inter-disciplinarity, something which this contribution from Scotland reflects and celebrates. In offering comment on current and past research activity on island matters this collection of chapters speaks to the wider range of Scottish island related themes, topics and issues evolving from research legacies that are rich, varied and buoyant, and from which there is much to yet discover and to celebrate more fully.

This edited collection of chapters offers a collective commentary on the islands of Scotland, or to be more precise Scotland's inhabited islands. Contributors variously invite exploration and reflection on examples of island history, community and culture, from the past and today. The collection offers some examination of key policies for the socio-economic well-being of viable communities and how a prescient context of strategies for sustainability in the local and global context of small island communities remains a source of debate, research, innovation and inspiration throughout Scotland's island communities. With this in mind, we have encouraged contributors to include sources and references that support claims but to also point readers towards further reading and critiques that may be of interest. We also hope that this small collection may add some value to the review and realisation of strategic interventions of both policymakers and practitioners working on and for small island communities locally, regionally and globally.

The 'emergence' of Scotland's islands?

History offers a key frame of reference for the understanding of Scotland's islands, both long past and recent. Interestingly the very idea of what constitutes 'history' in the context of researching and debating islands in social, cultural and economic contexts is worthy of further focus. As James Hunter (2007: 10) has written, speaking of the challenges of how marginality and peripherality have been attributed to the overall region of the Highlands and Islands of Scotland, it is both a historical yet reversible condition:

> What has marginalised the Highlands and Islands is not their location, but rather the way the world began to be organised in post-medieval times – when power, decision-making and, most of all, people were drained away from here and concentrated elsewhere. Today, thankfully, this process is reversible. In a way that has not been possible since the industrial revolution, new communications and other technologies enable us to envisage a more dispersed pattern both of economic activity and of settlement – a pattern reminiscent, incidentally, of the one familiar to Iona's monks. (2007: 10)

And as Hunter notes it was originally to Shetland that Scotland looked to see the opportunities for a new vision of development and confidence for the whole highlands and islands region. Individuals such as Robert (Bob) Storey of Zetland County Council[1] were pivotal, speaking particularly to the concern of an 'erosion' of Shetland cultural heritage and 'way of life'. Storey, with others drawn from across island and highland communities, and with academic and political champions, would lead the vanguard in Shetland on the underpinning of socio-economic development with a

1   Zetland County Council established in 1889 was replaced during local government restructuring by Shetland Islands Council in 1974.

vision that would place a sense of culture and place identity at the heart
of the region's development strategy. In 1965 the Highlands and Islands
Development Board (HIDB) was established, the precursory regional development body to the current Highlands and Islands Enterprise (HIE)
and became a policy scaffold for the socio-economic revitalisation of the
region.[2] Decades later HIE would be 'moved' to reassert and revisit some
of the underpinning ambitions of the area's socio-cultural development
with questions being asked over just how 'culture' and the integrity of
local place histories and cultures *were* being sustained and developed: a
reinvigorated (re-visioned) policy ensued (c.f. Brennan et al. 2016).[3]
Today, unquestionably, cultural enterprise, and the role of cultural capital in informing other sectoral development (via education, media, arts
and advocacy), is a central flagship of the wider region's success but 'long
views' and depth afforded by discipline dissection and critique are crucial
(c.f. Abrams (2005) on the gendered history of the material economies of
Shetland, for example).

The active countering of what has been long documented (and debated) the 'Highland Problem' (see Condry 1976; but more especially,
Burnett 2011; Perchard and Mackenzie 2013; McCullough 2018), by
policies and ambitions seeking development 'solutions' – arresting depopulation and 'social decline' – has fostered a steady and innovative
expansion of highland and island enterprise, innovation, community
activism and resolve. Today the highlands and islands exist, operate and
compete as an invigorated, confident and empowered region. Challenges
do remain, however: social inequalities, connectivity issues, 'isolation',
fragility of demographics, higher costs of living, for example, continue
to impact everyday life on islands. Furthermore, expectations of what
constitutes 'a good quality of life' shift, and new or alternative visions of

2   Highlands and Islands Enterprise 'timeline' of regional development, <http://time-
     line.hie.co.uk/stories/our-region/> accessed 10 December 2019.
3   The links between language, culture and the economic rationale for the support for
     Gàidhlig in the region included advocates such as Willie Roe (2005) 'Gaelic not
     only plays an essential and crucial part in this, but it also helps reinforce the culture
     of sustainable development across the region, which is at the heart of everything we
     do at HIE'.

social, cultural, economic and environmental priorities, compete within and beyond highland and island contexts more broadly. Research, debate and critical review from 'all quarters' remain key to documenting and resolving ongoing challenges in this regard (see Grydehøj (2011) on Shetland or Ford (2019) on Orkney's 'ecologies' and 'entanglements', for example). Agents and actors such as the education sector, not least the University of the Highlands and Islands (UHI), (the region's multi-campus university), development agencies, local authorities, consultancies, think tanks and pressure groups, media and journalistic expertise, as well as the myriad of island (and highland)-related social, economic and cultural organisations, groups and individuals each offer expertise, share opinion, provoke and challenge through debate. There are advocates of island and highland cause – politicians at all levels – but also, as it was in the past, celebrities who amplify the ideas and issues of places, people and practices to wider audiences to mostly good effect although such celebrification can bring a reification of island particularities that is (not always) helpful.

Remoteness and peripherality: A good place for debate?

We are 'not remote' here? What constitutes islands as peripheral or not remains a complex and contested terrain (Baldacchino 2005). The concept and framing of Scotland's islands as beyond, at the edge or indeed marginal remains meaningful to use within academic critique not least to challenge the premises upon which both factual or more fictionalised narratives of Scotland's islands and narratives of what might be termed 'islandness' are configured (c.f. Davis 2016; Reeploeg 2017b). One only has to peruse the 'new book' and bestsellers list, Sunday broadsheet property pages, 'adventure' tourism promotion, or the happy blogging of 'outward bounders', to realise that Scotland's offshore islands remain culturally and powerfully configured from outwith as 'remote'. VisitScotland promotes Scotland currently with '9 "must read" books about Scotland' that includes no less than six that directly reference highland and especially island places, island going and island product.[4] For those who work within the commodified economy of selling island place (product) experiences both off and on islands, remoteness is both real and imagined: articulated to position the experience of islandness as distinctive and different. The lure of the island 'sell' is well known, and it presents considerable economic leverage via tourism, via food and drink but also the arts, literature and film. In short, 'remoteness' as exotification persists but it also lends itself to creative responses that redefine, challenge and critique what is 'known' or assumed in the name of Scotland's island places and people.

Remoteness operates locally as an everyday signifier for island residents themselves, however. Island residents occasionally *will* position their lived experience as one of difference and a degree of distance to 'the mainland'. Skye with its bridge is one celebrated example where for many decades the island was served (arguably quite successfully in contrast to other island experience) by two regular ferry routes from 'the mainland' and in this day to day sense Skye might not be considered 'remote'. Yet, when overly pressured by tourism, or by second-home ownership demand, or by ferry and (notoriously) the initial (excessive) bridge crossing (toll) costs, an island's sense of remoteness may be complexly configured as a code of pilgrimage and attraction for some and one of frustration, 'defence', and anger for others. Impacts of change, as well as of not enough change, are tracked and traced deeply throughout island community accounts and memories of development, confidence and success. Remoteness culturally and socially is, by virtue of its lived realities and perception, an embodied and emotional frame of experience (Boon et al. 2018). Everyday island experience is to live regularly with the mundane particularity of relationships, home, work, school, health, leisure, transport, politics and culture, in the island environment and so, of course, (it needs to be said) weather. Repeated weather constraints on transport, travel (including the roads and rail, as

---

4   VisitScotland: '9 must read books about Scotland' blogpost by Sarah Clark, 26 April 2020, <https://www.visitscotland.com/blog/scotland/must-read-books/> accessed 10 May 2020.

well as air and sea routes) and supplies, for example, is to know and live 'remoteness'.[5] Again, remoteness may not be best argued as a literal geography but rather a policy and agency one informed by the consciousness of the various positions of island residents to counter and combat *feelings* of isolation, distance, being 'peripheral' or marginal' to things, or not (as the 2020 Covid (media) narratives pertaining to the islands have illuminated).

By 2020, more presciently within the theorising language of the 'archipelagic' (Stratford et al. 2011; Pugh 2013), what is of 'everyday' contention is where island residents are aware of and frustrated by (i.e. what often matters) the differing layers and modes of connectivity with other islands. Centralising governance and issues of misrepresentation, feelings of 'remoteness', 'far away' and 'not being listened to' occur regularly *within islands* as well as more broadly in reference to the 'central' powers of Westminster or indeed 'devolved powers' that reside in Edinburgh. Here we allude to the spatial slipperiness of (inter/intra) relationships where Inverness, Lochgilphead, Tobermory, Portree, Oban, Stornoway, Kirkwall and Lerwick, for example, are each in their own way 'remote' to other 'further' communities. Across Scotland her islands connections continue and are celebrated and embellished but these relations are also sometimes neglected, 'forgotten' or disowned. Each of Scotland's islands has a myriad of relations with other regions (not least historical continuities within the North Atlantic). In this, we draw on Pugh (2013) and his valuable critique:

> The key thrust of this ontology is therefore island movements; not a simple gathering of islands, but an emphasis upon how islands act in concert; or, as Deleuze and Guattari (1986) would say, through constellations; so that the framing of an island archipelago draws attention to fluid cultural processes, sites of abstract and material relations of movement and rest, dependent upon changing conditions of articulation or connection. (2013: 11)

As Pugh (2013: 12) points out, following Stratford et al (2011) it is the tropes of the archipelago – 'assemblages, networks, filaments, connective

5   In 2012 National Theatre of Scotland and Shetland Arts produced 'Ignition': a collaborative theatre performance with Shetland's resident community exploring the role of the car, energy (oil and renewable) and transport in rural context. See <https://www.shetlandarts.org/our-work/past-projects/ignition> accessed 19 December 2019.

tissues, mobilities, and multiplicities' – that offer a theorising framework for further investigation and reflection. In building on – and beyond – island studies we can appreciate what has been termed 'archipelagic relations' and a focus to better explore, understand and document the seeking out of 'disjuncture, connection and entanglement between and among islands' (Stratford et al. 2011: 124). In a Scottish context, then, we return again to James Hunter (2007) and the connectivity that history affords, namely that the Highlands and Islands past 'cannot be understood in isolation' and research and scholarship of the wider region can and should

> utilise linkages between this area and others: taking advantage of the way our history overlaps with that of Ireland; stressing the extent to which the medieval Earldom of Orkney, indeed the Viking period generally, connects the Highlands and Islands with Scandinavia and with the broader North Atlantic rim; capitalising on the fact that our countless emigrants provide entries into histories other than our own. (Hunter 2007: 11)

The economic and policy context of current and future island 'ways of life' and viability are inextricably meshed with deep historical legacies of ownership, governance, trade links, migration, cultural expression, social cohesion via the institutions of connection as well as distinction. Conceiving of the islands of Scotland requires and evokes a sense of place – space, history, society and geography – and its representation. The visuality, mapping and narration of islands is powerful. Scotland has its own complex history in this regard: it is to this we turn to now.

Ways of seeing: A visuality, mapping and narration of Scotland's islands

The islands of Scotland vary in size, resource, environment and imagining; it is also fair to say that in this varied landscape of representation some islands arguably figure more prominently than others in broader public consciousness, and for differing reasons (e.g. Iona, Skye, Islay, St Kilda or

Fair Isle).[6] The role of culture in placing islands into a wider consciousness and indeed keeping them there is an ongoing (essential) project that
shows little sign of abating. The 'project' has deep historical roots with a
myriad of accounts (although much is lost) documenting and asserting
island cultures, communities and environments, within Scotland as well
as beyond.

Taking a long view of history from observations based on several years
of archaeological and historical enquiry across Scotland and its islands,
Ewan Campbell (2019) has recently argued strongly against the persistence
of an old academic orthodoxy that Scotland is as peripheral in its historical
importance as it is in its geographical location. In this regard Campbell
(2019: 17) argues that 'to ignore or sideline Scotland runs the danger not
just of bad scholarship, but also of missing important questions which are
raised by comparing the achievements of a liminal society with those of
an economic core'. A long view of history remains useful to reiterate the
way of seeing Scotland's islands not least in terms of cultural expression.
The historical context Campbell refers to was Scotland in early medieval
Europe, a setting in which Campbell surveyed the range of intellectual and
artistic achievements across Scotland. With a particular focus on the island
monastic communities of the seventh century, Campbell maintained that
such was the imaginative and innovative depth and quality of the cultural
output of the era, it could justifiably be termed the age of 'the First Scottish
Enlightenment'. Firmly rejecting the notion of Scotland's peripherality
Campbell (2019: 14–15) asserted that, not least in its largely island-based
scholarship and artistry, Scotland was innovative precisely *because* it was in
a liminal, non-mainstream situation. As a counter to the external tendency

---

6   The stock of islands in broader media imagining can certainly go down as it can
     go up. Taransay, for example, had been diminished in even local reference (no
     longer inhabited) but it drew national attention when it was featured on the BBC
     Castaway 2000 television series; Eigg had also lain (indeed been laid) low for some
     decades until 'enough was enough' and the community activism to secure a 'buy-out'
     of the island from its landowning legacy placed it centre stage as a cause célèbre of
     community empowerment, a profile further enhanced with its innovative 'Green
     island' policy; currently Unst is gaining considerable media interest as the potential
     site for a space port.

to dismiss or ignore Scotland, and its significance, Campbell framed his response as an advocacy of what he termed: 'A view *from* the periphery, rather than a view *of* the periphery (2019: 1). Applying such a perspective to the multi-disciplinarity of island studies, is an approach which this collection seeks to implement and which it would warmly endorse.

It is not until the mid-seventeenth century that the first comprehensive accounts of *all* Scotland's island communities appear together in an all-Scotland context. In 1654 Dutchman Johannes Blaeu publishes his Atlas of Scotland, volume V of his major *Atlas novus* project: included within are some 250 islands, from the Isle of Man to North Rona and Sule Skerry. Bleau's Atlas is unrivalled in its detail. In addition to maps of Arran and Bute and the islands of the Firth of Clyde, it included no less than ten maps covering the whole of the Hebrides (Islay, Jura, Mull, the Small Isles, Skye, the Uists and Barra, Lewis and Harris). A further plate contained a map each of Orkney and Shetland. As noted in the background essays to the National Library of Scotland's digitised Blaeu collection, these island maps and their accompanying texts are remarkable not only for the detailed naming of individual islands but also for the wealth of local knowledge they contain. Provided as accompanying text to the maps and produced by several contributors, each map includes a chorographic representation ('regional description') that contains 'in one way or another, the essential features of the form: an interest in genealogy; the etymology of place names; summaries of the local economy; remarks upon natural features; qualitative judgements upon the airs and waters of places; poetic accounts and so on'.[7]

The sense of drawing on in situ observed, 'local' knowledge and expertise was essential here. To the north, a range of sources were drawn on for the Northern Isles; the text accompanying the maps of Orkney and Shetland being augmented by more vivid and detailed models of chorography provided by an anonymous native of Orkney, for example (Bleau NLS). For the Hebrides, the primary source of regional description is George Buchanan's *Rerum Scoticarum Historia* (1582), material which in

---

7   See 'A Vision of Scotland: Joan Blaeu and the Atlas novus', by Charles W. J. Withers, <https://maps.nls.uk/atlas/blaeu/vision_of_scotland.html> accessed 10 December 2019.

turn derived from an earlier unpublished manuscript, *Description of the Occidental i.e. Western Isles of Scotland*, compiled by Donald Monro in 1549 (Martin and Monro 1999). Monro, a churchman, was the first writer to give a comprehensive description of the Western Isles known to have been based on personal observation. Furthermore, in their successful collaboration with Blaeu and Europe, the Scottish enthusiasts behind the project achieved both their intellectual and political purpose, namely that Scotland's profile and identity as an ancient European country was asserted.

Only a few decades later, a similar intellectual and political impetus led Martin Martin (a native of Skye) to publish his own accounts of the distinctive history, natural attributes and customs of his own particular part of Scotland, the Gaelic-speaking islands of the Hebrides. He did so in two indispensable first-hand accounts of his travels: *A Late Voyage to St Kilda* in 1698 and *A Description of the Western Islands of Scotland ca. 1695* in 1703 (Martin and Monro 1999). Martin's works are significant, not just because as early traveller's tales each is an absorbing read but because of the nature of their authorship and the timing of their publication. As a native islander, Gael and a member of a longstanding Hebridean family, Martin was able to give an inside view of the community in which he lived and to whom he belonged. At the same time, he also wrote from the perspective of a natural scientist and antiquarian, someone with the same wider connections to the intellectual world of Edinburgh and beyond that had sustained the Blaeu mapping of Scotland project. Crucially, Martin made his tours and recorded his observations on the eve of a phase in their history when the Western Isles would be socially and culturally transformed (consumed) by external and eclipsing forces. In documenting the islands at this time, it fell to Martin Martin to portray (a way of seeing) island society, particularly the practices, beliefs and customs of the ordinary people, to borrow a founding phrase of island studies: 'On their own terms' (McCall 1994).

From the opening moment of the incorporating Union in 1707 through the '45 Jacobite Rising and its post-Culloden aftermath, to the profound intellectual and social engagement with Enlightenment ideas and Improvement practices in its final decades, the eighteenth century was a pivotal era for Scotland's islands. The way in which wider moments, ideas and practices impacted varied across the Northern and Western Isles, including the imperial fashioning of the 'old north' of 'North Britain' (c.f. Andersson Burnett and Newby 2008; Reeploeg 2017a, e.g.). It was events and outcomes in the Hebrides, however, that had a particularly enduring significance, most especially in respect of Gaelic culture and society. From Skye, Martin Martin had given the wider world an idealised portrait of Gaelic society. Some sixty years later, James MacPherson, a central Highland Gael[8] presented a similar portrait, not through description of the present but through the poetic voice of the bards of the ancient Gaelic social order from which the Highland society of the eighteenth century traced its descent.

Scotland's Gaelic culture included a rich oral tradition of tales and poetry[9] relating the exploits of the legendary figures of an earlier heroic age whose presence was also inscribed and remembered on an appropriately 'wild' and emotive landscape of misty mountains and distant islands. MacPherson's talent lay in presenting, or rather *re*-presenting the complex legacy of the Gaelic tradition through his own 'translations', claiming them to be the Homeric voice of *Ossian*, an old blind bard of the third century whose epic poems recalled the historical presence and passions

8   From a family and district heavily involved in the Jacobite Rising of 1745, MacPherson had first-hand experience of the brutal post-Culloden repression and the raft of government policies designed to eradicate the language, culture and way of life of Highland society. From his connections in Edinburgh literary circles MacPherson was also aware that several aspects of both the landscape and culture of the much-maligned Highlands contained the very features that the sensibilities and curiosity of the *literati* of Edinburgh found so appealing (Pittock 1999).

9   Although Skye, the 'Isle of Mist' features as the home of the warrior hero Cuchullin, the tales of *Ossian* were primarily set not in the islands but around the seaboard approaches to the isles, notably the hills of Morven on the Sound of Mull. Yet, MacPherson's project, his poems and the attached controversy were of considerable significance for the Hebrides. When collecting original material to work on, MacPherson had specifically gone to Skye, the Uists and Benbecula and to Mull because he felt that in these islands the surviving oral tradition was at its strongest, the language and content of the tales and heroic verse at its richest. The Hebrides, in short, were already being identified as the heartland of the culture. The evidence subsequently published after the Highland Society's own enquiry into the situation confirmed this to be the case. MacPherson's activities also ensured that a significant number of Gaelic manuscripts, not least from the islands, were saved for posterity.

of the Golden Age of Scotland's early Gaels. MacPherson's 'translations' also depicted the highland and islands landscape in verse, evocatively appealing to the fashionable literary tastes of Edinburgh, London and beyond. MacPherson's Ossianic works were a huge success. They aroused feelings of national pride in Scotland, circulated widely across Europe and rankled not a few in England for their perceived challenge to the 'natural order' of an English cultural superiority. Later, and controversially, MacPherson was accused of forgery, his work acrimoniously dismissed as hoax. Subsequent scholarship has been less dismissive, recognising his work not as literal translations but as 'creative interpretation' where MacPherson's own literary compositions sought to meet the tastes of his age and are best seen as neither Gaelic nor English works but rather an attempt to mediate between the two (Stafford 1988).

Across Britain and Europe, the 1770s were a new age of exploration with 'voyages of discovery' already taking place to lands and peoples as distant as the Pacific and the Arctic. When the Ossianic controversy put the spotlight so firmly on Scotland's Gaelic heartlands as the surviving living relic of an ancient society, a thirst for 'discovery' of the Hebrides through exploration and travel by curious observers from afar was unleashed. The earliest and most significant of these 'tours' was when Samuel Johnson, London's leading man of letters, and his Scottish companion James Boswell, lawyer and author, made an extensive tour of several of the Western Isles in 1773 (Black 2011).[10] In the impactful wake of MacPherson's *Ossian,* both Johnson's and Boswell's accounts marked what became an accumulating library of narratives of voyages to the Hebrides by a steady stream of visitors (Cooper 1979; Bray 2001). Though few had the enquiring minds, perceptive observations or literary capabilities to match those of their predecessors what did emerge in the years that followed was the delineation of Scotland's Hebrides as a distinct sub-set of the wider representational polity and an increasingly commodified entity of the Highlands; that is,

---

10   Johnson published his account in 1775, Boswell added his in 1785, a year after Johnson's death. Subsequently the two accounts have been regularly published together and are widely regarded as classics of travel writing.

as a distinctly *island* cultural landscape of place, practices and communities in its own right.

The Ossianic, romantic optic was not the only prism through which Scotland's islands were viewed in the late eighteenth century (Womack 1989), however. Alongside 'Romance' there was 'Improvement' and the voyaging visitor literature also included the observations and proposals of those who saw a promising economic future for the islands in diverse schemes for 'improved' land use, fisheries, planned villages and industry. The subsequent shift in land use, leading to removal and out-migration, sheep farms and deer forests, also generated its own strand of visitor accounts, a prolonged debate in newspaper columns and pamphlets over destitution, congestion, and the future viability of island communities. Boswell and Johnson's visit took place at a time when the Hebrides were undergoing a phase of voluntary mass migration, one that brought the experience of island exile to the fore in island culture and memory. Over the later nineteenth century this experience of exile and loss intensified as the Hebrides were afflicted by successive periods of removal and forced migrations when whole communities and sometimes whole islands were cleared of their population. Given this traumatic dislocation of people across almost the entirety of the Highlands, it is interesting to note that it was island poets, such as William Livingstone of Islay, whose verse most evocatively expressed the searing sense of loss, just as it was Mary MacPherson of Skye who emerged as the 'voice' of crofter resistance (MacLean 1985).

To the north, while involved in both the Jacobite politics of 1745 and the social and economic promotion of 'improved' agricultural practices, fisheries and commerce of subsequent centuries, the Northern Isles did not attract anything like the level of attention given to the Hebrides. The Hebrides and Gaelic language and culture had become synonymous with reflecting broader representations and understandings of Scotland's 'island' people and culture. This changed significantly in the nineteenth century with the ascription of a Norse identity to the people of the Northern Isles, as the living descendants of the Viking warriors of the Old Norse sagas (Smith 1988; Hall 2010). Once again literature and cultural ascription played a key role. In 1822 Sir Walter Scott's *The Pirate*, set in Shetland, raised an initial public awareness of this aspect of island history. An array of influential

scholars followed, notably the Orcadian, Samuel Laing, vigorously advo-
cating that the Orkney and Shetland islanders were essentially Norse /
Teutonic as opposed to Scots / Celtic. In the context of early Victorian
discourse around English superiority, this manufactured Nordic identity
was promoted as a key contributory strand in the belief in Teutonic su-
premacy that underpinned the Anglo British imperial project.

From the 1880s and through the early part of the twentieth century, as
the promotion of a Celtic and Gaelic profile of national identity emerged in
Scottish politics and culture (Gifford and Riach 2004), a 'Norse – Celtic'
debate developed with some unattractive racial undertones (D'Arcy 1996).
Ironically, it *polarised* the Gaelic Hebrides against the Nordic Northern
Isles at the very time that the idea of a joint archipelagic arc of creative
practice and shared attributes was being mooted, based not least on the
disproportionately high incidence of writers, artists and musicians resident
in Scotland's disparate island communities at that time (MacDiarmid 1939).
Brannigan (2015: 147) reinforces the early twentieth-century connective,
relational and material relations between islands (and nations) as important,
detailing a 'flurry of archipelagic literature' characterised by 'the circulation of people and ideas between islands, and is certainly marked by the
perception that the islands on the western edge, be they the Blaskets, the
Arans, or the Hebrides, represent peripheral extremes of mainland society'.

It was against this now established backdrop of 'far western edge' that
the cultural phenomenon of the 'Celtic Twilight' emerged; an aspect of a
wider Celtic Renaissance movement (initiating in Ireland), and broadly
mapped to the 1890s–1930s. Allied to a re-claiming of 'pre-modern' values
and practices, the 'Celtic Twilight led to a particular surge of interest in
the Hebrides. Welded to 'romantic' expressions and re-imaginings of both
Irish and Scottish Gaelic culture and by association with the mythological
otherworld of joy and eternal youth of early Gaelic tradition the Celtic
Twilight framed a particularly powerful (yet problematic) re-mediation
of the Hebrides as 'Celtic otherworld' (Burnett and Burnett 2011). One
example of how the 'remote corners' of the Hebrides was placed on a global
stage was through singer and composer Marjory Kennedy-Fraser and the
songs she collected on visits to the outer isles, particularly Eriskay and
which she 'translated' for an urban bourgeois audience. Coupled with

Kennedy-Fraser's compatriot Rev Kenneth Macleod (of Eigg), famous for his own penned collection *The Road to the Isles: Poetry, Lore, and Tradition of the Hebrides* (1927), such examples are emblematic of a modern cultural industry of the 'imagining' of the remote and rural communities of Scotland's islands (Blaikie 2010) and presents another layer in the cultural history that shaped the dominant vision of the Hebrides well into the twentieth century. Islanders themselves lived the remote modernity of things a little differently, perhaps. Ironically, while persistent motifs of Hebridean cultural alterity, that is as places and people 'at distance' and journeyed to via the literal and cultural 'Road to the Isles', were being presented as a retreat from advancing modernity, the island communities themselves were embracing the improvements to communications, croft work and domestic life that modernity offered with alacrity.

Islands as structural and sustainable: Agencies and ambitions

Through the prism of cultural and creative practices and the signifying processes – of arts and of media, for example – the islands of Scotland each offer deep-rooted, embodied and embellished histories which are nevertheless also representative of future trends, nuanced responses, varying ambitions and complex responsibilities. Scotland's islands are notable for the collective community efforts and energies to identify, protect and care for local histories, and tangible and intangible cultural heritage, and who is best placed to do it. Sustaining the islands' rich cultural histories has not been without challenge. The cultural services sector remains precarious, subject to budgetary constraints, and much of the community arts and cultural activism energies are contingent on the continued support and engagement of wider community support and volunteerism. Arts and cultural activities, so many of which form the intrinsic backdrop to 'island history and culture', are integral to sustaining people and place *in place* yet the success and future capacity of island cultural heritage in still 'small' and often dispersed communities can suffer from a degree of over-burdening on a few, coupled with the strain and expectation of sustained 'development planning'.

Rural (island and highland) communities in Scotland and elsewhere on the often imagined 'Celtic fringe' (c.f. Clancy 2015; Brennan et al. 2016) are still frequently framed as an 'ancient' and 'artisan' realm, and are well documented as sites of counter-urbanisation with its associated 'local' socio-cultural tensions and rural enterprise development politics. There is nonetheless a re-energised focus on the 'natural' resource futures that underpin social and private enterprise within remote areas such as the hills, coast and marine environments. The interface between the arts and island environments is an expressive and energised terrain in this regard. Poetry, literature, visual arts, music, performance and more are each variously meaningful, powerful and political frames of reference for all on and off islands.[11] Furthermore, the connectivity of island spaces to the local/global nexus is brought into sharp relief in regard of the quickening realities and impactful narratives of climate change (Baldacchino and Kelman 2014; Grydehøj and Kelman 2017) and the critical appraisal offered by scholars, such as Chandler and Pugh (2020) on the 'shifting stakes' of sustainability and resilience in regard of the Anthropocene and climate change, are crucial.[12]

So too are debates on 'the commons', a claim of rights and the relationality of identity and culture. Land – its use, ownership and representation – more generally remains a passionately debated topic in Scotland, not least as it informs narratives more broadly of Scotland's rural assets as resource, as sites for development and for identity claims and validation. It has been a relatively short period of time in which the discoursing of Scotland highlands and islands, and rural and remote regions generally, have

11   See, for example, the Scottish Centre for Geopoetics, for example, as a rich well of island related cultural expression, <http://www.geopoetics.org.uk/what-is-geopoetics/>, see also McFadyen (2018) 'Finding Radical Hope in Geopoetics', The Annual Tony McManus Lecture, <http://www.geopoetics.org.uk/mcmanus-geopoetics-lecture-mairimcfadyen/> accessed 10 April 2020.

12   See, for example, the archaeology climate change focus within UHI led from Orkney <https://archaeologyorkney.com/category/climate-change/> accessed 10 March 2020; see also Ford (2019), already cited.

noticeably shifted from an overwhelming framing of people and practices (culture work, economic development, social enterprise and environmental interface) heavily defined by the past to what is now unequivocally a wider narrative shift to championing that which is mapped to the future.[13] The diverse significance or acknowledgement of islandness in relation to the governance and public administration of Scotland's island communities over the centuries aptly reflects the complexities and indeed the contradictions of the situation. This is particularly noticeable in the broader comparison between the Northern and the Western Isles and the paradoxical position of the majority of island communities within the 'Western Isles' or Hebrides, themselves. From medieval times through to the late nineteenth century, the combined entity of 'Orkney and Zetland' were a distinct island jurisdiction. In contrast, with one exception, all of the Hebrides were incorporated in the sheriffdoms or shires of Argyllshire, Inverness-shire and Ross-shire, respectively. In the west, only the Isle of Bute as Bute-shire (including the Cumbraes and Arran) was a separate and distinct island jurisdiction. In 1889 with the formation of County Councils, Bute remained the only distinct island council on the west but in the north Orkney and Zetland were separated into two distinct island county councils. All the other Hebrides remained part of Argyll CC, Inverness CC and Ross and Cromarty CC, that is effectively under a *mainland* locus of governance (Grimble 1968; Magnusson 1968). In 1975 a major restructuring of local government abolished county councils replacing them with regional and district councils each with a different level of functions. Orkney, Shetland

---

13   Such a shift is not itself either 'good' or 'bad and it is worthy of critical review. It is also notable that 'islands' in Scotland are explicitly recognised as significant in themselves and as contributors and integral to the nation. Part of our interest lies in the scale of change within a rural and remote realm that has overwhelmingly been construed as ontologically defined by its history. Celebrated iconography and narratives of the region are variously both singularly 'homogenous' whilst actively seeking to define the regional in its mosaic of difference; (cultural) history as both a framing device and as a socio-economic 'truth' underpins these narratives. Commentaries and opinion pieces on Scottish island related issues on language, land, arts, environment, economy and history, from various contributors, including comments and social media engagement, can be found at Bella Caledonia, <https:// bellacaledonia.org.uk/all-articles/?all_keywords=islands>, for example.

and the Comhairle nan Eilean (the Western Isles Islands Council) were each established as multi-purpose island authorities. All other Argyll islands, the islands of Skye and Raasay, and the Small Isles, each remained within their respective mainland authorities at regional and district level. Although larger more 'unitary' authorities were restored in 1994, there was no change in the position of the islands. Shetland, Orkney and the Western Isles remain the only discrete island authorities and the majority of Scotland's inhabited islands actually lie within the combined administrative structure of their respective mainland/island or island/mainland authorities. Recent developments in island governance are now more fully asserted (although perhaps less clearly impacted) in the form of the Islands (Scotland) Act 2018.[14] There is also the issue of 'Europe', Brexit and tensions around what constitutes 'independence' more broadly within these islands. Currently there is a resurfacing of the Northern Isles 'independence' narrative where geopolitics (as well as geopoetics) – political and cultural identity narratives and resource competition critiques – variously frame who 'owns', 'speaks for', or lays claim to boundaries.[15]

The islands of Scotland vary in terms of both their actual and perceived isolation and distance from each other, and from the Scottish mainland, as well as Edinburgh, London or Bergen. Each island, certainly as they remain populated today, maps to a particular history of development and social policy. Notably Shetland's relatively recent 'living memory' economic 'turn of fortune' regarding the discovery and subsequent development of oil in the early 1970s makes it distinctive from other island groups of both its 'nearest neighbour' Orkney and the Inner and Outer Hebrides. In an attempt to counter the 'disruptive effects of rapid industrialization' (Hill et al. 1998: 16) brought about by the potential of an 'oil boom', the Shetland communities and the local authority sought to safeguard Shetland's 'distinctive way of life'. Furthermore, it was contested that the oil industry potentially risked negatively impacting on the increasing prosperity and

14   Scottish Government, <https://www.gov.scot/policies/community-empowerment/ empowering-our-island-communities/> accessed 19 January 2020.

15   See, for example, George Rosie's (2013) discussion on issues of Shetland and Orcadian 'independence' in 'The Shetland Card', 12 December 2013, <https:// bellacaledonia.org.uk/2013/12/12/the-shetland-card/> accessed 19 January 2020.

sustainability of growing island economics in fishing and tourism that had both been substantially supported and enhanced through the HIDB and other rural regeneration policy. The longer-view narratives of Scotland's twentieth-century island communities as struggling to contend with modernisation pressures were key to how future policy and representational practice developed (as already discussed). Island communities variously sought to both counter the ideas of 'peripheral' and marginal whilst contending with the reality of geographic and socio-economic contexts that nevertheless embodied a lived experience of peripherality, inequities and dis-proportionate living costs.

Scotland's islands have arguably undergone a marked acceleration of social transformation in the last decades of the twentieth century that are now consolidated as small island sustainability and successes, fuelled not least by significant underpinning of 'local' educational provision, where previously generations of children had to leave home and board to undertake required (and optional 'stay-on') schooling and training, improved digital connectivity, sustained transport provision albeit not without continual weather and other disruptive challenges, but also significant enhanced variation in employment opportunities and enterprise support. Such transition emerging from 'late modernity' as experienced in rural and remote Scotland is widespread yet variable and it nevertheless has offered an opportunity for both celebration and a countering of the processes and outcomes of change. As Duxbury and Campbell (2011: 112) have noted for rural and remote Canada, in 'the midst of transition, many communities are recognizing that the ways the community understands itself, celebrates itself, and expresses itself are major contributing factors to its ability to withstand economic, political, and cultural winds of change and transition'.

As with coastal communities worldwide, fishing and marine activity continues as key sectors for Scotland's offshore island communities. Today inshore and offshore marine activity and related processes and production is a high-tech expanding portfolio of businesses and enterprise supported by key interface with research and development policy. In the Inner Hebrides, and on a hyper-local scale but no less impactful, Tiree recently reappraised its 'Marine Resource' and set out future plans that build on the local economy of fishing, with an expansion of related food processing and production, but also the sea and marine environment more broadly as a valuable and attractive leisure resource further enhancing Tiree's reputation as an Atlantic water-sports destination. Islands, and Scotland is no small exception, must balance the demands of both production and consumption. The economies of small islands are often skewed to singular dominating industries and sectors, subjecting island economies, to a degree of boom/bust risk. In Scotland debates continue in terms of how economic development has impacted on island history and culture and vice-versa.[16] Communities have long sought to counter aspects of actual and symbolic impoverishment and exploitation (exemplified by debates and reactions to indigenous and minority language rights, crofting sustainability, resource 'extraction' such as the 'super-quarry' proposal on Harris or oil development in Shetland, fishing and fish farming across the islands and Scotland's north and west coastal communities, the protection of ecologies, and tourism).[17] The region offers a rich and complex field of scholarship in this regard. What, where and who constitutes 'remote' or 'too-close', what has been classed as 'margin', or 'periphery' and *further from* things became interestingly rearticulated during the Spring months of 2020 as the pandemic lockdown became established and debates formulated on accessing places, in what number and on whose terms. 'Remoteness', as nearness or distance then, is very much back in the spotlight.

16   See, for example, UHI's 'The Edge' seminar series <https://www.uhi.ac.uk/en/research-enterprise/res-themes/interdisciplinary-research-programmes/the-edge-call-for-contributions/seminar-series/>; see also Scottish Centre for Island Studies <https://scotcis.wordpress.com/about/>.

17   Most notably visitor tourism has caused particular concern in Skye with a global media focus circulating on the problematics of 'over-tourism'. Similar concerns over visitor pressures of cruise tourism in Orkney and remote communities more broadly, exacerbated not least by the emergence of the Covid-19 pandemic and related 'lockdown' concerns and restrictions of 2020, speak to longer-term tensions over economy, community and environment priorities in the islands.

The structure of the book

In addition to this introductory chapter, this collection of chapters offers a range of accounts, research and policy positions responding to and informing of Scotland's island communities, social histories and cultural representation. The evolution and transformation of Scotland's small island communities and its wider nexus is a rich and rewarding field of productive inquiry worthy of continued and expanding research, focus and debate that is deeply informing of Scottish cultural representation more broadly (see Brown et al. 2007). Scotland's islands are championed and celebrated through arts, culture and media yet they continue in many regards as remote and fragile economies. The policies of centralised (urban) government so often applied without recognition of the different requirements and challenges faced in the rural, never mind the particularities of islands, was addressed more fully by the Scottish Government's establishment of an Islands (Scotland) Act 2018. This collection offers a current review of these challenges and may help inform the strategic interventions of both policymakers and practitioners. The collection seeks to contextualise islandness for a range of readers drawing on the fields of history, social science, economy and the arts. The singular focus on Scotland is intended to offer readers a frame of reference by which key trends and debates pertaining to Scotland's small island communities and spaces can be explored and critiqued more widely.

Drawing on social history and related scholarship, Ray Burnett's chapter positions a longer view on ideas of how Scotland's islandness has been configured. Scotland's islands' history is a complex layered palimpsest where early ideas of Scotland's islands, and the identities and representations of 'islandness', circulated across Europe, and were variously configured within Scotland. The material and physical traces of people in place as expressive of their cultural and social condition is examined and offers a pivoting view to wider research legacies exploring key cultural and social expression. The next three chapters further expand on the cultural complexities of Scotland's islands. Hugh Cheape provides a 'deep dive' expert insight to the material culture of Hebridean island life and a regional ethnological view with a particular focus on the rich store that is Gaelic material culture. This chapter poses questions as to the future of shared knowledge, identities and how memory of a Hebridean community and its conversation (*seanchas*) is integral to its 'cosmos' and local word-view. Language and literary heritage pertaining to islands is a well-travelled expert researched field that island studies scholars have sought to enhance and exchange more widely. Turning to a different northern cultural focus, Andrew Jennings offers an 'ethnographic' consideration of Shetland's language and heritage to this end. Jennings adds wonderful illustrative weight to the research field on the nuanced distinctiveness of Shetlandic dialect and identity via notable legacies of Vikings and Victorians, and everyday Shetlandic onomastics. By way of further linking ideas of island cultural history, identity and heritage, Kathryn Burnett and Lynda Harling Stalker's chapter examines how arts, craft, creative industries, and cultural work more generally, play a signature role in framing ideas of island places. Commentaries that celebrate and frame small islands as 'special places' to live and work are inter-twined with the powerful positioning of island production and consumption as an 'enchanted' space that should remain subject to scrutiny.

As this introduction chapter has noted, in recent decades policy, research and planning with and from within island communities has become a central focus of Scotland's broader 'island-proofing' agenda. Mike Danson speaks to these histories of peripherality and 'margin' in the broader macro-context of northern Europe regional economies and Scotland's situated position to 'Nordic' and 'Atlantic' neighbours. Sharing good practice and the local particularities of small island economies and social contingencies has underpinned significant shifts in policy focus on aspects of remoteness, 'margin' and peripherality as well as the fragility of island and remote rural economies and social demographics. Danson's chapter highlights these key shifts in policy and critique, and contributors throughout this volume further exemplify these ambitions in practice. Successful policy reframing within Scotland to better empower communities, and by this ensure a greater demographic sustainability, remains an arena of critical debate and research focus. In focusing on a perennial rural social concern, Rosie Alexander draws on some of the extensive research on this in Scotland to position current understandings of the shifting nature of island demographics and, in particular, the experience of young people.

As with regions elsewhere[18], just what do Scottish islands' futures hold, is a fascinating environmental, socio-cultural and geo-political stage set to further interest and engage scholars across disciplines. Ownership and access to rural resources is a central pillar of how Scotland's island communities can and will underpin 'futures' and sustainable policy and practice. One of the most contested contexts of how Scotland's islands, and 'remote rural' communities more generally, have countered longer economic pressures and political disenfranchisement has been in the name of land ownership and its reform. Calum MacLeod invites consideration on some of this long condition with specific reference to the case study of West Harris but the chapter speaks to the broader context of Scotland's land reform and community ownership opportunities and challenges. Policy and practice have sought to respond to the similarities and its differences within island communities, to varying degrees of success. The complex and competing nature of socio-economic sectors within any resource space is noted here, as is the potential for growth and development synergies mindful of island particularities. The chapter by Mike Danson and Kathryn Burnett on island enterprise examines such synergies in more depth in regard of Scotland's small island enterprise contexts where history and culture are deeply inscribed on the narratives of entrepreneurial conditions, confidences and complexities.

Wider contexts of policy have been significantly ramped up in recent years with the Scottish Government's Islands (Scotland) Act (2018) and the wider policy focus on 'island proofing' and future proofing of all sectoral policy and ambitions. Francesco Sindico and Nicola Black contribute a useful commentary on this from their extensive fieldwork across the islands exploring how island residents view such an Act and the future it might hold. Finally, as a Sgitheanach, a Gael, with a strongly *situated* viewpoint of island emplacement, James Oliver provides this collection with a

---

18   See, for example, the Sustainable Island Futures research project at the University
      of Prince Edward Island, <https://projects.upei.ca/unescochair/sustainable-island-
      futures/> accessed 15 March 2020.

fascinating, concluding personal reflection on the relationality of islandness. In this final chapter Oliver offers readers a framing of islandness as an 'interaction of dialogues and dialect(ics)' that iterate and evolve between islandness 'on the ground' and islandness 'in the mind'. In conclusion, we hope this collection offers, as Oliver suggests, some thoughts on thinking *with* islandness that moves ideas of Scotland's islands beyond separation, or isolation. On reading we hope to invite further understandings of 'ways of seeing' all of Scotland's islands as informed by and informing of an ethical imagining of the places and peoples of all Scotland's islands and our collective sustainable futures.

Bibliography

Abrams, L. (2005). *Myth and materiality in a woman's world: Shetland 1800–2000*. Manchester: Manchester University Press.

Andersson Burnett, L. A., and Newby, A. G. (2008). 'Between Empire and "the North": Scottish Identity in the Nineteenth Century'. In S. Litonius, H. Litonius and T. Pettersson (eds), *Parting the Mists: Views on Scotland as a Part of Britain and Europe*, pp. 37–56. Helsingfors: Historicus.

Baldacchino, G. (2005). 'Editorial: islands – objects of representation', *Geografiska Annaler: Series B, Human Geography*, 87 (4), 247–251.

Baldacchino, G. (2008). 'Studying Islands: on whose terms? Some epistemological and methodological challenges to the pursuit of island studies', *Island Studies Journal*, 3 (1), 37–56.

Baldacchino, G. (2012). 'The lure of the island: a spatial analysis of power relations', *Journal of Marine and Island Cultures*, 1, 55–62.

Baldacchino, G. (ed.) (2018). *The Routledge International Handbook of Island Studies*. Abingdon, Oxfordshire: Routledge.

Baldacchino, G., and Kelman, I. (2014). 'Critiquing the pursuit of island sustainability: blue and green, with hardly a colour in between', *Shima*, 8, 1–21.

Black, R. (ed.) (2011). *Samuel Johnson's Journey to the Western Islands and James Boswell's Journal of a Tour*. Edinburgh: Birlinn.

Blaikie, A. (2010). *The Scots Imagination and Modern Memory*. Edinburgh: Edinburgh University Press.

Bleau, NLS National Library of Scotland digitised Blaeu collection and accompanying essays, <https://maps.nls.uk/atlas/blaeu/index.html> accessed 10 April 2019.

Boon, S., Butler, L., and Jefferies, D. (2018). *Autoethnography and Feminist Theory at the Water's Edge: Unsettled islands*. New York: Palgrave Pivot, Springer.

Brannigan, J. (2015). *Archipelagic Modernism, Literature in the Irish and British Isles, 1890–1970*. Edinburgh: Edinburgh University Press.

Bray, E. (2001). *Discovery of the Hebrides: Voyagers to the Western Isle, 1745–1833*. Edinburgh: Birlinn.

Brennan, S., Danson, M., and O'Rourke, B. (2016). 'Selling a Language to Save it? The Business-Oriented Promotion of Gaelic and Irish'. In W. McLeod, A. Gunderloch, and R. Dunbar (eds), *Cànan and Cultar (Language and Culture): Rannsachadh na Gàidhlig 8*, pp. 205–221. Edinburgh: Dunedin Academic Press.

Brown, I., Clancy, T., Manning, S., and Pittock, M. (eds) (2007). *The Edinburgh History of Scottish Literature: Modern Transformations: New Identities (from 1918)*. Edinburgh: Dunedin Academic Press.

Burnett, J. A. (2011). *The Making of the Modern Scottish Highlands, 1939–1965: Withstanding the 'Colossus of Advancing Materialism*. Dublin: Four Courts.

Burnett, R. (2013). 'Britain: The Fractured Island'. In Baldacchino, G., (ed.), *The Political Economy of Divided Islands, United Geographies, Multiple Polities*, pp. 228–245. Basingstoke: Palgrave Macmillan.

Burnett, R., and Burnett, K. A. (2011). 'Scotland's Hebrides: Song and Culture, Transmission and Transformation'. In Baldacchino, G., (ed.), *Island Songs, A Global Repertoire*, pp. 81–101. Plymouth: The Scarecrow Press.

Campbell, E. (2019). 'Peripheral vision: Scotland in Early Medieval Europe'. In Blackwell, A. E., (ed.), *Scotland in Early Medieval Europe*, pp. 17–33. Leiden: Sidestone Press.

Chandler, D., and Pugh, J. (2020). 'Islands of relationality and resilience: the shifting stakes of the Anthropocene'. *Area*, 52 (1), 65–72.

Clancy, T. O. (2015). 'How being Celtic got a bad name – and why you should care'. *The Conversation*, 13 July 2015. <https://theconversation.com/how-being-celtic-got-a-badname-and-why-you-should-care-44540> accessed 10 April 2020.

Condry, E. (1976). 'The impossibility of solving the highland problem', *Journal of the Anthropological Society of Oxford*, 8 (3), 138–149.

Cooper, D. (1979). *Road to the Isles: travellers in the Hebrides 1770–1914*. London: Routledge & Kegan Paul.

D'Arcy, J. (1996). *Scottish Skalds and Sagamen, Old Norse influence on Modern Scottish Literature*. East Linton: Tuckwell Press.

Davis, S. (2016). Book Review 'Islandology: geography, rhetoric, politics', *Social and Cultural Geography*, 17 (1), 140–141.

Duxbury, N., and Campbell, H. (2011). *Through Arts and Culture: A Literature Review*. Creative City Network of Canada, <http://www.creativecity.ca> accessed 18 October 2019.

Ford, R. (2019). 'Orkney Ecologies', *Humanities*, 9 (5), at doi:10.3390/h9010005 accessed 10 April 2020.

Gifford, D. M., and Riach, A. (eds) (2004). *Scotlands: Poets and the Nation*. Manchester: Carcanet.

Grimble, I. (1968). 'Unsceptered Isles'. In Thomson, D. C., and I. Grimble (eds), *The Future of the Highlands*, pp. 153–173. London: Routledge and Kegan Paul.

Grydehøj, A. (2011). 'Making the most of smallness: economic policy in microstates and sub-national island jurisdictions', *Space and Polity*, 15 (3), 183–196.

Grydehøj, A. (2013a). 'Ethnicity and the origins of local identity in Shetland, UK – Part I: Picts, Vikings, Fairies, Finns, and Aryans', *Journal of Marine and Island Cultures*, 2 (1), 39–48.

Grydehøj, A. (2013b). 'Ethnicity and the origins of local identity in Shetland, UK – Part II: Picts, Vikings, Fairies, Finns, and Aryans', *Journal of Marine and Island Cultures*, 2 (1), 107–114.

Grydehøj, A., and Kelman, I. (2017). 'The eco-island trap: climate change mitigation and conspicuous sustainability', *Area*, 49 (1), 106–113.

Hall, S. W. (2010). *The History of Orkney Literature*. Edinburgh: John Donald.

Hill, A. E., Seyfrit, C. L., and Danner, M. J. E. (1998). 'Oil development and social change in the Shetland Islands 1971–1991', *Impact Assessment and Project Appraisal*, 16 (1), 15–25.

Hunter, J. (2007). 'History: its key place in the future of the Highlands and Islands', *Northern Scotland*, 27 (1), 1–14.

MacDiarmid, H. (1939). *The Islands of Scotland: Hebrides, Orkneys, and Shetlands*. London: Batsford.

MacLean, S. (1985). *Ris a' Bhruthaich, The Criticism and Prose Writings of Sorley MacLean*. Stornoway: Acair.

Macleod, K. (1927). *The Road to the Isles: Poetry, Lore, and Tradition of the Hebrides*. Edinburgh: Robert Grant & Son.

Magnusson, M. (1968). 'Highland Administration'. In Thomson, D. C., and I. Grimble (eds), *The Future of the Highlands*, pp. 249–296. London: Routledge and Kegan Paul.

Martin, M., and Monro, D. (1999). Martin, M., *A Description of the Western Isles of Scotland ca 1695; A Voyage to St Kilda (1698)* and Monro, D., *A Description of the*

*Occidental i.e. Western Islands of Scotland, (*1549*)*, (intro., Withers, C.W.J. and Munro, R.W.), Edinburgh: Birlinn.

McCall, G. (1994). 'Nissology: a proposal for consideration', *Journal of the Pacific Society*, 63–64 (17), 93–106.

McCullough, K. L. (2018). 'Resolving the 'Highland problem': the Highlands and Islands of Scotland and the European Union', *Local Economy*, 33 (4), 421–437.

Nihtinen, A. (2015). 'Political change and reconstruction of the past in Shetland', *Northern Studies*, 47, 131–152.

Perchard, A., and Mackenzie, N. (2013). 'Too much on the Highlands?' Recasting the economic history of the Highlands and Islands', *Northern Scotland*, 4 (1), 3–22.

Pittock, M.G.H. (1999). *Celtic Identity and the British Image*. Manchester: Manchester University Press.

Pugh, J. (2013). 'Island movements: thinking with the archipelago', *Island Studies Journal*, 8 (1), 9–24.

Reeploeg, S. (2017a). *Between Scotland and Norway: Connected Cultures and Intercultural Encounters after 1700*, PhD Thesis. Open University/University of Aberdeen.

Reeploeg, S. (2017b). 'Peripheral visions: engaging nordic literary traditions on Orkney and Shetland', *Scandinavica*, 56 (1), 34–58.

Shima Editorial Board (2007). 'An introduction to island culture studies', *Shima*, 1(1), 1–5.

Smith, B. (1988). 'Shetland in Saga-time: re-reading the Orkneyinga Saga', *Northern Studies*, 25, 21–41.

Stafford, F. (1988). *The Sublime Savage: James MacPherson and the Poems of Ossian*. Edinburgh: Edinburgh University Press,

Stratford, E., Baldacchino, G., McMahon, E., Farbotko, C., and Harwood, A. (2011). 'Envisioning the archipelago', *Island Studies Journal*, 6 (2), 113–130.

Womack, P. (1989). *Improvement and Romance: Constructing the Myth of the Highlands*. Basingstoke: Macmillan.

RAY BURNETT

2. Little Islands on the Edge of the Ocean

This chapter undertakes to explore aspects of Scotland's island culture and society in two overlapping periods – the late Iron Age (500 BC– AD 500) and the overlapping Early Christian era (AD 500–900). Using thematic frames, and with reference to recorded history and scholar- ship, observations are drawn on ideas of islandness and 'ways of seeing' islands through a prism of accounts of and emerging within the islands of the west.

The earliest layers of a Hebridean sense of place and identity were, from its inception, inextricably linked to that of Scotland. This was the age in which 'the Hebrides' and their occupants first emerged into early history; when early kinship alliances evolved into Pictland and Dal Riata; and when the foundations were laid of an Early Christian church that evolved to play a critical role in the emergence of the kingdom of Alba (Woolf 2007; Fraser 2009). The historical relationship of the Hebrides to the wider context of Scotland over time has been distinctively different to that of the Northern Isles. Furthermore, the wider premise that a varie- gated yet bonded grouping of islands with a singularly distinct islandscape richly textured over time by layered accretions of shifting notion of residual meaning as to islands, island living, islanders and islandness is not unique to the Hebrides is noted. Nonetheless a focus on 'the Hebrides' offers an opportunity to expand on the particular accretion of aspects of island meaning in the two early historical periods explored informed by both historical record and more current dialogue.

In an early seminal island studies paper and its subsequent re-appraisal (Hay 2006, 2013), the case was made for an approach based on a phenom- enology of place, an approach involving both the valorisation of the speci- ficity of islands and what Hay called the 'irreducible particularity' of real islands (2013: 212). This involved the construction of island meanings in the unique terms of the 'emotional dialogue' between the individual island's environment and its residents. Developing David Harvey's theorisation of place as the locus of community and 'the site of collective memory' (1996: 310), Hay also made the important point as to the temporal axis of a particular island place: 'In order that cultural place meanings can accrue […] there must also be a capacity to layer up stories, so that a potent vernacular culture (or cultures) can exist and persist, welding past to present and ensuring a seamless passage of time' (Hay 2013: 32–33).

A temporal axis is not without its challenges, such is the palimpsest of island place. This chapter begins with a time frame of an Atlantic Iron Age with a brief foray into accounts of early classical writers describing the furthest reaches of the Roman empire, the northern fringe of the known world, for it is here in these sources that the islands lying to the west of Scotland first emerge in the historical record as a handful of names for individual islands and the collective name 'Ebudae', the 'Hebrides' (Breeze 2002). Split over two key time frames, aspects of settlement, place inscription imbrication and mythology, followed by the later voyaging tales (the immrama), accounts of Hebridean monasticism, and the scholarship of early Christianity, are all explored. These aspects examine and inform the cultural connectivity of the islands of the west to 'the known world' and the chapter concludes with some reflections on islandness as both 'real' and 'imaginative' and how ideas of the Hebrides circulate and inform our understanding of islands in Scotland and beyond today.

The Atlantic Iron Age

The late Iron Age (c.500 BC–AD c.500) is an important period in the history of the Hebrides. These are centuries of island past that emphatically shaped the island present. Behind the written classical references, the most important 'texts' to be read, interpreted and understood are not to be found in manuscripts but in the monumental stone legacy of each individual island, the archaeology of each discrete island landscape. Later, in this period the islands emerge in expressive cultural literary texts, in

the recorded tales and traditions of Gaelic mythology and early history
and the oral transmission of a collective memory of past associations and
meaning. What follows is some commentary on these differing yet interrelated temporal frames.

Archaeological evidence of a human presence across the Hebrides has
been traced back some 8,500 years, a protracted past that left its own residual legacy on the island landscape (Wickham-Jones 1994: 75–88). But
not until c.320 BC do the 'Ebudae' emerge in Pytheas of Marseille's *On the
Ocean,* a now lost text that was heavily drawn on by later classical writers.
Cunliffe (2001) has painstakingly shown how *On the Ocean* was based
on an actual fourth-century BC voyage made by Pytheas up the Brittanic
isle west coast to the Outer Hebrides and, with the aid of local maritime
skills and knowledge, on by Shetland to 'Ultima Thule' (Iceland). He also
demonstrates how the passage to the mythical 'Ultima Thule' was firmly
based on an actual voyage well within the ambit and seafaring reach of the
western and northern islanders of Scotland. A further insight into how a
later generation of islanders perceived their island landscape comes from
an account of a meeting at Delphi in AD 83/84 when the scholar Plutarch
was involved in a discussion about islands, the oracles and the gods. His
friend Demetrius, who had recently returned from Britain, reports

> many of the islands off Britain were uninhabited and widely scattered, some of
> them being named after gods and demigods. He himself had sailed, for the sake of
> learning and observation, to the island nearest to the uninhabited ones, on an official
> mission. This island had a few inhabitants, who were holy men, and all held exempt
> from raiding. (Burn 1969: 3)

Assessing the evidence available in presenting this extract from Plutarch's
essays, Burn concluded that Demetrius had been sent out on an
intelligence-gathering mission as part of Agricola's campaign in Roman
Britain, and that the islands he had visited were somewhere in the Inner
Hebrides. According to Demetrius it was the belief of the resident islanders that several of the uninhabited islands in the locality had once
been the home of supernatural beings. If one of them died, their death
was marked by storms and pestilence. It was their belief that these islands
were sacred to the gods or to the mighty dead. One island in particular

was where an old king of the gods still lay sleeping, guarded by a sea-monster and with many lesser deities in attendance around him. Other islands were described as the abodes of 'holy men', left to live alone and in peace. Burn equated these with the 'Druids as found in Celtic communities elsewhere: a learned order of 'wise men' with a knowledge ranged across astronomy, cosmology, theology, divination, magic and medical skills. Uninhabited island were ideal places for such learned men to retreat, contemplate and exercise the mind. More significantly, Demetrius had also observed that the islanders thought of these as *numinous* places, that is, islands that had a spiritual quality, marked by the presence of a divinity (Burn 1969: 5).

The classical accounts came from the early and middle decades of the late Iron Age era (500 BC–AD 500). Although they are scant, it is from these classical sources that we can begin to trace the earliest names of people and places along the western and northern seaboard of what would emerge as Scotland. It is, however, from the hallmark archaeological legacy of forts, duns, crannogs, wheelhouses and brochs across the evidently inter-linked Northern and Western Isles that we can begin to trace the social and cultural pattern of life across Scotland's island communities.

For all of Scotland's Western and Northern Isles, an excellent guide to the archaeological features of individual sites, including a guide to terms and definitions as well as a mapping facility to give location and context to each of these sites in its local island settings, is provided by Historic Environment Scotland's 'Canmore' portal (https://canmore.org.uk/). Substantial literature has also accumulated on both the dwelling structures in each of the principal island groupings and in the protracted debates as to classification, interpretation and chronology (Armit 1990, 1996; Nieke 1990; Harding 1997, 2000; Ballin Smith and Banks 2002; Mackie 2007).

What the evidence for the late Iron Age and Early History period underlines is the remarkable extent to which islands of various sizes and topologies are the sites of several distinct forms of island dwelling. There are large (Lewis, Skye, Mull, Islay), small (Harris, the Uists, Raasay, Lismore, Tiree, Jura) and smaller (the Barra Isles, Colonsay, Gigha) islands, each with a variety of distinct dwelling types. There are lochs within these islands with crannogs, island duns, or island brochs and there are tidal or deep-water islets or stacks wholly occupied by an island dun or fort. Each of these diverse locations raise the same fundamental question, as to why these specific sites were chosen at any particular time and how, if at all, did these sites of human settlement relate to each other? Developments within Scotland's archaeological circles increasingly help to provide a pertinent context in which these questions can be posed and addressed. Scotland's Archaeological Research Framework (ScARF) has drawn up national research agendas on each archaeological period including one on the Iron Age (2012). In a move away from seeing the environment as no more than background, the ScARF framework puts the focus on landscape as 'the arena in which every local aspect of human settlement and life takes place' (2012: 12). It invites a 'way of seeing' island settings from the perspective of their occupants, a landscape 'that exists by virtue of it being perceived, contextualised and experienced by people (Ashmore and Knapp 1999).

The Uists, Barra and the Barra Isles

Recent excavations and surveys on South Uist (Parker Pearson et al. 2004: 83–123) and on Barra and the Barra Isles (Branigan and Foster 2000) are good examples of the value of this approach. On South Uist the focus was on brochs and wheelhouses, with a line of enquiry that sought to address a series of questions as to occupancy, functionality, the pattern of locations and social relationships within the wider island community and beyond. Although left undeveloped, the findings as to the pattern of locations is of particular interest in relation to the issue of 'islandness'. Across all the principal islands with the exception of Barra, an inshore island in a freshwater loch was a favoured location and on South Uist, all twelve of the surviving broch sites are on such locations. Further north, North Uist provides even more intriguing evidence, not only of freshwater loch island broch sites, but of various brochs, duns and wheelhouses on tidal island sites (Lenfert 2011: 26–27; Canmore ID 10439). The reasons behind the choice of these island sites have yet to be determined although one recent survey has suggested that one of the most compelling reasons would have been to escape the Hebridean midges (Lenfert 2011: 12).

Further south the pattern of location is one of diversity. On Barra, in contrast to the Uists, for example, the locations of the island's six broch towers and other probable broch sites could hardly be more varied, from headlands, interior hillsides, to islands in freshwater lochs and offshore tidal islets (Branigan 2000a: 334–345). And on the Barra Isles, where there are the remains of a full array of Iron Age dry-stone dwellings, any assumption that ascribed group identity reflects a uniformity of settlement is not born out by the evidence. Indeed, the opposite is the case with each island's remains reflecting a marked degree of diversity in form, distribution and possible patterns of relationships. On Vatersay, the monumental landscape is broadly the same as on Barra, although in terms of its much smaller size Vatersay is actually more densely populated in each category. Smaller still is Sandray and it is also similar but with small roundhouses more numerous than large. South of Sandray, however, the picture seems very different. Pabbay has only one imposing broch and a few possible small roundhouses. Mingulay is the largest of the group yet is the only one with no broch or galleried dun, or small roundhouses, only five large ones, (two of which may be wheelhouses). Berneray, like Pabbay has only a solitary broch, perched on its spectacular Barra Head site, along with one small possible roundhouse. The only common feature extending across the islands are the promontory forts on Berneray, Mingulay and Biruaslum (off Vatersay). On Pabbay, and perhaps Sandray, there is important evidence that gives a 'brief glimpse' of late Iron Age Pictish occupation (Branigan 2000b: 347–348).

In short, as the most recent archaeological survey underlined, even in this distinct outlying island group there are noticeable distinctions in the Iron Age/Early History settlement patterns between the islands. These variations appear to reflect highly localised adaptations that were developed partly in response to the environment, and partly as statements of identity by small close-knit communities. And from this, Branigan (2000b: 346) concluded: 'All of us who have worked in these islands believe each island has its own distinctive character that is sometimes reflected in its archaeology'. Recent archaeological work from a specifically phenomenological perspective (Rennell 2010), primarily on North Uist, has concluded that Iron Age island living led not to isolation but connection, suggesting a degree of shared identity and/or cultural contact across the area:

> For Iron Age people then, being 'islanders' was potentially central to their society and social identity. It was the fact that these people lived on islands that brought these places together – facilitating the sharing of material culture. (2010: 51)

Paradoxically, within an individual island such as North Uist, the arch-aeological evidence in relation to settlement location was taken to suggest an inward-looking society with local rather than wider concerns. On North Uist, inland loch islets, mostly on hemmed in locations offered a very different experience of island life to that of dwellings on open coastal machair sites. This was taken to suggest that strongly localised, 'perhaps even island specific' identity may have existed alongside an Outer Hebrides or even an Atlantic province social identity (Rennell 2010: 53).

Gaelic mythology

How the islanders of the Iron Age/Early History settlements of island Dal Riata and maritime Pictland perceived the cultural and social associations of their inherited and lived landscape is not known. Only the early manuscripts and oral traditions of the 'sea-divided Gael' of Ireland and Scotland give us some degree of insight into how this landscape was peopled in the imagination. In this 'way of seeing', whether in the text or in the recitation, the islands are re-inhabited with the great mythical figures and legendary stories of an inherited past. On Islay, or Sanda and Gigha, we are with the Children of Lir turned into swans; on Dun Mhic Uisneachan, Loch Etive, we are in exile with Deirdre and the Sons of Uisnech; on Dun Scathaich, Skye, we are with Sgathaich as she trains CúChulainn; and across the islands, wherever the storytellers gather their audience, we are with Fionn mac Cumhaill and the exploits of the Fianna. A ninth-century tale graphically details the splendour in which the ruling kinships of island society were imagined to have lived:

Gartnán lived in Inis Mac Chéin (Skye). That island was covered with the best
buildings in the western part of the world … He had fifty nets for deer, and out
from the island were fifty nets for fishing. The fifty fish-nets had ropes from them
over the windows of the kitchen. There was a bell on the end of each rope, on the
rail in front of the steward. Four men used to throw (?) the first-run salmon up to
him. He himself in the meantime drank mead upon his couch. (Murphy 1961: 14)

As the voyage of enquiry of Pytheas confirms, by the fourth century BC
the inhabitants of the Hebrides had already accumulated considerable
maritime knowledge and navigational skills. These were communities in
which island-going, of an extensive and far-reaching nature, was an integral part of social and communal life. The Hebrides may have been 'on the
edge of the known world', but they were well-connected. And even from
a cursory survey it is clear that over this era, islands, of various types, were
a significant element in the choice of location for a range of dwellings. It
may well be that our understanding of island settlement over this period
would benefit by having the 'islandscape' being given the same consideration as the 'housescape' that already features as one of the prisms through
which the archaeological evidence from this era is considered (ScARF
2012: 48). The value of an 'islandscape' approach is further underlined by
the first-century AD evidence of Demetrius, the Greek *grammatikos*, as to
Hebridean islands that were homes of the pre-Christian gods, places with
spiritual or numinous qualities, or retreats for learned and holy 'wise men'
and this inherited 'way of seeing' has a particular relevance in the context
of the overlapping Early Christian era.

The Early Christian era

As with the Atlantic Iron Age, discussion of the sixth to eighth centuries
Early Christian era in the Hebrides also benefits from an awareness of
the significant paradigm shifts within the relevant fields of scholarship.
The most important of these is the sharp turn away from an established
historiography firmly underpinned by the notion of a small, independent
'Celtic church', encapsulated then eclipsed by the greater institutional

power of Rome. In reality, as Donald Meek (2000) has neatly summarised, the 'Celtic' saints whose presence was manifest across the islands of Dal Riata and of maritime Pictland were all part of the one universal Catholic church: a European mainstream presented and practised through a Gaelic and Pictish prism. At the same time, in relation to the turn of the century popular interest in notions of 'Celtic spirituality' and 'Celtic nature', Meek also expressed the general concern within Celtic and early medieval studies that the early Christian era was best understood through the beliefs of the era rather than the imposed constructs of the present (Meek 2014).

The other pertinent and more recent shift concerns what Fraser has termed: 'The revolution that has transformed early Insular history' (2009: 1). While this relates to the whole of Scotland, it is a 'revolution' that has particular significance in relation to the Hebrides. In essence it means that the context in which events such as the Christianisation of the Hebrides are understood and interpreted is no longer based on the traditional 'gaelocentric conceptions of this phase of Scotland's past' (Fraser 2009: 10). Instead a wider framework is put forward, one that is based on 'the emergence of a poly-ethnic and multicultural kingdom of the Picts' (2009: xi). For the interpretation of the early history of maritime Pictland, not least in relation to early monastic settlements in the islands and seaboard north of Ardnamurchan, it represents a major shift in context and approach (Fraser 2009: 94–115).

Early monastic settlements

When, in the sixth century, Christianity first presented itself in the Hebrides it did so in a particular form within Catholic Europe's own history and practice. Monasticism was a practice whose roots and route can be traced back through Ireland and Gaul to the Mediterranean and the vast deserts between the Nile and the Red Sea and the early Desert Fathers of Egypt (such as Anthony and Pachomius). As introduced to the Hebrides it was a combination and adaptation of the *cenobitic* (community) monasticism represented by Pachomius, and the *eremitic* (solitary) as exemplified by Anthony (Chitty 1966; Lawrence 2015). While firmly located within the doctrinal 'mainstream' of Western Latin rite Christendom, in effect it was the desert monasticism of the East that would develop through the Hebridean and essentially Gaelic prism of the West.

The role of the monastic foundations and in particular that of Iona, in maintaining the ecclesiastical and secular chronicles of the era has ensured that events within the Hebrides and the wider world were invariably presented in a predominantly monastic context. Over the sixth to eighth centuries, a dimly discernible but no less important diocesan and parochial structure also came into being, providing pastoral care to an increasingly Christianised island lay population. At the same time, the powerful kinship connections of Columba and several of his followers and abbatial successors, ensured that Iona soon emerged as the most pre-eminent of the early foundations, even although, as an island monastic settlement, Columba's Iona was neither first nor alone. Brendan of Clonfert established foundation on both Eileach na Naoimh (Garvellachs) and Tiree; Comgall of Bangor did likewise on Tiree while his pupil, Moluag, established a community further south on Lismore (Smyth 1984; Sharpe 1995). Whether due to its fertility, its location, or both, Tiree was unique in hosting a multiplicity of settlements. As well as the foundations of Brendan and Comgall, there was also 'Mag Luinge, founded by Columba as a daughter house of Iona. Adomnán, in his *Life* of the latter, also refers to the 'other monasteries of Tiree', but sadly further details have not survived (Sharpe 1995). Eigg was the site of a further monastic settlement although the annals detail its abrupt end on 17 April 617 with 'an attack and the killing of Donnán of Eigg with 150 martyrs' (Smyth 1984: 107–108). Eigg is seen as important for it was soon re-established and it has been suggested that the spread of subsequent dedications suggests that the cult of the martyred Donnan played an important part in the subsequent spread of Christianity into northern and maritime Pictland. This included the establishing of a community in Applecross by Maolrubha in 673 which has been described as part of the first real breakthrough of a Christian presence into maritime Pictland (Smyth 1984: 109–112).

The mapping out of the extent of this early monastic presence across the islands is most usefully traced through the meticulous field survey of simple incised crosses on the smallest and most insignificant of stones and other stone sculpture across a wide range of sites by Fisher (2001). The crosses had a crucial purpose and potency not least in their many small island locations. Found across a wide network of 'archipelago monasteries' the 'extreme simplicity' in which the symbol of the cross was displayed was a singularly apt testimony to the austere asceticism of the life of self-denial and exile chosen by those whose island monastic practice they both marked and defended. As Fisher (2001:1) observes this sense of the incised cross slab 'consciously protecting Christendom against the dark forces of the ocean' is a powerful feeling imbricated on the islandscape of every setting in which they appear, from Sanda to North Rona, Lismore to St Kilda. On some there is no more than a place name, or a ruined cell(s) with associated oral tradition while a few have more substantial remains, such as those of an early chapel, often with an attached burial ground. In the case of the Shiant Isles (the 'Holy Isles'), for example, it is a combination of such evidence that indicates some form of Early Christian monastic presence on all three of the Shiants island group (Foster 2001, 2004).

It would appear that the monastic life practised in the Hebrides followed that as developed in southern Gaul by John Cassian of Marseilles and Martin of Tours: a daily schedule of communal prayer, communal work, private study, private contemplation and the eremitic practice of retreat, solitude, ascetic self-denial and penance. The location for the latter could be on the same island but at a distance from the defined monastic policies, or in a separate daughter house on another island, under the guidance of an appointed prior (Clancy and Márkus 1995). Iona, for example, had a series of outlying penitential outposts on other islands, the most important being Mag Luinge on Tiree and the enigmatic *Hinba*. The identification of *Hinba* remains a subject of ongoing debate, with Jura, Colonsay and Canna being the most prominent contenders (MacQuarrie 1997: 91–102).

The monastic and eremitic 'way of seeing'

The spread and nature of these early monastic settlements suggests that the relocation of the practices and precepts of the desert to a Hebridean

setting was distinctive and imaginative (Dumville 2002). In their presentation of the poetic output of Iona and the Columban *familia*, Clancy
and Márkus (1995) have ably revealed the emotional intensity of the
monastic and eremitic life as a felt experience. Their outline of the intellectual milieu of Iona also underlines the achievement of Hebridean
monasticism in transforming the 'way of seeing' the natural and cultural
environment of the population at large (Clancy and Márkus 1995). For
those within these monastic communities there a prism through which
not just the islandscape of Iona and its associated islands could be viewed
but also the wider world. Márkus (1999) has observed how the stories told
in Adomnán's *Life of Columba*, reveal how 'a kind of mental map' was developed through which the lands and islands north and south of Iona were
seen. Dal Riata, the territory of Columba's own Christian people, was a
social space of amicable cultural and personal relationships. Pictland, and
maritime Pictland to the north, however, was replete with tales of danger,
hostility and the exercise of power while Iona itself was 'a little paradise,
a centre of harmony in a world of conflict' where the stories were all of
peace and a marked absence of conflict (Márkus 1999: 116–119).

Surveying Iona's archaeological remains, Macdonald has illustrated
how the members of the community viewed their own particular monastic
islandscape, one defined by a triple frame of boundaries: that of the shoreline defining the island, the *vallum* marking the community enclosure and
the inner *sancta sanctorum* of the chapel, the house of devotion and prayer
(1997: 29–30). The island and the monastery effectively seen as one and
the same, a sacred island: an 'earthly (here monastic) paradise restored as
a foreshadowing of the earthly paradise and realisable as long as the community perseveres in the monastic life and in the quest for Christian perfection' (Macdonald 1997: 26).

While self-denial and personal asceticism were integral elements in
the daily life of all the community, for many the path to perfection also
involved an additional element of individual retreat and reflective solitude. It had been an important part of Columba's life, some of his abbatial
successors were actually remembered as both abbot and anchorite, and
several of his followers were specifically noted for their distinctive pursuit
of the eremitic life. One such follower, a seventh-century saint known as

Beccan eremita, or Beccán of Rum, is of particular interest. While of the Iona community, Beccán lived the life of an anchorite on the isle of Rum. He was also a poet and a scholar. In Beccán's surviving praise poems commemorating Columba we gain a unique insight into the eremitic 'way of seeing' Columba's qualities as a seafaring saint in the islandscape of Iona and the Hebrides (Clancy and Márkus 1995: 129–163). Columba is profiled *not just* as a saint and scholar (Meek 2014) but also as a man who fully lived and experienced the elemental world of the seas of the Atlantic west. As Clancy and Márkus (1995: 131) observe Beccán the poet had himself 'the air of a man acquainted with sea journeys' – that is an elemental, emotional and experiential voyaging knowledge – such that when Beccán writes of Columba's voyage of self-exile from his Irish kin and homeland it is vividly presented: as 'a bold man over the sea's ridge'. From Beccán's account, it is as an intrepid island-going seafarer that Columba crosses 'the wave-strewn wild region', 'in scores of curraghs with an army of wretches' (Clancy and Márkus 1995: 147), to finally make landfall on Iona, the island from which the inspirational and powerful monastic community of the Hebrides will duly emerge.

For *Beccán eremita*, however, Columba is not eulogised, honoured and remembered for being a powerful abbot-scholar. In the eye of a committed follower of the ascetic and eremitic life Columba's greatest attribute is considered his commitment to penance and self-denial. And just as Adomnán's writings call to mind the community life of the Pachomian tradition, so Beccán's poetry evokes the life of Anthony and the ascetic call of the desert. It also foregrounds one other defining dimension of Hebridean monasticism – the quests of the voyagers.

The islands of the voyagers: The edge of the Ocean

From the sources they consulted in their libraries, the monastic communities on Iona and elsewhere in the Hebrides, were well aware that the seaways they regularly sailed were very different from those of the Mediterranean. In the Hebrides, of the early medieval mind, they were on the very edge of 'the Ocean', the limitless mass of water that was believed to

have surrounded the whole land mass of the earth, the primeval abyss and
'the very limit of inhabitable reality', the home of Leviathan, the abode
of demons, and Satan and the place where the apocalyptic beast would
arise to bring destruction to mankind at the end of time (O'Loughlin
1997: 12–14).

From its initial roots in the desert, the monastic life had always involved
an endless struggle with the Devil and his demons. For the monks of Iona
these same deadly foes were no less distant on 'the trackless wastes of the
Ocean' than they had been to any of their monastic forebears who had first
answered the earlier call of the desert (O'Loughlin 1997: 13). This was the
final challenge that those who were seen as the 'voyagers' sought out, well
beyond the western horizon, out on the wastes of the Ocean itself. One
such voyager, of the early Iona community of Columba, was Cormac Ua
Liatháin. Very little is known of Cormac beyond what Adomnán relates
in his *Life of Columba* which is important in itself as the first recorded reference to the 'voyaging' practice of the early seafaring saints to find their
ultimate place of retreat, their *terra deserta* out on the western Ocean.
Adomnán notes that three times Cormac set out to find his goal (Sharpe
1995: 118). Undeterred by initial failure, Cormac once more 'set sail over
the boundless ocean with his sails full' and on this occasion Columba
was absent from Iona, passing through the Great Glen and Loch Ness to
visit king Bridei of Pictland. Aware of the latter's authority over maritime
Pictland, Columba advised Bridei that some 'of our people have sailed off
hoping to find a place of retreat somewhere on the trackless sea' (Sharpe
1995: 196). Bridei was therefore asked to instruct the sub-king of Orkney
to give an assurance that no harm would befall them 'if by chance their
long wanderings should bring them to Orkney', which is exactly what hap-
pened. On his third attempt Cormac and his band were driven north and
west of the Outer Isles onto the open waters south of Iceland. For fourteen
summer days and nights, a prevailing and constant southerly wind drove
them north to a point where: 'They reckoned that they had passed beyond
the range of human exploration, and had reached a place from which they
might not be able to return' (Sharpe 1995: 196).

Here they encountered 'a source of terror' as a swarm of 'deadly loath-
some little creatures' covered the sea and proceeded to attack and pierce

the skin of their boat. Fortunately for them, although far away on Iona in person, 'St Columba was there in spirit, in the boat with Cormac' and foreseeing their unendurable danger, he called all the Iona community together to pray for their safe return. Columba's supplication for a favourable north wind was successful and they were returned safely to Iona (Sharpe 1995: 197–198). Despite Cormac's prominence in the Columba story as told by Adomnán and given the far-reaching nature of his voyaging exploits, it is perhaps surprising that there appears to be only one possible dedication to the persistent voyager saint anywhere in the Hebrides, and even that – 'St Cormac's Chapel' on Eilean Mòr – is in the inshore waters of the Sound of Jura, and probably commemorates someone else (Canmore ID 38634; SSPNP).

By the time Adomnán was writing of Cormac, it would appear that, notwithstanding its perilous nature, 'voyaging' was a well-established practice. For the most part those involved were anonymous, although significantly perhaps, three of the prominent named practitioners – Cormac Ua Liatháin, Brendan of Clonfert and Abban Mac hUí Chormaic (the voyager saint most probably commemorated on Eilean Mor) – were all associated by Adomnán with Columba and Iona. The numbers of voyagers involved appear to have been high. Notwithstanding poetic licence, a ninth/tenth-century 'Irish Litany of the Pilgrim Saints' refers to: 'Thrice fifty men of orders … who went on pilgrimage in one company with Abban Mac hUí Chormaic' (Plummer 1925: 61). It also evokes the dangers they faced and the price many paid. It ends with a commemoration of Brendan, those who had gone before him and the many others who did not return: 'All the saints who have perished in the isles of the ocean' (Thrall 2000: 20–21).

The extent of the presence of any of the voyager saints or their followers in the Hebrides is difficult to determine. Primarily it relies on the mapping out of dedications and traditions and in this respect the spread, density and locations are striking. With Abban and Cormac there is one possible commemoration each, on Sanda and Eilean Mor respectively. With Brendan, however, the dedications are unambiguous, extensive and in highly pertinent locations, ranging from Kilbrannan Sound off Arran, to Seil, the Garvellachs and Mull, then on across the Sea of the Hebrides to Barra, South Uist and, most significantly, to the remote outlier of St

Kilda (Barrett 1919: 79–81). Such was the predominance of the practice that it gave rise to a distinct genre of early Gaelic island-going voyager tales known as the *immrama*. Only a handful have survived, including the 'Voyage of Snédgusa and Maic Riagla', two of Columba's *familia* (Stokes 1888; Murray 2000). As tales of Christian allegory, primarily composed to serve a spiritual guidance purpose, the *immrama* are emphatically not to be regarded as historical accounts of actual voyages. They do, however, draw on a range of sources, including pre-Christian Gaelic notions of the 'marvellous otherworld' and the traveller's tales of a seafaring people (Clancy 2000). As Gaelic texts, the *immrama*, inevitably had a confined and limited audience. The tale of 'Brendan the Navigator' was different. Being in Latin, the *Navigatio Sancti Brendani* attracted a remarkable and enduring degree of interest across medieval Europe (Strijbosch 2000). For centuries it was taken to be the record of an actual sixth-century voyage. By the late nineteenth century, this was being presented as the earliest European transatlantic sea-crossing, an interpretation that has been comprehensively rejected by contemporary scholarship. As with the *immrama*, the *Navigatio*, is a work of Christian and monastic allegory (Carney 2000). At the same time, however, it is readily acknowledged that, as with the *immrama*, the compiler of the *Navigatio* would have been well aware of the seafaring exploits of the voyagers of the era. As a result, as Wooding (2000: 227) notes: 'It is likely that some geographical data derived from actual voyages *did* find their way into the setting of the tale'.

For an appreciation of just how much 'geographical data' there was to draw on it is necessary to turn to the work of Dicuil, another of the remarkable monk-scholars from Iona. In the late eighth century, doubtless as a result of the outbreak of violent Norse raids on the Hebrides, Dicuil sought refuge in Europe. He became a resident scholar at the Carolingian palace school in Aachen where, in 825, he wrote a treatise on the geography of the known earth. Referring to the islands lying to the west of Scotland, he stated: 'Among these I have lived in some, and have visited others; some I have only glimpsed, while others I have read about' (Tierney 1967: 75–76). It is a passage that led his modern editor to surmise that Dicuil 'was perhaps born there' (Tierney 1967: 12), that is, in the islands to the west of Scotland.

In his treatise Dicuil also referred to the first-hand accounts he had been given by clerics who had made passages to Orkney, Shetland and beyond. Dicuil gave the earliest recorded account of the Faroes, revealing that eremitic monks had been living there for nearly a hundred years but because of raiding Norsemen, the islands were now 'emptied of anchorites' and filled with only sheep and sea-birds (Tierney 1967: 77). Referring to Pytheas and the island of 'Ultima Thule' (Iceland), he also confirmed a monastic presence, stating unambiguously that it was now thirty years since clerics 'who had lived on the island' had described it to him, including their memorable depiction of the summer solstice: 'There was no darkness in that very small space of time, and a man could do whatever he wished as though the sun were there, even remove lice from his shirt' (Tierney 1967: 75).

Dicuil's work belongs to the eighth- to ninth-century era which has been described as the zenith of Hebridean monasticism's fame and achievement in Europe (Clancy and Márkus 1995: 16–18). In addition to his *Life of St Columba*, Adomnán's account *Of the Holy Places* had given the West its earliest map of Jerusalem (Meehan 1958). His *Law of the Innocents* was one of the earliest international treaties on the conduct of war and the protection of non-combatants (Márkus 1997). As knowledge of his work spread across Europe, Adomnán achieved the honour of a title bestowed on only a select few theological scholars and teachers when he became 'Adomnán the Illustrious' (O'Loughlin 2007: 198). In Iona and across the Hebrides, monastic and secular artists produced illuminated manuscripts, poetry and carved crosses of the highest order. And recent finds from the monastic site on Inchmarnock in the Firth of Clyde provides unique evidence as to the training of novices in literacy and artistic design (Lowe 2008).

Exile monk-scholars from the Hebrides also constituted a small but significant presence amongst the *peregrini Scottii*, the 'wandering Gaels' who formed such a distinct feature in the intellectual life of early medieval Europe. Cú Chuimne of Iona co-authored a comprehensive collection of canon law and early penitential codes that had an impact on church practice for centuries (Kelly 1995; Flechner 2019). Iona-trained Virgil, bishop of Salzburg, 'Apostle of Carinthia' and a scholar ahead of his time, played a key role in the introducing of anointment to the induction of Carolingian kings, a pivotal moment in the history of Europe (Enright 1985; Carney

2000). Adomnán had concluded his *Life* of Columba by noting how won-
drous it was that the reputation of Columba, 'one who dwelt in this little
island on the edge of the ocean' should have spread out across Europe,
reaching even Rome itself, 'the chief of all cities'(Sharpe 1995: 233). By the
early ninth century, the names of the departed abbots of Iona were remembered in the regular prayers for the dead in Salzburg and the martyrs of
Iona at the hands of the Norsemen were being commemorated in verse at
Reichenau in the heart of Europe (Carney 1964; Carey 2000).

An interim conclusion

Even a brief survey of this early period of recorded Hebridean history,
limited in scope and necessarily confined in depth, particularly one in
which an experiential perspective is deployed, teases out a range of contexts in which the tenuous notion of islandness emerges to contribute to
the everyday practice of island life, island-going and island identity. Some
are superceded and discarded but others evolved and were transformed
as they passed through the subsequent eras of Hebridean history. They
remain discernible strands in the layered palimpsest of residual culture
that is our own twenty-first-century inheritance and experience.

The most visible, thanks to judicious, informed archaeological enquiry, is the evident pattern of settlement, dwelling forms and monumental
structures related in some specific way to their island environment. They
evoke a clear sense of spatial knowledge in both domestic living and in the
collective exercise of power and authority within and across individual or
combined groups of islands and the wider seaways. The patterns suggest a
pragmatic and applied functional sense of islandness reflecting a stability
in social relations combined with the capability for collective defensive
or aggressive military capacity as deemed necessary. Another aspect of
this are the clear signs of a sense of intimacy and identification with local
place, reflective of an attachment to a familiar environment and a sense
of home in relation to both locality and individual dwelling. In a specific
island way, graphically illustrated by the island dun household on an

inshore island lochan of the pre-Christian period, or the solitary monk's individual anchoritic retreat in the Christian era, such material legacies underline that every 'real' island should be seen as 'a place of singular distinctiveness and identity' (Hay 2006), one imbued with a particular felt experience of 'islandness'.

A noted feature of the Early Christian era was the extent to which the sacral attributes of pre-Christian places, notably 'holy isles' or sacred locations on an island were not suppressed but transformed into Christianised sacred places. The sense of numinosity attached to individual islands was something that endured and was sustained across the cultural transition from one era to another. Accumulated layers of local secular knowledge as to island space were also retained and transmitted. In relation to the navigation of inter-island seaways and seafaring passages – an inherited experience – it has been suggested, was consciously drawn on in the Christian monastic era to inform and create a mental islandscape of 'spiritually memorized topographies' (Widell 2018). Even within its own time, practices and qualities associated with islandness of the Early Christian era were exported across space and time. Evidence from the excavation of a major Pictish monastic site far removed from Iona reveals how 'islandness' was an elastic and transferable concept. At Portmahomack, the layout of Columba's Hebridean foundation was effectively drawn on to delineate the boundaries of an 'island' monastic community not on an insular site but on the Tarbat peninsula of Easter Ross (Carver 2008, 2009).

What is perhaps most striking is the extent to which certain imputed attributes of 'islandness', vigorously promoted as part of the twenty-first century 'island experience', can be traced back to having roots in the late Iron Age/Early Christian period. This was the era in which monk-scholars made the first collections of Gaelic mythology with its location of the 'immortal isles; of the Otherworld in the Atlantic west; where Greek scholars also located the idyllic 'Isles of the Blest' of their own mythology. It is the era in which the roots of key tropes of commodified islandness, specifically Western Isles islandness are to be found. It was from this era that the notion of the Hebrides as distant places, remote island locations of timelessness entered the Western imagination. The eremitic practice of Hebridean monasticism confirmed islands as special places for solitary retreat and personal reflection; the association of the islands of the West with Idyllic utopias, lands of eternal youth, comfort and well-being took root.

This is the point at which the actuality of the 'real' island experience of island life comes up against the recreated constructs of an imagined islandness. For complex reasons of power, culture, politics and subalternity, it has been a mutated misrepresentation of aspects of island culture and practice that is still actively perpetuated rather than a promotion of cultural, social and intellectual achievement. The contribution of Hebridean monk-scholars to the intellectual and spiritual life of Carolingian Europe has been touched on. What space precludes is an addition of the extraordinary achievements of the subsequent era of a Norse Christian presence, one that led to a Norse and Gaelic presence across the North Atlantic, from the Faroes and Iceland to Greenland and 'Vinland' (Newfoundland). Taken alone or together, these contributions to the history of both Europe and the North Atlantic only serve to underline that, to borrow the seventh-century words of Adomnán: even the littlest of little islands on the outer Ocean, at the edge of the known world can have an enduring national and transnational significance.

Bibliography

Armit, I. (ed.) (1990). *Beyond the Brochs: Changing Perspectives on the Atlantic Scottish Iron Age*. Edinburgh: Edinburgh University Press.

Armit, I. (1996). *The Archaeology of Skye and the Western Isles*. Edinburgh: Edinburgh University Press.

Ashmore, W., and Knapp, A. B. (1999). *Archaeologies of Landscape, Contemporary Perspectives*. Oxford: Blackwell.

Ballin Smith, B., and Banks, I. (eds) (2002). *In the Shadow of the Brochs: The Iron Age in Scotland*. Stroud: Tempus.

Barrett, M. (1919). *A Calendar of Scottish Saints*. Fort Augustus: The Abbey Press.

Branigan, K. (2000a). 'The Later Prehistory of Barra and Vatersay'. In Branigan, K., and Foster, P. (eds), *From Barra to Berneray. Archaeological Survey and Excavation in the Southern Isles of the Outer Hebrides*, pp. 334-345. Sheffield: Sheffield Academic Press.

Branigan, K. (2000b). 'Barra and its Islands in the Prehistory of Northern Britain'. In Branigan, K., and Foster, P. (eds), *From Barra to Berneray. Archaeological Survey and Excavation in the Southern Isles of the Outer Hebrides*, pp. 346-354. Sheffield: Sheffield Academic Press.

Branigan, K., and Foster, P. (eds) (2000). *From Barra to Berneray. Archaeological Survey and Excavation in the Southern Isles of the Outer Hebrides*. Sheffield: Sheffield Academic Press.

Breeze, D. J. (2002). 'The Ancient Geography of Scotland'. In Ballin Smith, B., and I. Banks (eds), *In the Shadow of the Brochs: The Iron Age in Scotland*, pp. 11–13. Stroud: Tempus.

Burn, A. R. (1969). 'Holy men on islands in pre-Christian Britain', *Glasgow Archaeological Journal*, 1 (1), 2–6.

Canmore ID 10439. 'North Uist, Groatay, Dun Mhic Laitheann', <http://canmore.org.uk/site/10439> accessed 12 March 2020.

Canmore ID Mor 38634. 'Eilean Mor, St Cormac's Chapel and Burial-ground', <http://canmore.org.uk/site/38634> accessed 12 March 2020.

Carey, J. (2000). 'Ireland and the Antipodes: The Heterodoxy of Virgil of Salzburg'. In Wooding, J. M., (ed.), *The Otherworld Voyage in Early Irish Literature*, pp. 133–142. Dublin: Four Courts Press.

Carney J. (1964). *The Poems of Blathmac son of Cú Brettan*. Irish Text Society, Vol. 47. Dublin: Irish Text Society.

Carney, J. (2000). 'Review of *Navigatio sancti Brendani*'. In Wooding, J. M., (ed.), *The Otherworld Voyage in Early Irish Literature*, pp. 42–51. Dublin: Four Courts Press.

Carver, M. (2008). *Portmahomack, Monastery of the Picts*. Edinburgh: Edinburgh University Press.

Carver, M. (2009). 'Early Scottish monasteries and prehistory: a preliminary dialogue', *Scottish Historical Review*, 88 (226), 332–351.

Chitty, D. J. (1966). *The Desert a City: An Introduction to the Study of Egyptian and Palestinian Monasticism under the Christian Empire*. Oxford: Blackwell.

Clancy, T. O. (2000). 'Subversion at Sea: Structure, Style and Intent in the *Immrama*'. In Wooding, J. M., (ed.), *The Otherworld Voyage in Early Irish Literature*, pp. 194–225. Dublin: Four Courts Press.

Clancy, T. O., and Márkus, G. (1995). *Iona, The Earliest Poetry of a Celtic Monastery*. Edinburgh: Edinburgh University Press.

Cunliffe, B. (2001). *The Extraordinary Voyage of Pytheas the Greek*. London: Allan Lane.

Dumville, D. (2002). 'The North Atlantic Thallasocracy: Sailing to the Desert in early medieval Insular Spirituality'. In Crawford B. E., (ed.), *The Papar in the*

North Atlantic: Environment and History, St John's House Papers, No. 10. St Andrews: The Committee for Dark Age Studies, University of St Andrews.

Enright, M. J. (1985). *Iona, Tara and Soissons. The Origin of the Royal Anointing Ritual.* (Arbeiten zur Fruhmittelalterforschung, 17). Berlin/New York: Walter de Gruyter.

Fisher, I. (2001). *Early Medieval Sculpture in the West Highlands and Islands.* Edinburgh: Society of Antiquaries of Scotland.

Flechner, R. (2019). *The Hibernensis: (Studies in Medieval and Early Modern Canon Law)*, Vol. 1. A Study and Edition; Vol. 2. Translation, Commentary, and Indexes. Washington, D C: The Catholic University of America Press.

Foster, P. (2001). 'Shiant Islands Project (SHIP), Western Isles (Lochs parish)', *Discovery and Excavation in Scotland*, 2, 102.

Foster, P. (2004). 'The Shiants Project (SHIP) (Lochs parish), excavation; survey', *Discovery and Excavation in Scotland*, 5, 136–137.

Fraser, J. E. (2009). *From Caledonia to Pictland, Scotland to 795.* Edinburgh: Edinburgh University Press.

Harding, D. (1997). 'Forts, duns, brochs, crannogs: Iron Age Settlements in Argyll'. In Ritchie, J. N. G., (ed.), *The Archaeology of Argyll*, pp. 118–140. Edinburgh: Edinburgh University Press.

Harding, D. W. (2000). *The Hebridean Iron Age: Twenty Years' Research.* Edinburgh: Edinburgh University Department of Archaeology. <https://www.scottish heritagehub.com/content/1_1> accessed 15 January 2020.

Harvey, D. (1996). *Justice, Nature and the Geography of Difference.* Oxford: Blackwell.

Hay, P. (2006). 'A phenomenology of islands', *Island Studies Journal*, 1 (1), 19–42. <https://www.islandstudies.ca/sites/vre2.upei.ca.islandstudies/files/u2/ISJ-1-1-2006-Hay-pp19-42.pdf> accessed 12 March 2020.

Hay, P. (2013). 'What the sea portends: a reconsideration of contested island tropes', *Islands Studies Journal*, 8 (2), 209–232. <https://www.islandstudies.ca/sites/islandstudies.ca/files/ISJ-8-2-2013-Hay.pdf> accessed 12 March 2020.

Kelly, H. (1995). *The Irish Penitentials.* Dublin: Four Courts Press.

Lawrence, C. H. (2015). *Medieval Monasticism: Forms of Religious Life in Western Europe in the Middle Ages (The Medieval World).* London: Routledge.

Lowe, C. (2008). *Inchmarnock: An Early Historic Island Monastery and Its Archaeological Landscape.* Edinburgh: Society of Antiquaries of Scotland.

MacDonald, A. (1997). Adomnán's Monastery of Iona'. In Bourke, C., (ed.), *Studies in the Cult of Saint Columba*, pp. 24–44. Dublin: Four Courts Press.

MacKie, E. W. (2007). *The Roundhouses, Brochs and Wheelhouses of Atlantic Scotland c. 700 BC–AD 500: Architecture and Material Culture. Part 2: The Mainland and the Western Islands.* Oxford: Archaeological Reports British Series.

Macquarrie, A. (1997). *The Saints of Scotland, Essays in Scottish Church History*, AD *450–1093*. Edinburgh: John Donald.

Márkus, G. (ed. & trans.) (1997). *Adomnán's 'Law of the Innocents': Cáin Adomnáin: A Seventh Century Law for the Protection of Non-combatants*. Kilmartin: Kilmartin House Trust.

Meehan, D. (ed. & trans.) (1958). *Adomnán's De Locis Sanctis (Scriptores Latini Hiberniae 3)*. Dublin: Institute for Advance Studies.

Meek, D. E. (2000). *Quest for Celtic Christianity*. Boat of Garten: Handsel Press.

Meek, D. E. (2014). ' "Celtic Christianity" and St Columba', in *Passages from Tiree*. <https://meekwrite.blogspot.com/2014/01/celtic-christianity-and-st-columba.html> accessed 12 March 2020.

Murphy, G. (1961). *Saga and Myth in Ancient Ireland, Irish Life and Culture*. Cork: Mercier Press.

Murray, K. (2000). 'The Role of the *Cuilebad* in *Immram Snédgusa 7 Maic Riagla*'. In Wooding, J. M., (ed.), *The Otherworld Voyage in Early Irish Literature*, pp. 187–193. Dublin: Four Courts Press.

Nieke, M. (1990). 'Fortifications in Argyll: Retrospect and Future Prospect'. In Armit, I. (ed.), *Beyond the Brochs: Changing Perspectives on the Atlantic Scottish Iron Age*, pp. 131–142. Edinburgh: Edinburgh University Press.

O'Loughlin, T. (1997). 'Living in the Ocean'. In Bourke, C., (ed.), *Studies in the Cult of Columba*, pp. 11–23. Dublin: Four Courts Press.

O'Loughlin, T. (2007). *Adomnán and the Holy Places: The Perceptions of an Insular Monk on the Locations of the Biblical Drama*. London: Bloomsbury.

Parker-Pearson, M. Sharples, N., and Symonds, J. (2004). *South Uist, Archaeology and History of as Hebridean Island*. Stroud: Tempus.

Plummer, C. (ed. & trans.) (1925). *Irish Litanies*. London: Henry Bradshaw Society.

Rennell, R. (2010) 'Islands, Islets, experience and identity in the Outer Hebridean Iron Age', *Shima*, 4 (1), 47–64.

ScARF (2012). Hunter, F. and Carruthers, M. (eds). *Iron Age Scotland: ScARF Panel Report*. Scottish Archaeological Research Framework: Society of Antiquaries of Scotland. <http ://www.scottishheritagehub.com/sites/default/files/u13/ScARF%20Iron%20Age%20June%202012.pdf> accessed 12 March 2020.

SSPNP (n.d.) *Saints in Scottish Place-Names: Abbán maccu Cormaic on Eilean Mòr (maccu Cormaic)*, South Knapdale, <https://saintsplaces.gla.ac.uk/saint.php?id=4> accessed 28 March 2020.

Sharpe, R. (ed. & trans.) (1995). *Adomnán of Iona: Life of St Columba*. Harmondsworth: Penguin.

Smyth, A. P. (1984). *Warlords and Holy Men, Scotland* AD *80–1000*. Edinburgh: Edinburgh University Press.

Stokes, W., (ed. & trans.) (1888). 'The voyage of Snedgus and MacRiagla', *Revue Celtique*, 9, 14–25.

Strijbosch, C. (2000). *The Seafaring Saint, Sources and Analogues of the Twelfth Century Voyage of St. Brendan*. Dublin: Four Courts Press.

Tierney, J. J. (ed. & trans.) (1967). *Dicuili Liber De Mensura Orbis Terrae*. Dublin: Institute for Advanced Studies.

Thrall, W. F. (2000). 'Clerical sea pilgrimages and the *Immrama*'. In Wooding, J. M., (ed.), *The Otherworld Voyage in Early Irish Literature*, pp. 15–21. Dublin: Four Courts Press.

Wickham-Jones, C. R. (1994). *Scotland's First Settlers*. Edinburgh: Historic Scotland.

Widell, B. (2018). 'The monastic lifeworld: memories and narratives of landscapes of early medieval monasticism in Argyll, Scotland', *Landscapes*, 18 (1), 4–18.

Woolf, A. (2007), *From Pictland to Alba 789–1070*. Edinburgh: Edinburgh University Press

Wooding, J. M. (2000). 'Monastic Voyaging and the *Navigatio*'. In Wooding, J. M., (ed.), *The Otherworld Voyage in Early Irish Literature*, pp. 226–245. Dublin: Four Court Press.

3. Cha ghabhadh na b' fheàrr fhaighinn ('It couldn't be better'). Gaelic Perspectives on Island Cultural Heritage in Scotland's Hebrides

Island life offers opportunities and challenges which many have embraced in recent years. The urge to move or retire to Scotland's islands comes on strongly on occasions and must be part-responsible for a steadying of Hebridean population decline or even its reversal demonstrated in recent censuses; the districts of Skye and Lochalsh, for example, have turned the corner of continuous decline since the late nineteenth century and the population of Skye is now over 10,000. Living 'on the edge', it might be said, needs special gifts of resilience and inner strength which may not be *a priori* part of the expectations of the outside world or of the impression of 'islandness'. In circumstances where the individual is not a Hebridean by birth and might not have lived the island life over an extended period, it should be said that a need for special gifts is uppermost in the face of winter darkness and protracted seasonal North Atlantic weather patterns.

The exploration of islands is of compelling interest. A modern scholarly trend serves this well; and the assembling of a 'cultural biography' of an island may perhaps be slightly more compelling than the scrutiny of a mainland site, parish or 'estate' (e.g. Macdonald 1976; Storrie 1981; Burnett 1986; Caldwell 2018). Even where this is questioned in the promotion of an identity or 'character' of an island whose cultural landscape or cultural biography is being explored, description or scrutiny may fail to penetrate the human ecology to any significant depth or get 'under the skin'. Whatever treatment is adopted however, it tends to a more monolithic understanding of 'islandness'. This short study aims to open up the subject with a necessarily limited selection of points which are intended

to challenge the expectations of an outside world. A Hebridean colloqui-
alism as title, translating literally as 'a better couldn't be got', is adopted to
symbolise this approach (see NicNèill 2000: 360). The study looks briefly
at aspects of the culture and history of the Western Isles in order to offer
substantive insights into their cultural heritage against a background of
assumed stereotypes and expectations. Care is taken to respect the integrity of this heritage by leading with *sealladh a' Ghàidheil* or a Gaelic view
in exploring concepts such as identity. This offers a premise to counter-
balance or confront stereotypes or expectations that are nursed in the
outside world. The ways in which Hebrideans occupy and comprehend
their world within a world disinclines them to challenge the world outside islands. The following observations and descriptions might explain
why this is the case.

The annals of islands: A Scottish Hebridean context

Mention of islands in a Scottish context often summons up exceptional
examples; St Kilda beyond the Outer Hebrides is an intriguing subject
and offers an extreme example for the annals of islands. The 'ecology' of St
Kilda continues to offer a rich field of research for scientists and, *mutatis
mutandis*, keeps the island archipelago in the public eye. If, in the wider
literature, St Kilda is taken to represent Scottish 'islandness' – and it is
abundantly recorded for us by the outside world – we might respond that,
for a complex of reasons, this was a community, an economy and a culture that 'failed', the islanders having appealed to the Scottish Office for
their evacuation in 1930. Many other Hebridean islands, once inhabited,
are now deserted although 'failure' barely explains the process of abandonment. In many cases islands were populated or re-populated in recent
times under pressure of resources or clearance (Murchison 1959: 283–344;
Duncan 1995; Buxton 2016). The extent to which island sites are traded
in media terms suggests that failure or survival are not the first points
of interest. 'Castaway', one of the first reality television programmes, followed the fortunes of individuals spending the year 2000 on Taransay.

The views of 'real' islanders were rarely sought on this charade although the justifiably weary cynicism of Hebrideans in the face of 'Castaway' is well known. Island studies in the past (and into our own day) have too often played to stereotypes whereby the expectations of the outside world were more readily fulfilled, such is the impression of 'islandness' on the popular, cosmopolitan and 'continental' mind.

Language and dialect: Island cultural identity

The phrase 'cultural heritage' is widely used and readily traded. In the background is an understanding that the cultural heritage of the Western Isles is somehow different from that of Scotland as a whole and, for ease of definition, may draw its essence from the Gaelic language and an acceptance of a distinctive cultural identity that is deep-rooted. It is a given that Scottish Gaelic has suffered language attrition under the weight of English and it is a commonplace that English has come to dominate. Scottish Gaelic has moved in the Highlands and Islands from being a majority to a minority language and bilingualism has gone against the minority. Gaelic may be considered as 'old-fashioned' or thought of as a conservative language and, therefore, it is inferred that linguistically Gaelic may not have the resources to deal with ease and precision with certain subjects, for example, technological ones. A perceived conservatism (or 'failure to adapt') may have been coloured by the decline of high-register Gaelic and its literary language, and the view of Gaels themselves. It has been said that Gaelic suffices in its native context: 'Tha a' Ghàidhlig math gu leòr na h-àite fhèin – 's e sin ri ràdh, air latha fainge, no air a' chroit, no aig an iasgac' ('Gaelic is okay in its own proper place – that's to say, on a gathering day, on the croft or at the fishing').

This is a problem of linguistic attainment and diversity for a language that has been weakening in the face of an adjacent linguistic dominance. It has given rise to a field of scholarship in the sociology of language and an ideology of language planning under the leadership of Professor Joshua Fishman (1926–2015). With his interest in language contact and identity, Fishman devised programmes of intervention to soften the effects of

acculturation and assimilation by 'reversing language shift'. There is now
another side to the coin in so far as Gaelic-medium education is much
better established and our younger generations are competent and eager
to initiate and sustain conversations in the language. If you choose regularly to tune into *Radio nan Gàidheal*, you will be aware of a convincingly
complete and far-reaching Gaelic cultural environment – dialects and all.
This national radio station pursues the art of communication in proactive
fashion and rapidly disposes of suggestions that Scottish Gaelic may not
have a lexis to deal with, for example, modern and electronic technology.
Gaelic, in common with other minority languages, offers a language for
the digital age.

    Island identities take strength and character from their dialects and
Gaelic speakers are keenly aware of dialect differences at local and wider
levels. Scottish Gaelic dialect studies evolved in greater depth when the
'Linguistic Survey of Scotland' began collecting dialect material in the
1950s (Ó Dochartaigh 1997). Initiatives in dialect research had come from
Scandinavia, most notably in the study of Hebridean dialects (Borgstrøm
1937: 71–242; Borgstrøm 1940) and a study of the Gaelic of Lewis (Oftedal
1956). Research was then concentrated on phonology but has now broad-
ened out to consider and collect idiom and terminology. The concepts of
'material culture' and 'Regional Ethnology' have usefully informed this as
demonstrated by the current *Faclair na Gàidhlig* project; in this respect the
dialects of the Outer Hebrides and Skye and dialects of the Inner Hebrides
(as well as the mainland) display distinctive features of lexis (MacAskill
1963: 64–88; Cheape 2017: 16–20). Both dialects and material culture vary
in proportion and remind us that islands and groupings of islands such
as 'The Outer Hebrides' are far from homogeneous, most obviously with
different land structures but more subtly with different regimes of ownership and religious affiliations (see Meek 2000: 28–47).

    In spite of the decline in the number of speakers by the 1950s, Gaelic
was still a community language in the Hebrides and parts of the Mainland,
and sustained also by emigrant communities in cities such as Glasgow
and overseas in Nova Scotia. Perversely, the serious contraction of the
Gàidhealtachd or Gaelic-speaking areas of Scotland in the twentieth century has given greater prominence to the dialects of the Hebrides. These

are the voices, for example, heard in broadcasting. The Gaelic of Skye and the Outer Hebrides, therefore, has come to dominate in language use and has become a sort of standard dialect. Within this, the phonology and intonation in the Gaelic of Lewis is distinctive. While this is immediately recognised among most Gaelic speakers, they will cite individual items of vocabulary to describe the distinctive features of dialect. Distinctions in core vocabulary will be mentioned such as *bùrn* in Lewis and *uisge* in islands to the south for 'fresh water'. Dialects further to the south such as Tiree and Islay do not necessarily draw strength from this situation and their Gaelic may be regarded as 'peripheral' and somehow not meeting standards. Running counter to this is the recognition of differences and a need to sustain them, and a burgeoning pride building on this as a feature of a 'Gaelic revival'. Other distinctive features of dialect reside in tasks and tools, especially in an age before mechanisation while seasonal work was still a communal effort. Words and expressions illustrating every aspect of island life in Eriskay and South Uist were collected by Rev Fr Allan McDonald (1859–1905); the collection demonstrates the visual, concrete and epigrammatic speech of nineteenth-century Hebrideans speaking of their work, customs, strong religious sense and keen observation of animals and plants around them (Campbell 1958: 3; see also MacDonald 1936: 1–54).

If we move closer to our sources, and also draw on a different range of sources as typified by a cross-disciplinary 'Regional Ethnology', a more nuanced and deeper-seated understanding of the cultural heritage of islands can be demonstrated (see Fenton 1985: 43–54). In terms of the material culture (on which Regional Ethnology is predicated), most details emerging from research into locality challenge stereotypes. At a simple level, accounts of the Highlands and Islands will offer us a standard historical or sub-recent model of a population living in thatched houses of dry-stone construction, cultivating the ground with a *cas-chrom* and burning peat for fuel; as we move round the region these features can too often be challenged. There is evidence too that what might be perceived as hopelessly out-dated element of material culture in the *cas-chrom* earned plaudits as a 'modern' and relatively efficient tool (see below). Whether based on accounts of land-based economies or on the sea and fisheries, further dimensions can be added to the material culture through language, dialect and literature.

Even where these are rooted in Scottish Gaelic, it is evident that a different kind of stereotype is addressed that fulfils more of a 'Gaelic world view'.

Regional ethnology

The Outer Hebrides are an island chain stretching over 130 miles from the Butt of Lewis to Barra Head, with some 119 islands named and used for agricultural purposes though only sixteen are now permanently inhabited. The Inner Hebrides form a second island chain stretching about 153 miles from the north end of Skye south to the Mull of Oa in Islay. The population totals 46,632, distributed between the more highly populated islands of Skye, Mull and Islay, small towns such as Tobermory and Portree, and with a population of 8,100 in the town of Stornoway. Characteristically the population of the Hebrides lives in 'townships' or crofting settlements, generally positioned near the sea. The course of the nineteenth and twentieth centuries saw an 'abandonment' of the islands, perceived by many as lacking the essential services of a modern industrial economy and a welfare state. The nineteenth century itself so changed the face of the Hebrides, following the notorious era of the 'Highland Clearances' approximately between 1780 and 1880, that what went before is now hard to conceive – or to describe in a short chapter. An optimistic view would hold that we have relatively self-sufficient Hebridean agricultural economies today, a culture of self-employment, public sector employment, tourism and a well-worn tradition of working away. The statutory agricultural smallholdings created in the seven crofting counties are frequently questioned as to their viability and future, a by-product of the influence of growing administrative intervention regulating nature and environment.

In terms of 'islandness', the Hebrides seem to reach into a legendary past – a 'golden age' in our imagination. Grounding a 'golden age' in some sort of reality, our imagination may be fired by Martin Martin and his *Description of the Western Isles* of 1703 and his *Late Voyage to St Kilda* of 1698 (published in a single volume in MacLeod 1934). These were the beginnings of an historical record in the conventional and extended sense. 'Origins', often fallaciously conceived, continue to entice. There is a wealth of prehistoric remains and an extraordinary record of human occupation in the Hebrides, opening with a 'crannog' site on Loch Olabhat in North Uist constructed around 3,200 BCE. Among many prehistoric monuments, the most celebrated are the Stones of Callanish [*Calanais*] above Loch Roag on the west coast of Lewis and a complex archaeological landscape of standing stones, stone circles and stone alignments; modern scholarship has assigned a construction date of around 2,900 BCE and construction in several phases and uses until about 1,500 BC (Ritchie 1991: 185). It is an intriguing thought that this duration can be compared approximately with the veneration of Iona as a Christian site since its consecration by Calum Chille (HES Calanais Standing Stones). Less prominent but nonetheless significant are a scatter of sites identified with Mesolithic hunter-fishermen, their fireplaces and stone artefacts, offering a datum of c. 7,500 BCE. In generalised terms the hunting culture of the Mesolithic was succeeded by the farming culture of the Neolithic, probably occupying some of the same sites and districts, mixing farming with hunting and fishing and moving settlement more or less frequently in search of fresh stocks of wildlife, soil and pasture. The identity of these people, forbye their material culture and landscape, is beyond our reach and so Gaelic offers no insights apart from folk tales and legends about 'aboriginal' peoples or *tùsanaich*.

Closer to and opening up a sense of identity and contributing elements of a community memory, place-names and island names in the Hebrides have mixed Gaelic and Norse origins. The Hebrides were part of the Norse kingdoms for over 400 years until sovereignty was transferred to Scotland in 1266 under the terms of the Treaty of Perth. Beginning with waves of looting and settlement at the end of the eighth century, the Norse pioneers were generally vassals of the kings of Norway. A new factor recorded in Gaelic sources was a grouping referred to as *Gall-Ghàidheil* (literally 'foreigner-Gaels'), we assume a people of mixed Norse and Gaelic ancestry in Scotland and Ireland. The very extended northern commonwealth of islands between Norway and Iceland, with sub-kingdoms such as the Kingdom of Man and the Isles, favoured the emergence of local leaders such as Somerled, *Somhairle Mac Ghille Brighde*, in the twelfth century, exploiting a power vacuum left by the shrinking of Norse power. The Gaelic kingdom of the 'Lordship of the Isles' predominated in the fourteenth and fifteenth centuries under the leadership of Clan Donald who traced their descent from Somerled. A Gaelic status quo came under severe pressure and attack from a growing state under the Stewart dynasty and a feudal structure was imposed on the Highlands and Islands at the turn of the sixteenth century. The kings of Scots made expropriation into an art form and, with promises of rewards, set the leading families and kindreds against each other. Tensions and internecine warfare ensued, building towards stock definitions of Highlanders and Hebrideans as being unruly and barbarous. These coloured the literature and have contributed to stereotypes of clan history which were further defined in the eighteenth and nineteenth centuries and in the rosy glow of Romanticism.

The historian draws on the Archdeacon of the Isles, Donald Monro's description of the islands of about 1549, the accounts of travellers in the eighteenth and nineteenth centuries, and details in the *Statistical Account* of 1791–1799 and *New Statistical Account* of 1845 (Munro 1961). With the notable exception of many of the authors of the 'Statistical Accounts', the Hebrides are rarely described by any writer who was a native of them. Available to modern readership and scholarship, a great body of knowledge and statistical data dwarfs the literature of preceding generations but still often lacks the virtue of first-hand account. Early examples are rare but a 'Description of the Lewis' of about 1683 by an 'Indweller' is a happy exception. The tacksman of Bragar, *Iain 'ac Mhurchaidh 'ic Ailein* or John Morison, describes the use of *gibean* or grease from the gannet's stomach as form of poultice to heal the inflamed leg of a young friend: 'Yet in three weeks' time, being in my house, was perfectly whole by applying the said Oyle'. Personal observation is at a premium and his 'Description' includes a wide-ranging survey of all aspects of living in Lewis (Mitchell 1907: 210–215).

The history (and prehistory) of the Hebrides is predicated on the exploitation of the natural resources of land and sea, where fishing supplied a food protein to supplement the main food staples of oats and barley. The sea is naturally and powerfully part of Scotland's islands' identity. Much has been written about this and much remains to be written. The West

Coast and Hebrides were rich in supplies of fish. We learn about domestic and individual use of fishing in the late eighteenth century in the island 'Statistical Accounts'. We see that inshore fishing provided additional fresh food for the home and family, and a complement to the resources of the land. A Lewis saying was *dh'iarr am muir a thadhal* ('the sea wants to be visited') (Macdonald 1990: 92). Deeply ingrained in the island psyche is the awareness of the dangers and uncertainties of living by the sea. Loss of life by drowning was a constant threat that from time to time shattered communities. Storms and drownings such as in 1889 and 1895 are still recalled (Macdonald 1990: 99). The lives of fishing communities and of fisherfolks' families were riven with anxiety. The people of South Uist, for example, disliked fishing and avoided it; there was a practical reason that the population was settled on the western side with no natural harbours and a notoriously exposed coastline. Agriculture was perceived as a safer and more reliable livelihood.

Different kinds of fishing evolved to match the different fishing levels of the sea and the different habits of fish. 'White fish', such as saithe, cod, haddock and whiting, have always been an important source of food in the coastal zone, being taken with nets and lines baited with hooks. 'Small lines', *na lìn beaga*, were used mainly for winter work; and 'great lines', *na lìn mòra*, were for the spring and summer and in deeper waters. *Tha an sgadan fhèin os cionn nan uile* or 'the herring tops them all' was the mantra (Dòmhnallach agus Davenport 1987: 9). In terms of North Atlantic fisheries and of European trade, the herring has been of long-term importance. The herring were in the Minch in May and June and migrated round the coast to provide an autumn herring season as far south as East Anglia. For some decades in the second half of the nineteenth century, the Scottish herring industry was the biggest fishery in the world, dominating the main international market in Germany, Poland and Russia to the extent that Scottish herring had become a staple diet in the region. The shoals of herring were pursued farther offshore and larger boats such as the 'Fifie' and the 'Zulu' were built to meet this challenge. The boats needed bigger crews and the seasonal migration of the herring made for a longer season. The industry employed, it was estimated, about 100,000 people by the end of the century and a migrating workforce of men and women as crews, gutters and packers followed the herring round the coast from the Minch to Great Yarmouth. Women formed a landward side to this industry and followed the fisheries to gut and pack the herring into barrels. A significant economic and social role developed, still sealed into the communal memory as *Clann-Nighean an Sgadain*, although under-represented in the literature (Dòmhnallach agus Davenport 1987; De Fresnes 2010).

Shellfish are a source of protein and highly nutritious but shellfish were not appealing as food; traditionally this was a food of last resort. Runrig's song *Rubh 'nan Cudaigean* ('Cuddy Point') of 1980 brings this distaste into our own day. 'Rise up and take the bait [...] Come and eat the limpets and we'll eat the cuddies' (MacDonald and MacDonald 2000: 195). The song tells us that, and also that fishing with nets off shoreline rocks is a significant tradition (see also Fenton 2008: 85–89, 90–102). *Maorach* is used as a generic for shellfish but possibly with an earlier more specific meaning of 'mussel' (HSD 1828: 624, s.v. *maorach*); but 'mussel' is now replaced colloquially by *feusgan* which unequivocally refers to 'mussel' as bait. While *maorach* now serves to refer to fishing bait, it infers that people do not want to have a diet of 'bait'. The proverb *dèan maorach fhad 's a bhios an tràigh ann* ('gather shellfish while the tide is out') can be used to signal that an individual is enterprising but echoes the desperation of past times and a food of last resort. Other shellfish, figuring prominently in island dialects, are *faochag* 'whelk', *srùban*, 'cockle', *bàirneach*, 'limpet', and, of course, lobsters, crabs and scallops on which an inshore fishing economy and shellfish industry was built in the twentieth century. This grew out of the home-made *clèibh* ('creels') and *cliabh-ghiomach* ('lobster creel') which are embedded in Gaelic speech and demonstrate that, culturally, shell-fishing in small boats has been part-time and goes with crofting (Coull 2008: 374–388).

The famines of 1836 and 1845 in the Hebrides are recalled in the cold statistics that reflect mortality and emigration and increased state intervention but the searing memory of these years is part of island identity (see Henderson 1898: 57–62; Meek 2003: 158–169). Rev Dr Norman MacLeod, celebrated in his own day and since as *Caraid nan Gàidheal* ('The Friend of the Gael'), captured some of the pain in his writings in English for the outside world; he described how 'the poor ... had to resort to the shores for shellfish and dulse', and, crossing into South Uist in July 1847 in order to report to the Church on the state of destitution of the people, he wrote:

> The scene of wretchedness which we witnessed ... was deplorable, nay, heart-rending. On the beach the whole population of the country seemed to be met, gathering the precious cockles, hundreds of ponies with creels – men, women and naked children all at work. We met a crowd of people at the Fords. I never witnessed such countenances – starvation on many faces – the children with their melancholy looks, big looking knees, shrivelled legs, hollow eyes, swollen-like bellies – God help them, I never did witness such wretchedness. What would I not have given for twenty barrels of biscuits? I had money in abundance, but not one pound of meal could be got for the starving multitude. ... I was at a loss what to do; here was a population which I had ascertained to consist of 180 families in one wretched place, or about 1000 souls, and two-thirds of them without one grain of meal, and those who had most had not above three days' store. Many, very many, could not go to the shore from weakness, far less carry home the shellfish. Some were confined to bed, many suffering from severe dysentery from living exclusively on shellfish, or some wild mustard and wild spinach etc., and other herbs, and they have great abundance of spinach, or what they call *blanachan* [*bloinigean*]. I am persuaded that it has saved them from sea scurvy, as there were but few cases of that sad disease in this most wretched district. (MacLeod 1898: 125, 231–233)

The natural environment will inevitably be a part of our interest in islands and sea-birds bulk large in current conservation concerns. Sea-bird colonies were integrally part of the resources of islanders. Sea-bird fowling has been widespread in the North Atlantic region. Fowling traditions in Scotland are shared with countries such as Ireland, Iceland, the Faroes, Norway and Finland. Within Scotland, fowling was pursued in other areas of sea-bird colonies such as Westray, Foula, the Bass Rock and Ailsa Craig, but in the Hebrides the main sites were North Rona, Sula Sgeir, Sule Stack, Sule Skerry, the Flannans, Monach, the Shiants, Mingulay and St Kilda, islands where there are substantial bird colonies now rigorously protected by nature conservation legislation. Fowling was a way of life shared by coastal communities and a marked feature of their subsistence economies, to obtain food and other materials deriving from the birds. The taking of sea-birds and their eggs supplied seasonal fresh food and augmented the stores of preserved foodstuffs for winter and spring.

Against this, the harsh realities of harvesting birds from the nesting cliffs led to accidents and death, and the loss of 'breadwinners' to family and community. Given the scale of the activity within the individual communities, the work of fowling contributed to traditions of ingenuity, courage and tests of manhood, which were remembered as well as celebrated in song and story (Baldwin 1974: 60–103). A vestige of this way of life is to be seen in the annual expedition from Ness in Lewis to take young gannets from Sula Sgeir. Though not perhaps economically necessary, this is part of the culture and identity of the Lewis community and includes an appetite for the taste of sea-bird flesh and of the *guga* or young gannet. A taste for *guga* is a test of Ness-ness.

The natural resources on which the human population was finally dependent have been topography, soil and climate and in the Highlands and Islands these conditions generally favour animal husbandry. While the mainland Highlands, especially away from the east coast, is characterised as 'rough grazing' and do not offer opportunities for extensive cultivation and cropping, parts of the islands such as Tiree and Islay and the *machair* coastlands of the Outer Hebrides offer areas of land highly suited to cultivation. From time to time through recorded history, this relative abundance was being noticed as source of wealth for the Crown and State. Donald Monro listed 251 islands in 1549 for fiscal assessment. King James VI was convinced that wealth could be extracted from the Highlands and Islands and an anonymous account of the productiveness of the islands submitted to the king is witness to this covetousness (Skene 1880: 428–440; Munro 1961; Caldwell 2015: 355–362).

Seaweed in abundance has been a 'golden fringe' to island life. It is the most readily available manure and about 80% of the crofting townships have access to seashores. A twentieth-century comment by Catriona MacNeill of Barra offers a succinct and significant view from within:

> *Bha againn ri dhol don tràigh airson todhar a' buain 's a thoirt thun na croite airson leasachadh an talamh. Bha feamainn, às gach sheòrsa, cho glan, cha ghabhadh na b' fheàrr fhaighinn* ('We had to go to the shore to gather manure and to carry it to the croft to improve the soil. Seaweed of every sort was so pure, a better couldn't be got'). (NicNèill 2000: 360)

Rich in nitrogen and organic matter, seaweed is a 'food' that is of value for any soil. It is good for the sandy soils of the *machair* shorelines. The name *feamainn* applies to seaweeds of all kinds, whether growing on rocks or cast ashore. The importance of seaweed in the economy of Hebridean communities, as manure and in many other ways, cannot be over-estimated and is emphasised by the range of terms and terminology in Scottish Gaelic (Dwelly 1967: 421–422, *sv feamainn*). Every modern 'history' of the Hebrides and Northern Isles will include a large section on 'kelp' and the 'kelp industry', the calamitous era when the burning of seaweed employed huge numbers of men, women and children. The grim kelping period was at its height between 1790 and 1814 when landlords took vast profits (Hunter 1976: 32–41). The term *ceilp* was borrowed into Scottish Gaelic but has no such resonance as *feamainn* or seaweed as food source and fertiliser; how harvested, how cooked, how eaten, how composted, how laid on the land and with what expectations was held in the Hebridean mind, and the whole process illuminated by a huge glossary in Scottish Gaelic which far outstrips Linnaean botanical classifications.

Historically cattle were of overwhelming importance. This has been summarised for the Irish and Scottish *Gàidhealtachd*: 'The cow was the measure of everything; it was the unit of value; the ultimate in poverty was the man with only one cow, the wealth of the richest consisted of vast herds of them' (Lucas 1989: 4). Such a measure of wealth persisted and in the Statutes of Iona of 1609, families of substance in the islands were defined in terms of 'in goodis worth thriescore kye' (MacGregor 2006: 144–145). Thus assessed, they had to send their eldest sons to schools in the Lowlands and to learn Scots-English. A state of lawlessness was the official descriptor for the Highlands and Islands and the stealing of cattle was a symptom. The century after the forfeiture of the Lordship of the Isles was known as *Linn nan Creach* or 'The Era of Raiding', in which the fundamental form of warfare was the cattle raid (*creach*) in which such a test of manhood was a virtue rather than a moral slur. While raiding died out in the eighteenth century, cattle maintained their position as the mainstay of the traditional pastoral economy. Songs about cows and milking have survived in profusion as evidenced in a recent publication of about 300 songs with an insight into how the cows were viewed by the women who milked them (Ghriogair

2014). Milk products were important both as foodstuffs and as rent, butter
and cheese being commonly part of rent in kind (Grant 1995: 65–67). Most
of milk production was in the summer months, after cows had calved and
when grass was plentiful. Transhumance by which cattle were moved to
upland pastures – the 'shieling' or *àirigh* – was common across the high
ground of Scotland, began to disappear in the eighteenth century under
the influence of 'agricultural improvement' and survived, most notably in
Lewis, until after the Second World War. Fresh grass at higher altitudes
which were remote from the townships offered sites for the shielings to
which there was an annual summer migration of people and animals. This
kept cattle away from ground under cultivation and the growing crops and
was intimately linked with the functioning of pre-Clearance settlements.
Large flocks of new breeds of sheep were introduced progressively towards
the north and west of the Highlands from the 1760s and took over the
hill grazings. This commercial economy afforded huge value to a very few,
replaced an older indigenous sheep economy and forced Highlanders and
Hebrideans to emigrate (Hunter 1976, *passim*).

    The essential element of a self-sufficient economy was the successful
sourcing of food. Cultivation has left its mark on the landscape and where
it is no longer being pursued, the so-called 'lazy-bed' is a monument to
settlement and cultivation. This is a form of cultivation that seems to exemplify the traditional agriculture of the Islands and marks where crops of
oats and barley, and later of potatoes, were raised. It must be said that this
is not a mark of laziness but is a phrase that preserves an obsolete sense of
the English word for 'fallow' or 'untilled'. This refers to the way that the
lazy-bed is assembled; manure is laid in strips and the sods of earth are
turned up onto the manure for the rows of the crop, and the original soil
surface below the growing crop is not dug or tilled. This form of raised bed
is an ideal method of cultivation in wet, peaty soils and in a rocky landscape where potential areas of cultivation are small. In such areas where
the plough could not so readily be used, spade cultivation achieved the
intensity and results of horticulture. The tools such as the *cas-dhireach* or
'straight spade' and the *cas-chrom* or 'crooked spade' were the tools of the
small-scale cultivator where all work was done by the hands and feet and
more often as a communal activity. In this respect it must be significant

that Martin Martin commented that in Lewis about 500 people were said to have been employed for several months of the year in making lazy-beds. Donald Monro recognised this in writing of Taransay on the west coast of Harris that: '[…] all this tilth is delvit with spaidis, except sa meckle as ane hors pleuch will teill; and yit thay have maist abundant of beire, and maist myth of corn, store and fishing' (Munro 1961: 80).

The *cas-dhireach* with its blacksmith-made blade is close to a prehistoric cultivating implement. It was a simple and inexpensive tool and it is a historically self-effacing one; very few examples survive and the evidence of Gaelic suggests that, (the work of tillage being historically of low status compared with hunting and pastoralism), the tool has long-since been re-cycled and has disappeared. The *cas-chrom* is much more prominent in the historical and material record. It had a long wooden shaft (*cas*) with a wrought-iron blade (*caibe*) mounted on the 'head' or point of the shaft. On most examples, the head was a separate piece of wood which was nailed and strapped to the shaft for strength, and the final element was a foot-peg or *sgonnan* for pushing the blade and head under the turf. The *cas-chrom* was used as a substitute for the plough and especially in rocky soils where the plough could not operate (e.g. MacQueen 1793: 307–308). In these circumstances, it was an effective tool in the hands of a good operator and would achieve a good seed-yield ratio. The view of 'Enlightenment' observers, charged with designing a better future, is ambivalent and even supportive. Rev Dr John Walker, for example, admitted that *cas-chrom* cultivation in Skye yielded usually one third more crop than plough tillage, that the *cas-chrom* was a 'beneficial instrument' and 'it is also useful to the numerous small subtenants who having no horse cannot get their little patch of ground cultivated' (McKay 1980: 172, 211). Another enlightenment voice in the debate was that of Rev James MacDonald (1771–1810) of North Uist. This well-travelled multi-lingual young master of observation offers interesting comments, for example, that the tacksmen might be '… entitled to the honours and advantages of a civilised and polished life'. In describing the *cas-chrom* as the only implement of tillage in the parishes of Uig and Lochs, he claimed that it supported a population of about 5,000: 'All their corn and all their potatoes are raised with the caschrom […] a sort of proof, though not conclusive, that the instrument is not altogether contemptible' (MacDonald 1811: 77–78, 151). The *cas-chrom* may not have been an ancient tool and even the name, as distinguishing it from the *cas-dhireach*, suggests that it might have been an early modern adaptation, especially where holdings were being sub-divided from the late eighteenth century and intensive use of smaller plots was being made for grain and potato crops (Fenton 1974: 131–148).

The standard 'swing plough' of the 'agricultural revolution' spread across Scotland, Lowlands and Highlands, in the course of the second half of the eighteenth century. Towards the north and west and in the islands, where the real economic base lay in grazing, spade cultivation continued, and the uptake of the swing plough was less. In the parish accounts of the 1790s, the plough was used by tacksmen in Stornoway parish, a mark of wealth and status denied to most of the occupiers of the ground. For most, land was too limited to work a plough or maintain a horse. Though the agriculture literature recommended the advanced forms of tillage, only the lairds, tacksmen and ministers had access to the new south-country ploughs and 'improved' breeds of draught horse. In the Inner Hebrides the influence of mainland agriculture and technology was stronger. Where cultivation was easier, but resources were scarce, as in Tiree which in 1845 was described as having 350 ploughs, implements would be copied by local joiners and blacksmiths.

Cultural heritage and identity: Some thoughts in conclusion

Introducing a Gaelic point of view to a scholarly enterprise in island studies may have been pre-empted by others. A term often proposed in the literature is, typically, *dùthchas*, as offering an insight into Gaelic cultural identity; this refers to an instinctive trait denoting the individual's sense of belonging to a home place. For the Hebridean, *dùthchas* has dimensionality as a putative total field of understanding embracing landscape, a sense of geography, a sense of history and a formal order of experience in which all these are merged (Newton 2006: 29). Such an all-embracing definition rooted in a single word seems compelling rather than conclusive. It may serve to meet the expectations of the outside world but more could be offered for island studies. A further word that does not seem to have been much scrutinised is *seanchas* – similarly complex but a different order of response. The usage of *seanchas* occupies a spectrum of meaning between 'talk' or 'conversation' and access to a whole integrated cosmos of knowledge, perhaps too lightly translated as 'traditional lore'. *Seanchas* holds a key to the shared knowledge and memory of a community, and more significantly to a shared identity among Gaelic-speaking islanders, expressed also to the outside world in terms of song (see Gillies 2010). Exploring the inner life of subjects and the world of ideas may add a dimension. Is it impertinent to interrogate people's lives, their thoughts and feelings and how they see themselves, and to lay bare their experiences and pre-occupations? This is far beyond the scope of this chapter but a surrogate can be suggested from literature to achieve, arguably, a symbolic account of island 'cultural heritage'.

Tormod Caimbeul's inspired island novella, *Deireadh an Fhoghair* ('The End of Autumn'), is not going to supply either glib or structured answers but serves to represent the subject. It is a powerful work in cultural terms, and emotional without being the slightest sentimental. Set within the limited compass of a day and a night, the thoughts and feelings of three islanders are closely examined, moving from universal questions of love, life and death to sheep-handling and the merits of turnips. It is the 'end of autumn' of the lives of the three characters and of the world as they know it. Daily life seems to be defined by individual characters and past events that colour most conversations, and time, as conventionally experienced, becomes meaningless. It is evident that the knowledge that they have of their island world and its emblems of crops, animals and peats is still vast and detailed, a characteristic probably shared with all similar communities across the world. Their vocabulary is rich in idiom and terminology and 'true' to the tradition: *Bha feamainn ann a dh'itheadh iad, mircein, duilisg agus stamhan; bha feamainn ann a bhruicheadh 'ad dhan a' chrodh, 's bha feamainn ann a sgaoileadh 'ad air a' chlàr bhuntàta* ('There was seaweed that they would eat, badderlock [i.e. an edible seaweed], dulse and tangle; there was seaweed that they would boil up for the cattle; and there was seaweed that they would spread on the potato bed') (Caimbeul 1979: 29). The author, *Tormod a' Bhocsair* (1942–2015), belonged to Ness in Lewis from where the language and idiom is drawn. It demonstrates that Gaelic oral tradition still has great power and resonance and will contribute virtually immeasurably to cultural identity with these forms of *seanchas*. It offers a clear message that Gaelic island culture is distinctive and different.

This chapter adds to the study of islands, in this case of Scotland's Hebrides, by drawing on the repertoire of an indigenous language and 'mother-tongue', the records of a Regional Ethnology, conventional (documentary) history and the social sciences. The further aim is to reach a more nuanced account of island 'cultural heritage' by exploring a 'local worldview' and finding a sufficiency in those parts of islandness not reached by observers in the outside world. Modern scholarship bears a heavy burden of the need to push back on unspoken perceptions. Prevailing views continue to influence the discourse and, in turn, public opinion. An article in the journal *Antiquity* by a pre-war archaeologist, E. C. Curwen, was titled 'The Hebrides: a cultural backwater' (Curwen 1938: 288). The renowned post-war archaeologist, Professor Stuart Piggott, commented on crofting and the crofting landscape as expressions of ancient social and economic practices that had survived longer on the 'Celtic fringe' (Piggot 1982: 92). The recent excavation of a post-medieval site in Ness, Lewis, tempers the 'cultural backwater' notion with the case for a strong local identity operating historically in a northern European economic and political theatre (Barrowman 2019: 41). A material turn in academic discourses is tending to a widening of the disciplinary palette and assumptions of multi-disciplinary and cross-disciplinary capabilities. Intellectual trends in historical studies are now absorbing topics such as identity and memory, and show a readiness to accept a blending of archival research and oral tradition, blends that have surely become irresistible with the new wealth of material online such as the sound archives of Scottish Gaelic (see *Tobar an Dualchais*).

Bibliography

Baldwin, J. R. (1974). 'Sea bird fowling in Scotland and Faroe', *Folk Life. A Journal of Ethnological Studies*, 12, 60–103.

Barrowman, R. C. (2019). ' "A Cultural Backwater": the 'localness' of Dùn Èistean, Ness, and its place in the wider maritime world of Northwest Scotland', *Journal of the North Atlantic*, 12, 32–43.

Borgstrøm, C. Hj. (1937). 'The Gaelic of Barra in the Outer Hebrides', *Norsk Tidsskrift for Sprogvidenskap*, 7, 71–242.

Borgstrøm, C. Hj. (1940). *The Dialects of the Outer Hebrides. A Linguistic Survey of the Gaelic Dialects of Scotland I*. Norsk Tidsskrift for Sprogvidenskap Supplementary Volume I. Oslo.

Burnett, R. (1986). *Benbecula*. Torlum: The Mingulay Press.

Buxton, B. (2016). *Mingulay. An Island and Its People*. Edinburgh: Birlinn Ltd.

Caimbeul, T. (1979). *Deireadh an Fhoghair*. Dun Eideann: U & R Chambers.

Caldwell, D. H. (2015). 'The Sea Power of the Western Isles of Scotland in the Late Medieval Period'. In Barrett, J. H. and S. J. Gibbon (eds), *Maritime Societies of the Viking and Medieval World*. Society for Medieval Archaeology Monograph 37, pp. 350–368. Leeds: Maney Publishing.

Caldwell, D. (2018). *Mull and Iona: A Historical Guide*. Edinburgh: Birlinn Ltd.

Campbell, J. L. (ed.) (1958). *Gaelic Words and Expressions from South Uist and Eriskay collected by Rev. Fr Allan McDonald*. Dublin: Dublin Institute for Advanced Studies.

Cheape, H. (2017). 'Cultar Dùthchasach: a Gaelic approach to material culture studies', *History Scotland*, 17 (1), 16–20.

Coull, J. R. (2008). 'Shellfishing'. In Coull, J. R., Fenton, A., and K. Veitch (eds), *Boats, Fishing and the Sea. Scottish Life and Society. A Compendium of Scottish Ethnology Volume 4*. European Ethnological Research Centre, pp. 374–388. Edinburgh: John Donald.

Curwen, E. C. (1938). 'The Hebrides. A cultural backwater', *Antiquity*, 12, 261–289.

De Fresnes, J. L. (2010). 'Image and Identity. The Lives of the Scots Herring Girls, 1900–1950'. Unpublished PhD Thesis. The Open University.

Dòmhnallach, T. C., and Davenport, L. (1987). *Clann-nighean an Sgadain*. Steòrnabhagh: Acair.

Duncan, A. (1995). *Hebridean Island. Memories of Scarp*. East Linton: Tuckwell Press.

Dwelly, E. (1967). *The Illustrated Gaelic-English Dictionary*. Sixth Edition. Glasgow: Alex. Maclaren and Sons.

Fenton, A. (1974). 'The Cas-chrom. A review of the evidence', *Tools & Tillage*, II (3), 131–148.

Fenton, A. (1985). *The Shape of the Past. Essays in Scottish Ethnology*. Edinburgh: John Donald.

Fenton, A. (2008). 'Craig Fishing'. In Coull, J. R., Fenton, A., and K. Veitch (eds), *Boats, Fishing and the Sea. Scottish Life and Society. A Compendium of Scottish*

Ethnology Volume 4. European Ethnological Research Centre, pp. 85–89. Edinburgh: John Donald.

Ghriogair, S. (2014). *Ri Luinneig mun Chrò. Crodh ann am Beatha agus Dualchas nan Gàidheal*. Grace Note Publications.

Gillies, A. L. (2010). *Songs of Gaelic Scotland*. Edinburgh: Birlinn Ltd.

Grant, I. F. (1995). *Highland Folk Ways*. Edinburgh: Birlinn Ltd.

Henderson, Rev Dr G. (ed.) (1898). *Leabhar nan Gleann*. Edinburgh: N MacLeod.

HES [Historic Environment Scotland] Calanais Standing Stones – Statement of Significance <https://www.historicenvironment.scot/archives-and-research/publications/publication/> accessed 30 August 2019.

HSD [Highland Society Dictionary] (1828). *Dictionarium Scoto-Celticum. A Dictionary of the Gaelic Language Compiled and Published under the Direction of The Highland Society of Scotland*. Volume I. Edinburgh: William Blackwood and London: T. Cadell.

Hunter, J. (1976). *The Making of the Crofting Community*. Edinburgh: John Donald.

Lucas, A. T. (1989). *Cattle in Ancient Ireland*. Studies in Irish Archaeology and History. Kilkenny: Boethius Press.

MacAskill, A. J (1963). 'Differences in dialect, vocabulary and general idiom between the islands', *Transactions of the Gaelic Society of Inverness*, 43 (1960–1963), 64–88.

Macdonald, D. (1990). *Lewis. A History of the Island*. Edinburgh: Gordon Wright Publishing.

MacDonald, D. (1936). 'Some rare Gaelic words and phrases', *Transactions of the Gaelic Society of Inverness*, 37 (1934–1936), 1–54.

MacDonald, Rev J. (1811). *General View of the Agriculture of the Hebrides or Western Isles of Scotland*. Edinburgh.

MacDonald, C., and MacDonald, R. (2000). *Flower of the West. The Runrig Songbook*. Ridge Books.

MacGregor, M. (2006). 'The Statutes of Iona: text and content', *The Innes Review*, 57 (2), 111–181.

MacLeod, D. J. (1934). *A Description of the Western Islands of Scotland c. 1695 by Martin Martin*. Stirling: Aeneas Mackay.

MacLeod, J. N. (1898). *Memorials of the Rev Norman MacLeod*. Edinburgh: David Douglas.

MacQueen, Rev A. (1793). 'The Parish of North Uist'. In *The Statistical Account of Scotland*, 13, 300–325. Edinburgh.

McKay, M. M. (ed.) (1980). *Rev Dr John Walker's Report on the Hebrides of 1764 and 1771*. Edinburgh: John Donald.

Meek, D. E. (2000). 'God and Gaelic. The Highland Churches and Gaelic Cultural Identity'. In McCoy, G., and M. Scott (eds), *Gaelic Identities: Aithne na nGaidheal*, pp. 28–47. Belfast: Queen's University Belfast, Institute of Irish Studies, Ultach Trust.

Meek, D. E. (ed.) (2003). *Caran an t-Saoghail. Anthology of 19th Century Scottish Gaelic Verse*. Edinburgh: Birlinn Ltd.

Mitchell, A. (1907). *Geographical Collections Relating to Scotland Made by Walter Macfarlane*, II. Edinburgh: Scottish History Society.

Munro, R. W. (1961). *Monro's Western Isles of Scotland and Genealogies of the Clans, 1549*. Edinburgh: Oliver and Boyd.

Murchison, T. M. (1959). 'Deserted Hebridean Islands: notes and traditions', *Transactions of the Gaelic Society of Inverness*, 42 (1953–1959), 283–344.

Newton, M. (ed.) (2006). *Dùthchas nan Gàidheal. Selected Essays of John MacInnes*. Edinburgh: Birlinn.

NicNèill, C. (2000). 'Na h-Eilthirich', *Gairm* Àireamh, 192 (Am Foghar 2000), 359–363.

Ó Dochartaigh, C. (1997). *Survey of the Gaelic Dialects of Scotland*. Dublin: Dublin Institute of Advanced Studies, School of Celtic Studies, 1–5 (1994–1997).

Oftedal, M. (1956). *The Gaelic of Leurbost, Isle of Lewis. A Linguistic Survey of the Gaelic Dialects of Scotland III*. Norsk Tidsskrift for Sprogvidenskap Supplementary Volume IV. Oslo.

Piggot, S. (1982). *Scotland before History*. Edinburgh: Edinburgh University Press.

Ritchie, G., and Ritchie, A. (1991). *Scotland. Archaeology and Early History*. Edinburgh: Edinburgh University Press.

Skene, W. F. (1880). *Celtic Scotland. Volume III. Land and People*. Edinburgh: David Douglas.

Storrie, M. C. (1981). *Islay. Biography of an Island*. Second Edition. Islay: Oa Press.

Tobar an Dualchais, <http://www.tobarandualchais.co.uk/gd/> accessed 10 September 2019.

ANDREW JENNINGS

4. 'Da Norn is lang gien, but hit's left a waageng,': The Distinctiveness of Shetland Cultural Identity

'Da Norn is lang gien, but hit's left a waageng,':
from the poem *A Shuttle o Soonds* by Christine de Lucca (2002)

Islands are often home to culturally rich and distinctive communities. This is undoubtedly the case with Shetland and the Shetlanders, who, although they have been connected to Scotland since 1469, still maintain their unique regional identity. Arguably the process of *Scottification* has not yet been entirely completed. This identity manifests itself in a number of ways, from the oft heard profession that, 'I'm not Scottish' and the commonplace statement about taking the ferry to Scotland, to the distinctive voting patterns in recent referenda. Although a majority of Shetlanders supported Scottish devolution in the 1997 referendum, which reflects a shift in opinion since the previous referendum in 1979, when 73% of Shetland voters rejected a Scottish Assembly, Shetlanders seem less keen on Scottish independence. 63.7% voted 'No' in the Scottish independence referendum in 2014, against 53.4% for the Scottish population as a whole (Jennings 2017: 66–68).

There are sound linguistic and cultural reasons for this attitude. As the late Jo Grimond, MP for Orkney and Shetland said in a parliamentary debate culminating in The Zetland County Council Act 1974, which gave the new Shetland Islands Council extraordinary powers, '[Shetlanders'] traditions are largely Norse in origin and differ from the traditions of much of the rest of Britain.' Grimond was not being fanciful. Norse cultural heritage is a vital part of Shetland identity, and indeed was used by an identifiable group of Shetlandic intellectuals in the nineteenth century to construct a nordophile, Shetlandic identity, distinct from that of the

Scots. These figures worked with real evidence. For example, with regards to Shetlandic folklore, the great Swedish folklorist Bo Almqvist has stated, 'the Norse character of Shetland can hardly be over-rated' (Almqvist 1991: 3). Shetland also had a Nordic language called Norn, which was very similar to Faroese, and although this may have lost its last speakers in the late eighteenth century, as the poet Christine De Lucca (2002) says, it left a *waageng* 'after taste'. The Faroese scholar Jakob Jakobsen collected c.10,000 Norn words still current in the local dialect at the end of the nineteenth century, publishing them in a dictionary which is still a must-have for any serious Shetlander. These salvaged words continue to appear in poetry, on the lips of locals, in modern house names, and in the name for Shetland's music, cinema and creative industries centre, *Mareel*.

This chapter has a simple premise, to present the extent to which Norse cultural heritage is extant in modern Shetland and to show where it is used both consciously and unconsciously to support a distinctive identity. I am also not making a value judgement about the materials, and I am shying away from value loaded terms such as authentic or romantic. Rather I am presenting, I hope, an impartial ethnographic view, based on residence in Shetland over a fourteen-year period.

Viking visions

When Shetland appears in the media, it is often accompanied by a stereo-typical picture of a Viking, perhaps the current Up Helly Aa Guizer Jarl in full costume with winged helmet and wielding an axe, or by Vikings burning a galley. Shetland and the image of the Viking are intimately en-twined in the popular imagination. Of course, there is more to Shetland than its Viking connections and the average Shetlander is no more a Viking than an inhabitant of Edinburgh. Nonetheless, many, probably most, Shetlanders feel a connection of some kind with their Viking and later Norse past (although admittedly a survey has not been undertaken). Of course, there are some Shetlanders who do not. Presumably these include those Shetlanders who complained to the island studies scholar

Adam Grydhøj (2013) that it was people outwith Shetland who associated Shetlanders with Vikings. However, he does not seem to have believed them, and he points out, 'there is no doubt that the Vikings play a strong role in local discourse and that any present-day association of this sort by outsiders results from the importance of the Vikings to the community's self-image' (Grydhøj 2013: 41).

The historian Bruce Lenman felt that the Viking connection could be problematical for Shetland, as he claims

> Shetlanders do indeed have one of the few vital ... identities left in the regions of the United Kingdom. However, this does pose problems because it expresses itself in the glorification of a largely mythical Viking past about as relevant to the historical experience of the community as the ancient Celtic twilight so beloved by the average middle-class English-speaking Catholic nationalist in Dublin. (1987: 501)

However, in what sense is it a problem? The glorification of a largely mythical past is not restricted to Shetland, as Lenman points out. The Viking and later Norse past, when Shetland was part of the Norse world, serves to symbolically distinguish the islands from mainland Scotland, and helps in the building of the imagined Shetland community. As Silke Reeploeg (2017: 214) argues, Shetlanders use the Norse part of their heritage to bolster, support and provide a boundary around their local, unique identity. As she says, 'Shetland's Nordic heritage is thus not just a nostalgic look back to times past, but a continuous chorographic activity that resists, or subverts, being a British or Scottish 'national outpost'. It can be defined as an intercultural interpretation by the islanders themselves of their unique 'otherness', or regional cultural identity'. The gender historian Lynn Abrams, who has provided Shetlanders with a detailed examination of the unique place of women in Shetlandic society in her study *Myth and Materiality in a Women's World, Shetland 1800–2000* (2010), commented on the islanders' current identity and its Norse associations. She states that, 'Shetland's sense of otherness and distance from the mainstream and mainland Scotland is accentuated by its Norse heritage' (Abrams 2010: 3) and further, 'Norse tropes are present throughout the popular cultural construction of Shetland identity' (Abrams 2010: 34). A particularly strong case for the importance of the

Viking past to Shetlanders was made by Callum G. Brown (1998: 18) who found, in his study of the historical origins and contemporary signifi-cance of the annual Up-Helly-Aa fire festival, that, 'for Shetland children, the Norse were their forefathers – if not literally in all cases, then cer-tainly the precursors of the islands' contemporary community ... it is the Norse heritage of heroic sagas, individual bravery, and mighty struggles with enemies which dominates the Shetlander's sense of identity'.

Thomas Simchak (2008: 95) noted, in his exploration of how the con-struction of the Sullom Voe Oil Terminal and other oil support infrastruc-ture impacted on Shetland's perceptions of its identity, a similar focus on Norse heritage, that, 'The Norse connection is certainly one of the most overt elements of constructed Shetland identities'. However, he added a rider: 'Exactly how connected modern Shetland is to its Viking heritage is debatable, depending on who one speaks to – Shetland is outwardly far more Scottish than it is Norwegian ... but one can actually offend certain Shetlanders by discounting the islands' Norse heritage' (2008: 95). I would argue that modern Shetlanders have been connected to the Viking past through the efforts of the *Shetland Amenity Trust*, a charitable organisa-tion created in 1983 to preserve and enhance Shetland's natural and cul-tural heritage.

The *Shetland Amenity Trust* has overseen a number of Viking projects, which have boosted an awareness of Shetland's Viking heritage both at home and within the Nordic world. The *Trust* managed the *Viking Unst* project, which surveyed and mapped around sixty Norse longhouses, the densest concentration of such houses anywhere. They also collaborated in the ex-cavation of three of these houses and produced a glossy book detailing the project and its findings. This volume found an enthusiastic Shetland audi-ence. The Trust also organised the international *17th Viking Congress*, held in Lerwick in 2013. The proceedings entitled *Shetland and the Viking World* (2016) include a number of important papers on Shetland's Viking past. The *Trust* was also the lead partner in the *Creative Europe* funded *Follow the Vikings Project*, which ran from 1 July 2015 to 30 June 2019. It included a *Follow the Vikings International Roadshow* which, with a professional cast and accompanied by the Shetland *Hjaltibonhoga* fiddlers, retold the story of the Icelandic poet, Egil Skallagrimsson. All these efforts have publicised to the Shetland public the extent to which Shetland has a rich Viking heritage and is at the heart of modern Viking activities. The subjective perception by Shetlanders of their Norse identity is of greater importance than any objective measure. The Shetlandic scholar John Stewart, whose research has, among other things, been fundamental to an understanding of Shetland's Old Norse place-names, commented, in his important collection of the folklore of Whalsay and Shetland, that the people of the island of Whalsay were clear in, 'the knowledge (it is stronger than tradition) … that they are not Scots and came from Norway' (Stewart 2005: 9). It is interesting to note that Stewart was a native of Whalsay, so spoke with an insider's perspective.

Victorian imaginings

The existence of a current Shetlandic identity, which valorises its Viking and Norse associations, and occasionally denigrates its Scottish connections, was largely the work of a group of nineteenth-century autochthonous, nordophiliac intellectuals, such as the authors Jessie Saxby and J. J. Haldane Burgess and the antiquarian Arthur Laurenson who, inspired by the European intellectual currents of their time, undertook a successful process of sub-national identity imagining, although these intellectuals did have materials to base their romantic imaginings upon. This fascinating microcosmic example of contemporary European cultural trends has been minutely researched by Bronwen Cohen in her PhD Thesis (1983) 'Norse Imagery in Shetland: An Historical Study of Intellectuals and their use of the Past in the Construction of Shetland's Identity, with Particular Reference to the Period 1800–1914', and more recently by Adam Grydhøj (2013) in his paper on 'Ethnicity and the origins of local identity in Shetland, UK'. Of course, much of the identity building was couched in racial terms. For example, Jessie Saxby (1910), in her book *The Cradle of Our Race*, referred to Shetlanders' Norse 'virile virtues', and wrote that when she was on a boat crewed by Shetlanders, she was surrounded by 'faces and accents belonging to the old Norsemen,

conserved in the Shetland Isles – as in Iceland – through the ages, and
exist now to prove how strong is the force we inherit from the most virile
race that ever existed'. J. J. Haldane Burgess (1896: 3) in the preface to
his *Lowra Biglan's Mutch* stated forcefully the distinctive racial identity
of the Shetlanders as he saw it: 'We are not Scotch. We have never been
Scotch. And besides, we never will be Scotch, just in the same manner as
Britons never, never, will be slaves […] We repudiate utterly all connection with the Scotch.'

However, in addition to promulgating now dated racial hypotheses
concerning the origins and merits of the Shetlanders, Cohen (1983: 491)
points out that this group of intellectuals were particularly significant
because their emphasis upon Shetland's Norse identity was widely com-
municated outwith their group to the Shetland population at large. The
most important result of this engagement with the Shetland population
was undoubtedly the development of Up Helly Aa, which, 'through the
influence in particular, it would appear, of J. J. Haldane Burgess, became
and remains, an annual celebration of Shetland's Norse past, an annual
affirmation of the islands' Norse identity, an illustration of the effectiveness of such cultural symbols and performances' (Cohen 1983: 492).
A particularly interesting element is the annual choice of the Guizer
Jarl's name. The names are chosen with great care and each has a back
story. For example, in 1981 Harry Jamieson took the name of Thorvald
Thoreson, a real Norwegian chieftain who figures in Shetland folklore and
thirty-seven years later, his son Stewart chose to depict his son Thorvald
Thorvaldsson, who was based on the island of Papa Stour in Shetland
in the fourteenth century. Lerwick's Up Helly Aa has inspired ten other
areas of Shetland to hold their own Viking fire festivals, so almost every
weekend from the beginning of January to the middle of March one can
be experienced. These events have a huge effect on the children who are
involved at an early age and will presumably want to carry this tradition
on into the future.

There were other tangible results. In 1890 Zetland County Council
adopted Arthur Laurenson's design for the County Seal. This included
a longship on the obverse side and, on the reverse there was rock

representing 'The Old Rock' of Shetland surrounded by a band with the inscription *Hjaltlands Althing* and outside of this instead of a typical Latin motto, there was a maxim from the medieval Icelandic *Njál's Saga*, which reads *Með lögum skal land byggja* [By law is a land built up]. This has been subsequently adopted by Shetland Islands Council. This motto is prominently displayed on a large welcome sign at Lerwick Harbour and catches the eye of locals and cruise ship passengers alike, endowing an aura of Norseness to the scene. Laurenson was also intimately involved in the decoration of Lerwick Town Hall, which dominates the centre of the town. He chose the subject matter of the stained-glass windows. These feature Norwegian kings such as Harald Fairhair, who supposedly visited Shetland in the ninth century, and the Norse jarls of Orkney, like St Magnus, who ruled Shetland in the medieval period, although King James III of Scotland also features, as he was the Scottish king under whom the impignoration, or mortgaging, of the islands to Scotland took place in 1469. In 1883 *The Shetland Times* recognised the importance of the new hall and its role in supporting the identity of the islanders: 'The building of our Town Hall marks an epoch in our history. It serves to show that, as a community, we have a public and national life, and that we have arrived at that stage when a people recognise the continuity of its history, and desires to perpetuate the memory of the historic past of an ancient race' (29 December 1883). Laurenson was also involved in the creation of another public symbol of identity, a county flag. However, the history of vexillology is littered with flags that did not become popular on and this was one of them. Nonetheless, visitors to Shetland are likely to be frequently confronted with a modern blue and white Shetland flag broadcasting a visual connection with the Nordic world. This was created by Roy Grønneberg and Bill Adams in 1969 to commemorate 500 years since the impignoration and 500 years of Scottish rule. It uses the same colours adopted by Laurenson, blue and white. These reflect the colours of the Scottish saltire. However, the cross is the offset Nordic cross, as seen on Scandinavian flags. The flag was officially recognised by the Lord Lyon King of Arms in 2005 in time for Shetlanders to use it at the Island Games.

Onomastic oddities

It is not only on the County Seal that visitors are confronted with Old
Norse. A number of communities in Shetland have requested bilingual
road signs with their name, not in Gaelic as happens on the Mainland,
and which would cause consternation in a non-Gaelic speaking territory,
but in Old Norse. These signs also provide the interested reader with an
etymology of the name. Some of the etymologies are more hypothetical
than others. For example, it is uncertain that Veensgarth, although clearly
one of the 95% of Shetland names with an Old Norse origin, derives from
Víkingsgarðr, although it is not impossible. However, the motivation
is clear – place-names undoubtedly identity Shetland as a Nordic area,
which shares names with Norway, the Faroe Islands and Iceland. For example, Lerwick 'Clay Bay', also occurs as Leirvik on the island of Stord in
Norway, and as Leirvík on Eysturoy in the Faroe Islands.

Shetland's rich placename heritage has attracted scholars from both
Scandinavia, such as Jakob Jakobsen and more recently Peder Gammeltoft
(2005), who has written on Shetland island names, and Shetland, most notably Doreen Waugh, who produced an extensive body of work, including the
delightfully named 'Drongs, hjogelbens, pobis and skoreks: Jakobsen recorded
them all' (Waugh 2010). In 1998 she came up with the idea of a *Shetland Place
Names Project* and convinced *Shetland Amenity Trust* to establish it. This
unique project has been ably led and developed by Eileen Brooke Freeman,
who has done a great deal to keep place-names in the public consciousness.

Onomastics might seem a rather arcane subject with a small number of
devotees, however, the symbolism embodied in names is readily understood
by Shetlanders. This was observed by the Norwegian politician Jon Leirfall
who visited Shetland in the 1970s. He noted in his book *Vest i havet*, which
explored the historical connections between Norway and the islands in
the Atlantic, that, 'Det er blitt ei motesak å gi heimane sine norske namn'
[It has become a fashion to give their homes Norse names] (1976:168).
A short survey of the names that Shetlanders have chosen for their homes
reveals a strong desire to express an affinity with Shetland's Norse heritage,
unlike on the mainland of Scotland where there are few Gaelic names. This

desire is manifested in a number of different name types. Some Shetlanders have chosen Shetlandic place-names such as *Valaberg, Fivlagord, Trola, Winjarø, Da Sneug* and *Winyadepla*. Others have chosen dialect words of Norn origin, mostly scavenged from Jakobsen's dictionary, like *Mareel* 'Sea Phosphorescence', *Shoormal*, 'High-water mark', *Da Haaf* 'The Deep Sea', *Hjarta*, 'Term of Endearment', *Bonhoga*, 'Childhood's Home', *Voar* 'Spring', *Daalamist* 'Dale-mist' and the unique *Vaegapiddi*, an exclamation used by a fisherman when his oatcake was washed overboard! Connections with Norway, sometimes referred to as the Mother Country, have inspired some to use Norwegian place-names. The following appear: *Andoya, Geiranger, Ulvik, Svolvaer, Torghatten, Tonsberg, Roros, Holmenkollen, Hammerfest, Trondheim* and *Øvredal*. Then there are a number of names indicate a surprising knowledge of the sagas, runes and Norse mythology, such as *Brattahlid*, Eirik the Red's farm in Greenland, *Jorvik*, the Norse name for York, *Geirhilda*, after Flóki Vilgerðarsson's daughter reputed to have died in Shetland, *Dagaz*, the proto-Germanic name for the D-rune, *Mjölnir*, Þórr's hammer, *Aegirsta*, an invented name which means the 'Place of Aegir' who was god of the sea, *Vanaheim*, the home of the Vanir gods, *Glitnir*, the hall of Forseti, the Norse god of law and justice, Valhalla, the home of the gods, which not surprisingly occurs at least four times, and *Ragnarok*, the doom, or twilight of the gods, surely an unusual name for a house!

Leirfall (1976: 168) also noted that, 'overalt møter du norske symbol, i … reklame og i forretningsnamn' [overall you meet Norwegian symbols, in advertising and business names]. Again this is undoubtedly true. For example, the inter-island ferries which operate on Yell Sound are the *Dagalien* 'Beginning of Twilight' and the *Daggri* 'Dawn', while the ferry that operates to Papa Stour, the *Snolda*, takes its name from a sea-stack. A look through the Shetland business listings reveal a number of businesses with Norse connections. On the island of Whalsay the charity shop, which is famous throughout Shetland, is called *Shoard*, a word of Norse origin meaning a support. On the mainland there is a physiotherapy clinic called *Yasp*, a dialect word of likely Norse origin which means lively or energetic. Other businesses include a café called *Faerdie-Maet*, which appropriately means provisions for a journey, a riding club called *Filsket*, meaning frisky, a gallery called *Bonhoga*, childhood home, a pub called *Da Noost*, a noost being a place where a boat is drawn up, a local housing association *Hjaltland Housing Association Ltd* which takes its name from the Old Norse name for Shetland, a former restaurant called *Osla's*, a Norse female personal name still current, and a hotel called *Kveldsro*, which is Norwegian for evening calm. The Vikings also put in an appearance: there is *Viking Energy*, which is planning to build a large windfarm in the centre of Shetland and the *Viking Bus Station* in Lerwick.

Shetland produces a comparatively large number of musicians and, given that their appeal is partly in presenting themselves as representatives of Shetland's culture, they often choose evocative names. These include *Da Fustra*, called after a sunken rock off the coast of Unst, *Haltadans*, a stone setting on the island of Fetlar, and *Hjaltibonhoga*, the fiddle group who perform every year at the Royal Edinburgh Military Tattoo, and who bear a name which is claimed on their website to be from the Old Norse for 'Shetland, my spiritual home', but more interestingly is actually a new coining.

When it comes to anthroponomastics Shetland also has unique features with Norse associations. There are personal names such as the aforementioned *Osla*, from Old Norse Áslaug, which it must be said is no longer common, although the song by Eddie Barclay *Muckle Osla's Flittin* is sung. A more common female name would be *Vaila*, an Old Norse island name, or *Astrid* and *Ingrid*. Male names include *Hance* or *Hansie*, *Magnus* and its diminutives *Magnie* and *Mansie* and *Rasmie*, short for Erasmus. The latter is infrequent, although J. J. Haldane Burgesses' poem *Rasmie's Büddie* is well known. There are many Shetland surnames which are fossilised patronymics and therefore fit the Scandinavian pattern. Examples include *Jarmson*, or *Jeromson*, *Herculson*, *Erasmuson*, *Georgeson*, possibly Sigurd's son, *Laurenson*, *Ollason* and *Manson*, Magnus's son. Clearly in many different onomastic ways Shetland has a pronounced Norse appearance.

Dialectal dimensions

As noted with the choice of house and business names, the Shetland dialect is a clear marker of a distinct identity. Its existence cannot fail to be noticed by visitors to the islands. Despite warnings, like that voiced in *The Scotsman* newspaper on 11 October 2016 that the dialect might have died out by 2045, it is still resolutely alive, although undergoing linguistic change. A recent study did find evidence of dialect obsolescence amongst younger speakers in Lerwick (Smith and Durham 2012: 80). However, as an incomer, the writer was struck by the richness and distinctiveness of the dialect when he arrived to live in the village of Scalloway in 2007. He noted the reaction of tourists on hearing the locals in his bookshop, and their often-bewildered looks as they heard the dialect for the first time. Unusually for a dialect, one can hear it on BBC Radio Shetland, sometimes even in the evening news bulletin, marking its normality within the community, although Smith (1996: 41) suggests these tend to be the more frivolous new items, standard English being used for serious announcements. There are a good number of publications available in dialect, including translations like *Alice's Adventirs in Wonderlaand* (2012) and *Da Gruffalo's Bairn* (2016), and books of poetry, like those by Christian Da Lucca and Robert Allan Jamieson. The widely read and much-admired quarterly magazine the *New Shetlander* has been publishing dialect material since its inception in 1947. There is also an organisation dedicated to encouraging and promoting dialect use called *Shetland ForWirds*, which was formed in 2004 and has subsequently published amongst other things the *Craigsaet* CD full of 'rhymes, sangs and stories for peerie bairns'. They present awards for the use of dialect and they maintain an excellent website with a large range of resources, including teaching materials for primary and secondary schools. However, it is interesting to note that the words Norse, Nordic or Norn are noticeable by the absence. *Shetland ForWirds* is keen to promote the dialect as it exists today and not focus merely on its Norse component. In an excellent paper available on their website describing the history of the dialect, the Shetland archivist Brian Smith discusses and dismisses the belief that the current dialect is in any sense inferior to Norn, a belief which owes its origin to Jakobsen. As Smith (1996) says, 'The reason I dwell on these matters is that Jakobsen had a huge impact here, in his own day and afterwards. He fell in love with Shetland, and Shetland fell in love with him. [However] Jakobsen's account of Shetland's linguistic history has two aspects. On the one hand he paints a picture of a golden age, the era when Shetlanders spoke Norn. And the other side of the Jakobsen coin is that the modern Shetland dialect is a vastly inferior version of the old language.' This hankering after a golden age is likely to be the reason that some do appear to valorise the Norn component in the dialect. In the recent Shetland dialect dictionary by the Christie-Johnstons (2010) all words of Norn origin are in blue so that they cannot be missed. Of course, whether valorised or not, the dialect is heavily influenced by Norn. The extinct Scandinavian language of Shetland still exerts its influence.

According to Robert McColl Millar (2008: 237), the present dialect developed in the nineteenth century, 'from the supraregional koiné of the original sixteenth and seventeenth century Scots-speaking settlers and the heavily Norn-influenced Scots of the first and second generations of islanders who no longer had Norn as a mother tongue'. Van Leyden (2004) has described it as, 'a conservative variety of Lowland Scots with a substantial Scandinavian substratum'. This substratum consists of both linguistic and lexical features. Regarding Norn linguistic features in the dialect, Van Leyden noted in her study of the *Prosodic Characteristics of Orkney and Shetland Dialects* that the dialect has, 'retained its Scandinavian temporal organisation, while Orkney has apparently lost this feature … [confirming] … the general assumption that Shetland dialect has maintained its Norn substratum to a greater extent than Orkney'. The very notable practice of assigning gendered pronouns to inanimate objects is likely to be a Norn influence, because, although in one study when Shetland dialect genders were compared by Ljosland (2012) to Old Norse genders, the correlation seemed to be no more than what might be expected from random chance, in another more recent study by Villupilai (2018: 28), it was found that the genders did in fact, 'pattern significantly with the Old Norse genders'.

Despite Michael Barnes (2010: 27) suggesting that the dialect contains only, 'a small Scandinavian element, and one that is steadily diminishing', lexically the small Scandinavian element is in common use and seems remarkably stable. Gunnel Melchers (1981) describes how these Norn words tend to survive in the semantic fields of emotions, homely activities, flora and fauna. The Christie-Johnstons' dictionary contains hundreds of examples of words still known and understood. Here are a few of the specimens that the writer has encountered in everyday conversation: *affrug* 'a backwash of waves after having hit cliffs or the shore', *cloor* 'to scratch', as in the phrase 'da cat cloored da cooch', *oag* 'to crawl, as in 'oagin hame', *helly* 'the weekend', as in 'have a good helly', *Voar* 'Spring', as in 'the voar red up (clean up)', *kline* 'to spread', as in 'I klined my toast, *troitle* 'mutter', as in 'she troitled to herself', *spaegie* 'stiffness', as in 'I'm spaegied from the football', *dratsie* 'an otter', *shalder* 'an oyster catcher', *dunter* 'an eider duck', *sparls* 'a type of sausage from Burra' and the phrase *Joost vargin awaa* roughly 'just messing about'.

Research into the Shetland dialect is not merely the province of academics. On Facebook the *Wir Midder Tongue* page currently has 1954 members. It is a hotbed of activity ranging from etymologies to chats about usage, such as, 'Whit aboot a stowen dunt? Do you use dat?'. However, it is clear from the discussions that words of Norn origin are of particular interest, particularly if they have Norwegian, Faroese or Icelandic cognates.

Legal niceties

It is surely no coincidence that *Með lögum skal land byggja* became the slogan to represent Shetland – law and identity are intimately connected. For example, Scotland's national identity owes much to the protection of its legal system provided by the 1707 Treaty of Union. A figure such as Arthur Anderson was well aware that Shetland still had some vestigial legal distinctiveness. In 1611, the 'foreyne lawis' of Orkney and Shetland, local versions of the Norwegian thirteenth-century Law Code of King Magnus VI Lawmender, were formally abolished by *Act of the Privy Council of Scotland* (Smith and Ballantyne 1994: 261–262). The laws of Scotland were to replace them. However, despite this, elements of Shetland's legal identity survived to a much later date. Some of the laws were recodified in the *Old Country Acts of Shetland* (1814), and Udal land tenure, with its laws about inheritance and various landscape rights, survived. Udal comes from the Old Norse word *Óðal* 'property held in allodial tenure', which means ancestral land not held of a feudal superior,

and therefore not owing feudal duties of any kind, although a tax called
scat was owed to the Crown. In the nineteenth century, Sir Walter Scott
started the trend of romanticising this form of landholding in his novel
The Pirate (1821). It still has an aura of romance and represents the Golden
Age, when all Shetlanders were small-scale landowners, before feudalism
and greedy Scottish interlopers spoiled everything. However, in actual
fact, like all Golden Ages the reality was rather different, and throughout
most of Shetland's history the majority of Shetlanders were tenants rather
than peasant proprietors (Smith 2000: 68).

Michael Jones (2011: 71), in a study of the significance of Udal Law,
states with justification that even today, 'awareness of Old Norse legal rights
has survived 540 years of Scottish and British rule'. He shows how Udal
Law continues to be referred to in public debates, including in 2001–2002
when it came up in disputes about possible changes to foreshore rights
(Jones 2011: 78). He argues that, because Udal Law is a significant part
of Shetland history, it serves as an important marker of identity, even if
it does not now have much legal reality (Jones 2011: 81). It is a sort of tal-
isman brought out when local rights are believed to have been ignored
and there have been a number of notable occasions when there has been
an dispute with the Crown where Udal Law has been brandished, most
notably in the case of the St Ninians' Isle Treasure, Scotland's finest early
medieval silver hoard found on St Ninian's Isle in 1958 – did it belong to
the Crown or did it belong to the landowner and by extension Shetland?
Unfortunately, as far as Shetland is concerned, the Crown won, and the
treasure was removed to the National Museum in Edinburgh. Udal Law
was mentioned in the recent debate about the transfer of the Crown Estate
to the Scottish Parliament in 2018, and it will no doubt continue to play
its part in the future.

Folklore and freuteries

Shetland has a rich folklore heritage and it plays its part, as folklore
has done in other places and at other times, in creating a sense of

Shetland distinctiveness with its roots firmly connected to the past. This heritage is celebrated in the islands in several ways. In 1945 the *Shetland Folk Society* was founded, and since then it has published a number of important works, including the series of *Folk Books*, a veritable cornucopia of folklore riches, such as the telling in dialect of the tale about *Katherine Asmundder* 'da hidmist queen a Foula', who was, according to the storyteller, descended from a Norseman called Guttorm (1995: 47–52). The last volume was published in 1995, although the society itself continues. The magazines *New Shetlander* and *Shetland Life* have regularly published folklore material. In a piece on 'Gygrs, guykerls and other grotesque females in the landscape', Jennings (2009: 31–38) explored Norse hags infesting the Shetland countryside. A visit to the bookshop will present the visitor with a number of folklore themed books. There are recent publications such as *Da Book o Trows* (2007), a delightful collection of stories about Shetland's faery folk, *Folklore from Whalsay and Shetland* by John Stewart, *Shetland Folk Tales* by the late, great Shetland storyteller Lawrence Tulloch, and *Guddicks: Traditional Riddles from Shetland* by Amy Lightfoot and Laurie Goodlad. There are also reprinted antiquarian collections, set to confuse the unwary, like John Spence's *Shetland Folk-Lore* (1899), and the *County Folklore Vol. III Orkney and Shetland Islands* (1903). One can experience Shetland's folklore at the *Shetland Museum*, which has a customs and folklore zone, where, under a circle of dialect words, visitors can sit in traditional chairs and listen to traditional stories. There is even a *trowie knowe* 'fairy hill', where one can encounter Shetland's diminutive supernatural beings. The word *trow*, as all Shetlanders know, comes from Old Norse *troll* 'magical being'. Another exhibit is a beautiful *skekkler's* costume made from straw, *skekklers* being guizers, another word of Norse origin from *skekkill* 'a stretched out animal skin', which at one time would have been worn to hide the guizer's identity.

There is no doubt that Shetland's folklore is of Norse origin, and as such it has attracted the interest of scholars from across Scandinavia. As the Swedish folklorist Bo Almqvist (1991: 5) said, 'a survey of the Scandinavian folklore of Orkney and Shetland would fill several thick volumes'. In a study of the *Uglier Foot* motif he discusses the clear connection between the Shetland folktale about *Jan Teit and the Bear*, recorded in the nineteenth century, and the story about *Þórarinn Nefjólfsson* from Medieval Iceland (Almqvist 1991: 86–91). Terry Gunnell (2007) has studied Shetland's mumming tradition and shown its intimate connection with mumming in the Faroe Islands and Iceland, while Vilborg Davíðsdóttir (2010) has studied the stories of two great Shetland storytellers, Brucie Henderson and Tom Tulloch. In a recent publication Jennings (2016: 27–56) explored the supernatural tales and beliefs from the island of Fetlar. Once these were collected together it became clear just how Nordic the material was. There was a *landnám* 'land taking' story about the coming of the first settlers, there was a version of the migratory tale ML6070 'Fairies send a message', which has not been collected on mainland Scotland but occurs widely in Norway, and there were several stories about Finns, the Old Norse word for the Sami. I concluded that the island had an, 'identifiably Nordic folklore dialect' (2016: 32).

Shetland has a thriving folk music scene, and the fiddle tradition is particularly strong. Peter Cooke in his masterly study of Shetland fiddlers and fiddle music described how Scottish music traditions came to replace indigenous ones of Norse origin. Nonetheless, he pointed to a number of fiddle tunes such as the *Muckle Reel o' Papa* which are strikingly similar to the Norwegian *Halling*, dance tunes in the Hardanger fiddle tradition of western Norway. Although he suggested that the *Muckle* or *Aald reels* were unlikely to be revived (Cooke 1986: 58), in fact they do feature in performance, and when they are played listeners are exposed to music with distinctly Nordic musical traits. Similarly, if Shetland songs are performed, listeners might well hear the *Unst Boat Song*, which is in a broken form of Norn. It features on the CD *Across the Waters* by the Fair Isle group *Friðarey*. The Norse folklore of Shetland is not confined to books, museums or scholarly discourse; it can still pop up unexpectedly. I was told an anecdote by an inhabitant of Lerwick about *Minnie Grülie*, a bugbear who haunted the coal shed when she was a girl. *Grülie* is the Old Norse *grýla* 'an ogress' with a penchant for eating children! She still haunts Iceland at Christmas.

Conclusions

In 1733 Thomas Gifford, one of the most important figures in Shetland of his day, published an *Historical Description of the Zetland Islands*. As one might expect, this is an extremely valuable resource, providing a rare insight into the way of life of Shetlanders at the time. It contains passages which describe their cultural identity. Although the Norse element was clearly in decline, it was still evidently extant. In one passage Gifford reports that

> The islands and places in them are all Danish, and continue so for the most part to this day; and the customs, manners, and language of the old Zetlanders, with their way of living, were the same as in Norway, even down to the time of some old men yet living; and the greatest part of the vulgar inhabitants, and some of considerable note here, still reckon themselves of Danish extract, and are all Patronymics, whereby they are distinguished from those that have come from the continent of Britain ... Still these old Danish inhabitants value themselves much upon their antiquity ... particularly one Patrick Gilbertson, of Islesburgh, an old man about ninety years, alive at writing hereof, reckons himself the 22nd generation, in a lineal succession, possessors of Islesburgh.

One is struck with the parallels today. The place-names continue to be of Old Norse origin. Although modern Shetlanders no longer speak the language of the old *Zetlanders*, the modern Shetland dialect has more than a smattering of Norn words still used in everyday speech. Many still reckon themselves of Norse descent. A conversation with a Scalloway local procured the information that he was not really Scottish but rather part Norse and part Spanish, from the Armada no less. Many proudly bear surnames which are in origin fixed patronymics. Like Patrick Gilbertson, there are many with an intense interest in family history. The Shetland writer Malachy Tallack (2007) has described *reddin up kin* – working out exactly who you are related to – as the most popular of island sports. The *Shetland Family History Society* has its own premises in Lerwick, publishes a regular magazine and maintains a very useful website.

The Scottish poet Hugh MacDiarmid, who lived on the Shetland island of Whalsay from 1933 to 1942, noted

The insistence that the Shetlanders are Scandinavians is stirring and represents a tendency which I think ought to be encouraged by all possible means, and especially by a recovery of the Old Norn tongue, and an effort to build up a vigorous cultural movement on that basis, since that can only help them to preserve and develop a distinctive life. (1939: 59)

However, like much of what MacDiarmid wrote, this is taking things to the extreme, because despite the interest in Norse connections, the surviving Norn lexicon in the dialect and the popularity of Norwegian night classes, there is no great movement to reinstate a dead language, although there is a website which explores the potential for recreating it and is a valuable resource of extant Norn materials. However, such a project, even if it had popular support, is a vain exercise, because Norn is no longer recoverable in any meaningful sense; too much has been lost. Nonetheless, as we have seen, Shetland does have a rich Norse heritage, a heritage which has been recognised by many Nordic scholars. The Shetland community engages with its Norse heritage in its own way – flying the Shetland flag, consciously using dialect words of Norn origin, choosing a Norse housename, visiting a Viking archaeological site or indeed taking part in Up Helly Aa or one of the other local Viking festivals and singing hopefully, 'Worthy sons of Vikings make us'.

Bibliography

Abrams, L. (2010). *Myth and Materiality in a Woman's World*. Manchester: Manchester University Press.

Almqvist, B. (1991). *Viking Ale: Studies in folklore contacts between the Northern and Western worlds*. Aberystwyth: Boethius Press.

Anderson, B. (1983). *Imagined Communities*. London: Verso.

Barnes, M. (2010). 'The Study of Norn'. In Millar, R. M., (ed.), *Northern Lights, Northern Words*, pp. 26–47. Aberdeen: FRLSU.

Brown, C. G. (1998). *Up-Helly-Aa: Custom, Culture and Community in Shetland*. Manchester: Manchester University Press.

Christie-Johnston, A., and A. (2010). *Shetland Words: A Dictionary of the Shetland Dialect*. Lerwick: The Shetland Times Ltd.

Cohen, B. J. (1983). *Norse Imagery in Shetland: An Historical Study of Intellectuals and Their Use of the Past in the Construction of Shetland's Identity, with Particular Reference to the Period 1800–1914*. PhD Thesis. University of Manchester.

Cooke, P. (1986). *The Fiddle Tradition of the Shetland Isles*. Cambridge: Cambridge University Press.

De Lucca, C. (2002). *Plain Song*. Lerwick: The Shetland Library.

Gammeltoft, P. (2005). 'Shetland and Orkney Island-Names – A Dynamic Group'. In Millar, R. M., (ed.), *Northern Lights, Northern Words*, pp. 15–25. Aberdeen: FRLSU.

Gifford, T. (1879). *Historical Description of the Zetland Islands in the Year 1733*. Edinburgh: Thomas George Stevenson.

Grimond, J. (1974). *Zetland County Council Debate, 30 April 1973, Vol. 855 cc.860–902*. London: Hansard.

Grydhøj, A. (2013). 'Ethnicity and the origins of local identity in Shetland, UK – Part I: Picts, Vikings, Fairies, Finns, and Aryans', *Journal of Marine and Island Cultures*, 2 (1), 39–48.

Grønneberg, R. (2001). 'The origins of the Shetland flag', *The Flag Bulletin*, 40.

Gunnell, T. (2007). 'Masks and mumming in the Nordic area'. In Gunnell, T., (ed.), *Masks and Mumming in the Nordic Area*, pp. 275–326. Uppsala: Kungl.Gustav Adolks Akademien för svensk folkkulture.

Haldane Burgess, J. J. (1896). *Lowra Biglan's Mutch*. Kirkwall: Leonards.

Jakobsen, J. (1985). *An Etymological Dictionary of the Norn Language in Shetland*. Lerwick: Shetland Folk Society.

Jennings, A. (2009). 'Gygrs, guykerls and other grotesque females in the landscape', *New Shetlander*, Issue 249 – Hairst, 31–38.

Jennings, A. (2016). 'Memories and Metamorphoses: A Short Introduction to the Supernatural Tales and Beliefs from Fetlar in Shetland'. In Kuusela, T., and G. Maiello (eds), *Folk Belief and Traditions of the Supernatural*, pp. 27–56. Copenhagen: Beewolf Press.

Jennings, A. (2017). 'Our Islands Our Future: Purposeful Opportunism at Its Best'. In Brinklow, L., and R. Gibson (eds), *From Black Horse to White Steeds: Building Community Resilience*, pp. 62–85. Charlottetown: Island Studies Press.

Jones, M. (2011). 'Landscape and Legal Rights in Orkney and Shetland'. In Egoz, S., Makhzoumi, J., and G. Pungetti (eds), *The Right to Landscape: Contesting Landscape and Human Rights,* Farnham: Ashgate Publishing Ltd.

Leirfall, J. (1976). *Vest I havet: Vesterhasøyane gjennom tusen års norsk historie*. Oslo: Samlaget.

Lenman, B. P. (1987). 'Review of Shetland Life and Trade 1550–1914 by Hance D. Smith', *The English Historical Review*, 102 (403), 501–501.

Ljosland, R. (2012). 'I'll cross dat brig whin I come til him': grammatical gender in the Orkney and Shetland dialects of Scots', *Scottish Language*, 31, 29–58.

MacDiarmid, H. (1939). *The Islands of Scotland: Hebrides, Orkneys, and Shetlands*. London: Batsford.

McColl Millar, R. (2008). 'The origins and development of Shetland dialect in light of dialect contact theories', *English World-Wide* 29 (3), 237–267.

Melchers, G. (1981). 'The Norn element in Shetland dialect today – a case of 'never accepted' language death'. In Ejerhed, E., and I. Henrysson (eds), *Tvåspråkighet*. Umeå: University of Umeå.

Reeploeg, S. (2017). 'Peripheral visions: engaging Nordic literary traditions on Orkney and Shetland', *Scandinavica*, 56 (1), 34–58.

Saxby, J. (1910). *The Cradle of Our Race: Souvenance of a Cruise on Northern Seas*. Edinburgh: J. and H. Lindsay.

Scott, W. (1821). *The Pirate*. Edinburgh: Constable and Ballantyne.

Simchak, T. (2008). *Oil, Culture and Economy: The Reinvention of the Shetland Way of Life*. MLitt Thesis. University of Oxford.

Smith, B. (1996). 'The development of the spoken and written Shetland Dialect: a historian's view', *Northern Studies*, 31, 30–43.

Smith, B. (2000). *Toons and Tenants: Settlement and Society in Shetland, 1299–1899*. Lerwick: The Shetland Times Ltd.

Smith, B., and Ballantyne, J.H. (1994). *Shetland Documents, 1580–1611*. Lerwick: The Shetland Times Ltd.

Smith, J., and Durham, M. (2012). 'Bidialectalism or dialect death? Explaining generational change in the Shetland Islands, Scotland', *American Speech*, 87(1), 57–88.

Smith, M. R. (2006). *The Literature of Shetland*. Lerwick: The Shetland Times

Stewart, J. (2005). *Folklore from Whalsay and Shetland*. Lerwick: Shetland Amenity Trust.

Tallack, M. (2007). 'Coontin kin', *New Statesman*, 23 July, p. 4., <https://www.newstatesman.com/blogs/malachy-tallack/2007/07/cousins-third-anyone-times > accessed 30 October 2019.

The Shetland Folklore Development Group. (2007). *Da Book o Trows*. Lerwick.

Van Leyden, K. (2004). *Prosodic Characteristics of Orkney and Shetland Dialects: An Experimental; Approach*. Utrecht: LOT.

Vilborg Davíðsdóttir (2010). MA Thesis. *'An Dat's de Peerie Story': Rannsókn og túlkun á sögnum tveggja Hjaltlendinga*. Háskóli Íslands.

Villupilai, V. (2018). 'Gendered Inanimates in Spoken Shetland Dialect'. Abstract for The Forum for Research on Languages of Scotland and Ulster 12th Triennial

Conference 23–25 August 2018 English Language & Linguistics, University of Glasgow, 28, <https://frlsuupdate.files.wordpress.com/2018/08/frlsu-2018-abstracts1.pdf> accessed 30 October 2019.

Waugh, D. (2010). 'Drongs, hjogelbens, pobis and skoreks: Jakobsen recorded them all'. In Sigurðardóttir, T., and B. Smith (eds) *Jakob Jakobsen in Shetland and the Faroes*. Lerwick: Shetland Amenity Trust and the University of the Faroe Islands.

5. Scotland's Islands and Cultural Work: The 'Specialness' of Place

This chapter discusses island places as literal and symbolic sites of cultural work and examines the textual nature of narratives and accounts that are suggestive of island cultural work as 'special'. Our discussion is informed by a growing research focus on the emotional, embodied and material aspects of making contemporary creative forms, from across the arts – including literature, visual culture, music and dance – and of craft-making and design, as both an aesthetic but also notably a commercial activity, in and on Scotland's islands (Lu 2015; Harling Stalker and Burnett 2016; Burnett and Harling Stalker 2018; McHattie et al. 2018). The wider context of Scotland's islands as sites of successful creative and cultural industry (Highlands and Islands Enterprise 2014) is well documented but not without debate. We note the complex interface between arts and crafts with other creative and cultural work activities and sites of cultural production and consumption, namely media, museums and galleries, and heritage and tourism but also education, and other sectoral policies, for example, around food and drink, land and landscape, and the expansion of 'island technologies' (Bevan and McLean 2013). We are mindful of the complexity surrounding research attempts to capture the material and everyday lived experience of island places and environments (Butler 2012; Vannini and Taggart 2012; Stratford 2017; Boon et al. 2018; Bates et al. 2019).

Our own experiences of living and working in small island communities in Scotland and in Canada, as well as our good fortune to exchange and share in the expertise, research and knowledge of colleagues across both island studies networks and cultural work exchanges, has unquestionably informed our 'take' on examining cultural work within Scotland's island context. Cultural work is typified by a capacity to create and circulate symbolic, aesthetic or creative goods and services (Banks 2007; Banks et al. 2013) and in considering *how* we explore island cultural work we recognise that attempting to explain cultural work experience is a shifting and contingent process, not least in reference to Scotland's various and layered island *localisms*. *Why* we are interested in examining Scotland's islands as sites and spaces of cultural work is more prosaic. Creative and cultural industries are championed across Scotland. Scotland's island authorities and enterprise bodies target and support culture and creativity as key drivers for economic growth, promotional confidence and socio-cultural well-being (Burnett and Danson 2017). Our contribution to this collection of chapters presents an opportunity to scan the horizon of cultural work theorisation generally and use our bearings to comment on Scotland's islands' contexts more particularly.

Islands: Places of enchantment

Islands are often articulated as unique, enchanting and transformative but also as challenging and limiting; *conditioned* (not least here in Scotland) both by the physicality and the socioeconomics of island places. The materiality of both islandness and cultural work for us is situated within the broader celebratory narratives of small islands as creative and cultural 'making' places (Abrams 2006; Macdonald 2010, 2018; Brannigan 2015; Bevan and Downes 2017; Carden 2018a, 2018b). Island cultural work is increasingly commonplace, ambitious and confident yet we argue here that such work is nonetheless informed by and informing of precarity, marginality and a further embedding of 'islandness' as complex.

Cultural work is always undertaken in places and in islands this placeness of creative and cultural island activity is significant. As Smith articulates, place is a setting for 'interactions which are, in turn, reproduced by action itself [...] interpersonal actions are attuned by the symbolic meanings attached to a locale [...] action within a place will be influenced by the myths and narratives of the locale' (Smith 1999: 14–15). This sociological definition of place demonstrates that through action (indicative of agency) and interaction (indicative of things social) a place is *known* to people. It is embedded with meanings that are produced and reproduced. These meanings are important because they come to shape how people are motivated to act and attach meanings to what they do (and where they are). Place *specificity* is important to identity formation as Massey elaborates

> Places are collections of those stories, articulations within the wider power-geometries of space. Their character will be a product of those intersections within that wider setting, and of what is made of them. And, too, of the non-meetings-up, the disconnections and relations not established, the exclusions. All this contributes to the specificity of place. (2005: 125)

Massey demonstrates how place becomes not only about the stories that are told but also about boundary-building. Whose stories can be told and whose are left silent? Who is part of the place and who is not? This boundary-building through narrative is especially salient when examining islandness. Consequently, claiming islandness identity is itself highly contingent. Islandness as an analytical concept is suggestive of the way that islanders – 'as people living on islands' – are seen to possess certain qualities as Conkling claims where they

> share a sense of islandness that transcends the particulars of a local culture. Islandness is a metaphysical sensation that derives from the heightened experience that accompanies physical isolation [...] it amplifies a sense of place that is closer to the natural world because you are in closer proximity to your neighbours [...]. Islandness thus helps maintain island communities in spite of daunting economic pressures to abandon them. (2007: 191)

This islandness is seen as transcending the mundane. 'Islanders' embody qualities that *condition* them to live in places that should almost not be inhabitable and yet are places where people stay and come to live, guided by the narratives and myths of island life and work. We should take care to step away from tendencies that essentialise islanders or indeed islandness, however. Not all people resident on islands claim islander identity nor is it conferred upon them. The 'fixedness', or otherwise, of islandness as an idea, a *sensation*, or indeed a *condition* has been critiqued across island studies and within other arenas. Nonetheless, a sense of island 'specialness' remains deeply rooted to images, accounts, narratives, texts and cultural expression. Of note to us here is how current narratives of experiencing islandness persist as an alluring, embodied lived experience of both distance and proximity whereby the spaces and practices of islandness offer a heightened 'metaphysical sensation' that is suggestive of what Bennett (2001) has termed an 'enchanted orbit'. Enchantment offers us a useful terminology by which we can further interrogate Massey's ideas of a specificity of place not least in the particular regard of the situated experience of island cultural work such as art, craft and other creative expression. As Bennett (2001: 37) claims, enchantment 'requires a cultivated form of perception, a discerning and meticulous attentiveness to the singular specificity of things'. Furthermore, enchantment is most likely to occur through tangible items, things, or what she would later call vibrant objects. One can never be sure when this object will appear and strike us; 'provoked by a surprise' (Bennett 2001: 104). In our two examples of island cultural work expression (*Harris Tweed* and *Shetland Wool*) we examine how the mediatised and promotional accounts of island cultural production highlight and reinforce such enchantment aspects. Island things are imbued with a mystical quality, a vibrancy, a specificity and a capacity to surprise: enchantment is made, worked upon, yet imbued with an ethereal 'beyondness'.

In applying Bennett's enchanted orbit to islands – where an economic logic within culture will see 'special places spiral down from their enchanted orbits unless their extraordinary nature is continually reproduced' (Smith 1999: 22) – there needs to be a concerted effort to ensure that places maintain and indeed fulfil enchantment expectations (Vannini and Taggart 2012; Bates et al. 2019). Weber argued that while disenchantment is never reversible, it is never complete and Bennett claims that we can seek and find 'fugitive experiences of magic [...] within the calculable world. This results in an increased interest among rational, calculating selves in mysticism, eroticism, and other curiosities of the "cultural" field' (2001: 65). Modern cultural life offers various pathways and encouragements for us to seek out a life of *ataraxy*, that is, a life embodied as blessedness, contentment and tranquillity, characteristics that seem to mirror Conkling's suggestion of islandness (and somewhat problematically *islanders*) being 'beyond the mundane'.

Arts and crafts too have often been claimed as a realm of work that is beyond the mundane where, as Luckman (2015) argues, the 'aura' lies not so much in the artefact itself but 'more in the process of making'. For Luckman making reminds us of our agency within the physical world and while our re-enchantment 'may be most obviously manifest in the object, it is for these reasons that I argue that the deeper, more powerful sense of enchantment here lies in the making process itself'(Luckman 2015: 83). As we have already noted the interplay of the specialness aspects of distance and proximity that island places often seem to most especially signify is well recognised in the 'fugitive' and enchanted symbolism of island cultural worker accounts of their art and craft-making: notably islands are *special* and 'good places' to make 'good work' (c.f. Harling Stalker and Burnett 2016; Burnett and Harling Stalker 2018). We turn now to explore aspects of making on islands as *island making*, with some comment on cultural industries, cultural work and the representation of these more generally.

Making islands: Cultural industries, cultural work and cultural representation

Creative and cultural industries are defined variously but for our purposes here we adopt the claim that these are 'segments of the economy concerned with the generation of intellectual property, the production of 'aesthetic' or 'symbolic' goods or services' (Luckman 2012: 11). Artists, craftworkers and creatives, as 'islanders' and 'not islanders', each contribute and engage with island cultural work by virtue of their residency, and their situated claims to and engagements with island cultures and environments. What is of particular interest to us is the positioning of cultural workers in relation to doing islandness and 'island work', across island places of Scotland. The affective relationship to island places is widely circulated and island studies scholars, amongst others, seek to critique this more fully: 'If we think of islandness through the minutiae of affect or feeling, we can begin to examine more critically the connections between our selves and our islands' (Boon et al. 2018: 118).

Cultural representation and its mediatisation has powerfully under-pinned global discourse and visual narratives of small islands as spaces and sites of *enchantment* and of *enhancement*: islands as interesting, alluring, celebratory, productive and 'other'. Furthermore, this sighting, citing and site-ing – is undertaken (consciously, or not) by an expanding body of *island cultural workers*: artists, designers, media professionals, marketing and others variously underpinned by the term *creatives* who live and work on islands. Islands are accessed, facilitated, enjoyed, appropriated and ex-ploited to serve the interests and demands of audiences and consumers both within and outwith an island's shores. Cultural workers across a range of sectors and enterprise inform, stimulate, entertain, engage and facilitate a wider consumption of island culture and environments that is rewarding, celebratory and validating. Cultural work is variously co-operative, edu-cational, critical and transformative. It is also recognised to be highly con-tingent on social and cultural capital, frequently precarious and sometimes debilitating for one's self (Gill and Pratt 2008; Banks 2009, 2010; Luckman 2012; Taylor and Littleton 2012). Demands are made of its 'specialness' and for cultural work to be understood as 'good work'. There are intense expectations of cultural work's flexibility, creative freedom and inherent expressiveness, not least as being particularly identity *affirming* for the worker, for the work and for the site of cultural labour production and its consumption (place).

The same affirming aspect is often expected of islands (especially small and 'remote') too. The interplay between remote and rural island sites as special spaces that attract special kinds of work is reinforced in different ways. Islands have increasingly occupied a special space in late modern narratives as sites of freedom and expression and, as discussed elsewhere (not least in this volume), island spaces, sites and places confer, and have conferred upon them, *specialness* via literature, visual culture and the arts more widely (Macdonald 2010, 2018; Brannigan 2015; Burnett 2017; Holt et al. 2018). But also important and impactful are the ways in which islands (and in Scotland, the remote rural more generally) are framed as key sites of certain kinds of production and consumption: powerfully established via the cultural economies of tourism, heritage and media but also figuring in other key sectors such as food and drink production, life sciences and energy (e.g. car adverts, digital media tech, health products, or energy production) that utilise the iconography of remote island spaces as *useful* selling platforms of 'alternative' modernity, sustainability and well-being that each in their own way speak to aspects of distinctiveness and 'enchantment'.

Island cultural production is a growth sector in Scotland. To make on islands is to express identity: of place, of people and of process and this has been attractive to consumers but also to producers as a reinforcing of work location choice and identity affirming (enhancing). Our interest as island studies scholars then is to further highlight and critique the valuing, and the status of islands – as a resource, as a set of material and symbolic assets, as capital – within the broader realm of cultural work narratives in remote and island Scotland, and beyond. By way of illustrating this island cultural work specialness, as production and promotion, and as variously enchanting and enhancing, we present two established examples as indicative of broader tropes and trends: firstly, an account of Harris Tweed, made in the Outer Hebrides and secondly, Shetland wool and its associated knitting and textile heritage.

Harris Tweed: 'Our land, our people, our home'

As we reflect in this chapter on island arts and craft as both a material and symbolic textual landscape, we have chosen to highlight Harris Tweed as a celebrated expression of such a textuality. The creative documenting and the interface of arts, crafts, and economy and culture reflect more fully the voices or narratives of Scotland's island art and craft celebration more widely. Harris Tweed is mapped to the particular geographies of the Outer Hebrides, the island communities of 'Harris, Lewis and the Uists' (Moisley 1961; Pike 2015; McClellan 2017; Harris Tweed Authority 2019) not least in terms of the establishing, the survival and the mediated construction of an 'island industry'. As McClellan (2017: 90) states succinctly: 'When it comes to tweed, and especially Harris Tweed, place

inherently and passionately matters.' Various commentaries – journal-
ists, fashionistas, policy champions, politicians, entrepreneurs and researchers – have promoted (circulated) the 'specialness' and enchanting
qualities of Harris Tweed as both process and product:

> Harris Tweed is unlike any other, romantic and luxurious, the landscape of the Outer
> Hebrides rendered in cloth. Up close, the secret of the subtle shades is revealed: a
> blending of many colors, a pointillist adventure in wool, available by tradition in
> 8,000 designs. This tweed is luster, patina, fresh air, and northern light. (Harper
> and McDougall 2012: 86)

Following the takeover in 2006 of the *Kenneth Mackenzie Ltd.* business
(the mill was established in 1906), by a Yorkshire-based entrepreneur a
business decision to focus on only a handful of tweed patterns dramat-
ically impacted on the iconic mill's fortunes. Already 'in crisis', the tweed
industry was unquestionably struggling in an era of global market tur-
moil. The decision to effectively reject the island craft industry's rich
heritage by selecting only a few patterns (and to consign the mill's rich
and varied tapestry of tweed colour and design to the past heritage 'bin')
was seen by island communities and tweed aficionados alike as disas-
trous: economically, socially and culturally. Harper and McDougall speak
of the despondency of those tweed workers linked to the Mackenzie mill
who lost their tweed and weaving employment as a people who had lost
much more than just their livelihoods. The scene is described of weavers
and mill workers drifting away from tweed making to take 'steadier employment' in occupations such as taxi-driving or the new call-centre in
Stornoway: 'For people who have spent their lives with cloth, born and
bred to the production of Harris Tweed, and whose very identity comes
from it, these soulless alternatives are hard labor' (Harper and McDougall
2012: 92). In a 'good news' story more recently, the owner gifted the Lewis
based Mackenzie mill enterprise to the local mill management, effectively
securing a local say in a local industry for a local workforce on the islands
and generally Harris Tweed and its resurgence is a successful and going
concern. But the narratives are powerful and speak of a specialness of
place and the people working 'in, and of, place' as particular, and set apart
from *other* work.

McDougall, cited above, is a London based textile designer with island 'roots' and someone who it can be claimed *knows* both the place and the craft, and speaks of and for the legacy and the ambition of the industry as an integral part of a locality and environment: 'Harris Tweed is wholly produced on the island and its identity is intrinsically bound up in the landscape and heritage of its makers both visually and in its tactile qualities; thick, rough and protective' (Harper and McDougall 2012: 97). Elsewhere, digital journalist Kathryn Macleod (2017) in a recent BBC commentary again reinforces the particular placeness of Harris Tweed: 'What makes Harris Tweed so desirable at the cutting edge of fashion is the fact that the process by which the cloth is made is not "trendy" at all, but timeless – resulting in a luxury fabric that is deeply rooted in tradition, heritage and place'. The specialness conferred is that of an island product, but one produced of the 'DNA' (MacLeod 2017) of islanders in island place.

Sustainability is an inherent focus for the cultural and islands work of cloth weaving and mills and the protected status of the islands' tweed production's cultural environment is seen as key to longer term futures; so too is its continued requirement to champion its place brand. Harris Tweed is a unique product with enviable protected status governed, championed and protected through the Harris Tweed Authority. In 1993 a British Act of Parliament was passed to protect the cloth's production and quality trademark status:

> The mark of the Orb, pressed onto every length of cloth and seen on the traditional label affixed to finished items, guarantees the highest quality tweed, dyed, spun and handwoven by islanders of the Outer Hebrides of Scotland in their homes to the laws outlined in the Harris Tweed Act of Parliament. (Harris Tweed Authority 2019)[1]

Understanding how cultural work is entwined with the placeness of Scotland's islands such as in the crafting of tweed in the Outer Hebrides, and how this powerfully confers and reinforces cultural work as islandness, is perhaps best displayed by the account (quoted in full) provided by the official 'guardians of the orb' themselves, the Harris Tweed Authority:

---

1   Harris Tweed Authority <https://www.harristweed.org/about-us/guardians-of-the-orb>, accessed 20 July 2019.

The long, barren archipelago on the far north west tip of Europe is home to every dyer, blender, carder, spinner, warper, weaver, finisher and inspector of HARRIS TWEED. No part of the process takes place elsewhere.

As such, the land and people are woven into the very fabric of the cloth, reflecting as it does the colours of the landscapes, the beauty of our vistas and the values of our people.

To the north of the remote string of islands lies Lewis, a rugged and bleakly beautiful land of heather and moor, loch and stream and home to the three main mills and the main harbour town of Stornoway. Lewis is connected by a narrow isthmus of land to Harris in the south. More mountainous than its northern brother, Harris has some of the world's finest beaches of golden fine shell sand, shallow azure blue seas and a myriad of hidden crofts and villages. South of this main body a string of smaller islands tails off to the south, the machair meadows and loch-laden isles of the Uists and beautiful Barra at the furthest tip.

For hundreds of years these islands have produced a special tweed … HARRIS TWEED.

(2019)

By way of a celebration of the crafting of tweed as identity, particularity, survival and expression, Ian Lawson's book deriving from his exhibition *From the Land Comes the Cloth: Harris Tweed* (Lawson 2013), documents (mediates) the Harris Tweed industry, in aesthetic richness. The exhibition and book are works of art that in turn have elicited further creative response such as this example from an online retail blog:

It is clear when viewing these extraordinary, dramatic natural scenes how closely connected the Harris designs are with the landscape. Lawson's saturated colours, stark contrasts and wide angled views illustrate the diverse, vibrancy of the Outer Hebrides and reinforce a sense of integration between the islands and the making process. In his book, Lawson has said of his work that it is in celebration of all he has seen, that it is 'graced with the timeless beauty of this ancient craft'.[2]

Another narrative speaks for the elusive quality of any island essence yet notes too that by adopting a certain disposition it will *reveal* itself: 'It is a

2   Blue and White Company blog <https://www.blueandwhitecompany.com/ journal-entry/weaving-the-landscape>, accessed 20 September 2019.

rare thing to capture the essence of the Outer Hebrides. The true nature of life here, set within season after season of an ever-changing landscape, is elusive, only ever truly revealed to those with time, patience and a quieted soul. Harder still is to understand the profound relationship between is-landers and the land here, exemplified by the deep connection between our weavers and the Clò Mòr' (i.e. the 'big cloth'). Praise for the book is unequivocal in terms of it being an epic and 'deeply immersed realisa-tion' of the islands weaving heritage: 'It is a work of stunning originality and power, exhibiting a deeply personal poetry through his wonderful photography, intertwining his unique life and world-views with that of our own. Uncommonly, he has sought out and found so many of those rare and radiant things that represent our collection of destinies, defines who we are as islanders and presents a unified portrayal of our cherished homeland'. In just these few examples signifying Harris Tweed's island and cultural work, we can appreciate how the circulation of such narra-tives is powerful. The highly visual, accentuated message is symbolic of an enhanced and enchanted place, process and product that can in turn confer such qualities to its audience, its consumer but also *its maker*. We return to this later but let us turn now to our second example of island making: the wool and textile work of Shetland.

Shetland wool: Popularity, protection and life-affirming productivity

The women of Shetland have long been known for their knitting skills and ingenuity (see, e.g. Fryer 1995; Abrams 2005, 2006) and illus-trated in the excellent collection of Shetland textile essays curated by Laurenson (2013);[3] and interest continues to grow in doctoral work, such as Chapman (2015). While the mythology around knitting on the islands harkens back to the 1588 wrecked Spanish ship the *El Gran Griffon* (Compton 1983), we do know that in the 1580s Dutch fishermen would

3   See blog on the importance and interest to the related archival curation, research and commentaries generated on Shetland wool, knitting and textiles <https://kddandco.com/2014/01/29/shetland-textiles-800-bc-to-the-present/>, accessed 18 April 2020.

come ashore to purchase handknit stockings and mittens from Shetland women. Knitting was quickly established as a craft that would long be vital to the local economy and intriguingly stem some of the out-migration that many isolated islands face. It was in the mid-1800s that we see the distinctive and recognisable forms of knitting known as Fair Isle knitting and Shetland lace. Fair Isle knitting is allover stranded knitting with designs on jumpers and accessories 'influenced' by the aforementioned mythic Spaniards, and the knitted Shetland lace is to be so fine it could pass through a wedding ring. The quality and fashionability of the knitting reached greatest popularity when in 1914 the then Prince of Wales wore an allover Shetland jumper to play golf. The popularity for Fair Isle knitting has not waned. As Laurenson (2013: 100) makes clear it was 'the demand for a recognisable product' that allowed for 'sustained production of a relatively stable style. Essentially, Fair Isle knitwear became a sort of souvenir that epitomised rural Scotland. Associations with the everyday lives of fishermen fed into romantic notions of Scottishness.' Laurenson (2013: 102) continues that it was by the 1860s that we see Fair Isle knitting becoming as a distinct brand whereby histories of Fair Isle knitwear have been shaped by 'marketing stories which do not necessarily fit with the ideas and identities of people in Fair Isle and throughout Shetland. However, these stories have driven the commercial success of the style. Without them there would be no Fair Isle knitwear'.

The knitting techniques and stylings of Shetland have continued in popularity through to today. On *Ravelry.com*, a website for knitters and crocheters, there are 5,393 Fair Isle patterns and 1,358 Shetland patterns[4]. Many of the 'most popular' patterns are not written or created by those from Shetland. Those on the islands have tried to control the monikers and the idea of these forms of knitting but this is difficult to do. As Butler (2015: 132) reports, the EU did not grant protection for the patterns due to 'the widespread (misuse) of "Fair Isle." ' This illustrates the tension that can exist with non-tangible heritage for islands, and indeed rural and remote areas more generally. In 2015, the Cowichan tribe of Vancouver Island made claims against *Ralph Lauren* about the fashion

---

4   < https://www.ravelry.com/> accessed 27 October 2019.

house's misrepresentation of a sweater as being authentically Cowichan in origin.[5] The claim would not be upheld in court, due to the fact that the tribe had not trademarked their name and that they were located in Canada. However, *Ralph Lauren* did need to change to 'Cowichan-inspired' on their label[6] most likely to avoid public scrutiny. Shetland and Fair Isle have not fared so well.

As mentioned earlier, knitwear designers use patterns with lineage from Shetland and Fair Isle without concern. With much of the knitwear being exported Shetland has long been negotiating the whims of physically distant markets and fashion and by way of a proactive claim of island creativity and cultural work, Shetland developed an event that brings knitters (crucially also a revenue as 'visitors') to them and allows for perhaps more influence over the way that the patterns are appreciated. *Shetland Wool Week* (SWW) has become a primary feature on the Shetland calendar, second only now in scale to Up Helly Aa local wool brokers and retailers *Jamieson and Smith*, the *Shetland Amenity Trust* and the *Shetland Museum and Archives*, partnered together to showcase the first SWW, celebrating Shetland's wool craft and cultural heritage and in partnership with the wider UK *Campaign for Wool*. What started as a local celebration of textiles and the wool industry, has blossomed into an international attraction, drawing hundreds of textile enthusiasts, particularly knitters, from around the globe and the event's specialness (niche, island and place-embodied) and its success is widely celebrated. The *Woolly Round Up* (2018) organisers' report states that they have noticed that 'many visitors are now coming for longer, seeing it as an opportunity to learn new skills, holiday with friends, make new friends, travel, socialise, knit, spin, weave, and make memories. In fact, SWW has been described by some as a "life affirming experience"'.

In order for SWW to be 'life affirming' organisers effectively undertake to manage enchantment. Craftwork (particularly knitting) and 'the islands' (Shetland) come together to create this affirmation. As already noted, research such as Luckman's (2013, 2015) has underlined how craftwork has

5   <https://www.thefashionlaw.com/home/ralph-lauren-has-offended-a-canadian-tribe-with-this-sweater> accessed 16 December 2019.
6   <https://www.ralphlauren.com/women-clothing-sweaters/cowichan-inspired-zip-sweater/454113.html> accessed 16 December 2019.

an aura about it derived not just from the finished product but through the process of creation. SWW taps into the aura by having those attending not only view and purchase completed crafts but to also engage in knitting while on the islands. The programme is packed with workshops and demonstrations, visits to artists' studios and crofts, tours of the college and wool mill. Visitors are not observers but participants who take part in what is seen in various degrees as the ordinary yet 'enchanted' work, of Shetlanders. Shetland's culture is invoked through the making in place opportunities where 'traditional' crafts and contemporary art beyond knitting have made their way onto the programme, and Shetlandic (the islands *Shaetlan*, the modern Shetlandic Scots dialect) is woven into the discussions and promotions of SWW. Words like *makker* (maker), *peerie* (small) and *haps* (shawls) are widespread, all instinctive local place affirmations but also reinforcing for visitors of having entered a distinctive realm, where the words speak to the island's cultural confidences of difference and the specialness of Shetlandic place and history.

Managing enchantment: The cultural labour of island work

The 'remote rural' island settings of Scotland are particularly positioned (framed through narratives) to offer a version of what Banks (2010) and others refer to as the 'workshop' model of creative labour. The physical setting and island environment (isolation, beauty, 'wildness' is compounded by social authenticity of community and integrity of history and culture) and the particular possibility of both isolation and face-to-face interaction (arts enclaves). Remote islands can offer a temporary escape, for others a deep rootedness to place; some born of it and others borne by it. In any case rural and remote contexts of work, not least cultural work undertaken by artists, craftworkers, media professionals and the like, demand a celebration of and a commitment to, the (island) context.

This island context of cultural work is *materially* and *emotively* conditioned (c.f. Williams 1961) whether this is textile work, (for example, see especially Lynn Abrams excellent work here on Shetland's gendered history in this regard, 2005), or visual cultural archives, or the immense literary traditions and related cultural economies (see, e.g. Blaikie 2010; Macdonald 2010, 2018). Hollett writing in *Art North* (2019) 'On islandness' speaks of how the materiality of islandness and the 'labour of rural life is imbued in the work' of artists Ross-Smith and Walker. Echoing our own and others work on island and remote rural cultural work, Hollett speaks of the artists and their work as expressive of this sense of islands being 'good places to live' and to do 'good work', as he says, as 'worth being in':

> Oceans are often perceived as negative space; we don't recognise their silhouettes the way we know the shapes of continents. The Atlantic is a vast expanse we pass over or overlook. Similarly, materials such as burlap, linen and lichen are easily discarded, so plentiful they are almost valueless. [...] The artists take these historically under-valued materials and experiences, these 'negative' spaces, and remap them. Their work draws lines through these spaces because they are places worth being in. (2019: n.p.)

The subtext of Scotland's remote rural and island spaces as being 'worth being in' raises a number of interesting questions and concerns some of which are touched on elsewhere in this chapter collection. A re-valuing of the rural and remote spaces is widely recognised now where cultural consumption, industry and expression has sought to address the view that rural spaces are not inherently 'beyond' and at the margins of cultural economies. Rather studies have emerged that recognise and explore more fully the nature of remote and rural cultural work, not least from the accounts of cultural workers themselves. Nevertheless, city spaces (the urban) dominate national creative industries and arts, and the rural remains overwhelming positioned *at the margin*. Furthermore, rural spaces are not all equally, or indeed similarly, creative. Luckman argues that certain spaces are singularly more 'desirable' as both tourism and in-migration sites and that this is in 'no small part informed by rich artistic and cultural histories that continue to intersect with the contemporary local creative cultures' (2012: 11). This might not appear surprising or problematic at first glance – we expect difference – but it is clear that across rural and remote communities there is an extended reach of 'creative place making' and cultural enterprise development that increasingly asks of all rural places to be creative (and increasingly to be different too; islands are competitive economies in their own right). Creativity is therefore positioned as an asset, a resource of cultural and social capital, a driver of enterprise and a securing frame of distinction.

Nonetheless, islands are undoubtedly subject to a degree of fetish-isation where mediatisation of island brands and the commodification of island goods, products and services privilege particular iconography, images and narratives (Castree 2001; Baldacchino 2010). This promotion and re-lated consumption of islands – the privileging of islandness – is widespread and an established modernity trope. It has served some islands' promotional image very well, as it has their economies (Islay's whisky cultural heritage is world famous and Orkney has been especially proactive in positioning the Orkney Islands enhanced cultural product *offer* – archaeology, cultural tourism, food and drink, the arts and crafts). Other Scottish islands are all well-disposed to similar strategies and cultural products are promoted and enhanced through policy and enterprise that relies on the expertise, effort and excitement of cultural workers in turn to champion, to reinforce and to innovate cultural resources and expression locally and globally. Yet, despite confident commentaries this is not an even landscape of resources, expertise, marketplace or policy support across all Scotland's small islands. Furthermore, fetishisation is never wholly fixed but is subject to drift and reframing as market's demand novelty and cultural economies, innovation and each island place must compete, as indeed must the arts and craft, and all other cultural work island enterprises, whether single individuals to whole community industries, to survive and to succeed.

In island communities, cultural workers are often actively engaged with the possibilities that enhanced digital connectivity can offer. More usually it is the concerns of a lack of connectivity and digital marginality that have quite understandably preoccupied some rural policy champions and made the 'islandness as problematic difference' headlines. Digital con-nectivity is now well understood as a basic social necessity, underpinning media and digital literacy for all, as well as integral to business develop-ment, growth and success. Nevertheless, such connectivity is not without its counter-impact. Digital economies and creative industries demand en-gagement of particular kinds of labour that require skills, knowledge and self-investment. As already noted, cultural work – cultural labour – is an expanding and contested realm of identity and image making, of precarity and of self-management. That is, the 'marginal' status of such work, its risks and uncertainty, and the demands on the cultural worker to labour variously within art, creative and craft contexts is now well established within media accounts, policy and research cultures (Gill and Pratt 2008; Banks 2010). As Luckman and Andrew (2018) have noted for rural artists in Australia, the expanding demand for certain types of self-brand work to be undertaken as a given in creative and cultural industries impacts on the time available for the actual 'making work' of the cultural artefact itself. The remoteness of islands is no guarantee of 'removing oneself' from demands on time, engagement and circulation however special the island place may be as we have discussed elsewhere (Harling Stalker and Burnett 2016; Burnett and Harling Stalker 2018). In short, cultural work however special or enchanting is 'hard work', as much as any other 'island work'.

Conclusion

Island culture and the cultural work pertaining to it cannot be limited to just one identity group; rather claims are made variously by island residents, 'locals', 'islanders', 'visitors', and many others living on and off the island, as well as 'consumers and producers' of islands – as culture, as place and as practice. All of which involves the creation and circulation of narratives and expressions of cultural work as tangible and intangible products and practice. In writing this chapter, it is clear to us that any attempt to summarise the expressions and experiences of any or all of Scotland's islands cultural work is an impossible task but rather reinforces the complexity of an enticing and expanding field of further research debate and inquiry. Our brief focus on just two island cultural celebrations of 'specialness' and enchantment – Harris Tweed and Shetland wool have offered a loose frame within which further examples might be considered and expanded upon. To *contain* an account of Scotland's islands' arts and cultural activity and expression would be ambitious not least as the very terminology of cultural work is itself a shifting landscape of research, debate and policy. So too, of course, is the very idea of islandness. Having worked previously on narratives of cultural work in Scotland's islands and in Canada's maritime provinces, we are aware of the expanding range of helpful and insightful commentaries on these issues. Both contemporary and more 'classic' research commentaries on the economic, cultural and social aspects of Scotland's island places have informed this essay's account, as has a sense of textual appreciation of interpretations of data sources of media, documentary, archive, policy and promotion narratives to recognise cultural work as a key frame that expresses and positions images, ideas and understandings of what is understood and expressed as Scottish island life, cultural work and identity more widely (see especially Carden 2018b; McHattie et al. 2018). We hope to have provided some small account here of why research and critical exploration in this cultural field of cultural work, island making as 'modern enchantment' and identity crafting, remains 'special' and worthwhile, not least for Scotland but also for small island experience elsewhere.

Bibliography

Abrams, L. (2005). *Myth and Materiality in a Women's World: Shetland, 1800–2000.* Manchester: Manchester University Press.

Abrams, L. (2006). 'Knitting, autonomy and identity: the role of hand knitting in the construction of women's sense of self in an island community, Shetland, c. 1850–2000', *Textile History*, 37 (2), 149–165.

Baldacchino, G. (2010). 'Island brands and 'the Island' as a brand: insights from immigrant entrepreneurs on Prince Edward Island', *International Journal of Entrepreneurship and Small Business*, 9 (4), 378–393.

Banks, M. (2007). *The Politics of Cultural Work.* London: Palgrave MacMillan.

Banks, M. (2010). 'Craft labour and creative industries', *International Journal of Cultural Policy*, 16 (3), 305–321.

Banks, M., Gill, R., and Taylor, S. (eds) (2013). *Theorizing Cultural Work: Labour, Continuity and Change in the Cultural and Creative Industries.* London: Routledge.

Bates, L., Coleman, T., Wiles, J., and Kearns, R. (2019). 'Older residents' experiences of islandness, identity and precarity: Ageing on Waiheke Island', *Island Studies Journal*, 14 (2), 171–192.

Bennett, J. (2001). *The Enchantment of Modern Life: Attachments, Crossings and Ethics*. Princeton, NJ: Princeton University Press.

Bevan, A., and Downes, J. (2017). 'Wilder Being: Destruction and Creation in the Littoral Zone'. In Jokela, T., and G. Coutts (eds), *Relate North: Culture, Community and Communication*, pp. 154–166. Rovaniemi: Lapland University Press.

Bevan, A., and McLean, R. (2013). 'Northern field: a landscape of morphology and mythology', *Visual Studies*, 28 (3), 249–261.

Blaikie, A. (2010). *The Scots Imagination and Modern Memory*. Edinburgh: Edinburgh University Press.

Boon, S., Butler, L., and Jefferies, D. (2018). 'Home: Islandness'. In Boon, S., Butler L., and D. Jefferies (eds), *Autoethnography and Feminist Theory at the Water's Edge*, pp. 117–122. Palgrave Pivot: Cham.

Brannigan, J. (2015). *Archipelagic Modernism: literature in the Irish and British Isles, 1990–1970*. Edinburgh: Edinburgh University Press.

Burnett, K. A. (2017). 'Place apart: Scotland's north as a cultural industry of margins.' In T. Jokela and G. Coutts (eds), *Relate North: Culture, Community and Communication*, pp. 60–83. Rovaniemi: Lapland University Press.

Burnett, K. A., and Danson, M. (2017). 'Enterprise and entrepreneurship on islands and remote rural environments', *The International Journal of Entrepreneurship and Innovation*, 18 (1), 25–35.

Burnett, K. A., and Harling Stalker, L. (2018). 'Shut up for five years: locating narratives of cultural workers in Scotland's islands', *Sociologia Ruralis*, 58 (2), 239–257.

Butler, R. (2012). 'Islandness: it's all in the mind', *Tourism Recreation Research*, 37 (2), 173–176.

Butler, R.W. (2015). 'Knitting and More from Fair Isle, Scotland: Small Island Tradition and Micro Entrepreneurship'. In Baldacchino, G., (ed.), *Entrepreneurship in Small Island States and Territories*, pp. 83–96. London: Routledge.

Carden, S. (2018a). Shetland hand knitting: value and change. Centre for Rural Creativity, UHI. <https://pureadmin.uhi.ac.uk/ws/portalfiles/portal/3275629/Shetland_Hand_Knitting_Carden.pdf> accessed 18 April 2020.

Carden, S. (2018b). 'Introduction: Island textiles and clothing', *Island Studies Journal*, 13 (2), 3–8.

Castree, N. (2001). 'Commodity fetishism, geographical imaginations and imaginative geographies', *Environment and Planning* A, 33, 1519–1525.

Chapman, R. (2015). *The history of the fine lace knitting industry in nineteenth and early twentieth century Shetland*. PhD Thesis. University of Glasgow.

Conkling, P. (2007). 'On islanders and islandness', *The Geographical Review*, 97 (2), 191–201.

Gill, R., and Pratt, A. (2008). 'In the social factory?: immaterial labour, precariousness and cultural work', *Theory, Culture, and Society*, 25 (7–8), 1–30.

Harling Stalker, L., and Burnett, K. (2016). 'Good work? Scottish cultural workers' narratives about working and living on islands', *Island Studies Journal*, 11 (1), 193–208.

Harper, C., and McDougall, K. (2012). 'The very recent fall and rise of Harris Tweed', *TEXTILE*, 10 (1), 78–98.

Highlands and Islands Enterprise (HIE) (2014). *Creative Industries Strategy 2014– 2019*. Highlands and Islands Enterprise, <http ://www.hie.co.uk/growth-sectors/creative-industries/our-focus.html> accessed 5 February 2019.

Fryer, L. (1995). *Knitting by the Fireside and on the Hillside: A History of the Shetland Hand Knitting Industry c.1600–1950*. Lerwick: Shetland Times Ltd.

Hollett, M. (2019). 'On islandness', *ART NORTH*, 1 (Spring), 21–22.

Holt, Y., Martin-Jones, D., and Jones, O. (eds) (2018). *Visual Culture in the Northern British Archipelago*. New York and London: Routledge.

Laurenson, S. (2013). 'Fair Isle Knitting, Past and Present'. In Laurenson, S., (ed.), *Shetland Textiles: 800 BC to the Present*. Lerwick: Shetland Heritage Publications.

Lawson, I. (2013). *From the Land Comes the Cloth: Harris Tweed*. Penrith: Ian Lawson Books.

Lu, Y. T. (2015) *Lost in Location: Arts Development and Policy in Rural Scotland*. PhD Thesis. University of Glasgow.

Luckman, S. (2012). *Locating Cultural Work: The Politics and Poetics of Rural, Regional and Remote Creativity*. Basingstoke: Palgrave Macmillan.

Luckman, S. (2013). 'The aura of the analogue in a digital age: women's crafts, creative markets and home-based labour after Etsy', *Cultural Studies Review*, 19 (1), 249–270.

Luckman, S. (2015). *Craft and the Creative Economy*. Basingstoke: Palgrave Macmillan.

Luckman, S., and Andrew, J. (2018). 'Establishing the Crafting Self in the Contemporary Creative Economy'. In Luckman, S., and N. Thomas (eds), *Craft Economies*, pp. 119–128. UK: Bloomsbury Publishing.

Macdonald, M. (2010). 'Art as an expression of Northernness: The highlands of Scotland', *Visual Culture in Britain*, 11 (3), 355–371.

Macdonald, M. (2018). ' "A hesitation of the tide": Lindisfarne, Iona, Venice'. In Holt, Y., Martin-Jones, D., and O. Jones (eds), *Visual Culture in the Northern British Archipelago*, pp. 69–81. New York and London: Routledge.

Macleod, K. (2017). 'Harris Tweed from island cloth to cutting edge fashion', <http://www.bbc.com/travel/story/20171122-harris-tweed-from-island-cloth-to-cutting-edge-fashion > accessed 12 May 2019.

Massey, D. (2005). *For Space*. London: Sage.

McClellan, K. E. (2017). 'The British national costume: of Tweed and tension', *TEXTILE*, 15 (1), 86–107.

McHattie, L. S., Champion, K., and Broadley, C. (2018). 'Craft, textiles, and cultural assets in the Northern Isles: innovation from tradition in the Shetland Islands', *Island Studies Journal*, 13 (1), 39–54.

Moisley, H. A. (1961). 'Harris Tweed: A growing highland industry', *Economic Geography*, 37 (4), 353–370.

Pike, A. (2015). *Origination: The Geographies of Brands and Branding*. Oxford: Wiley-Blackwell.

Shetland Wool Week (2018). *Woolly Round Up*. <http://www.shetlandwoolweek.com/woolly-round-up-2018> accessed 10 December 2019.

Smith, P. (1999). 'The elementary forms of place and their transformations: a Durkheimian model', *Qualitative Sociology*, 22, 13–36.

Stratford, E., (ed.) (2017). *Island Geographies, Essays and Conversations*. London: Routledge.

Taylor, S., and Littleton, K. (2012). *Contemporary Identities of Creativity and Creative Work*. Abingdon: Ashgate.

Vannini, P., and Taggart, J. (2012). 'Doing islandness: a non-representational approach to an island's sense of place', *Cultural Geographies*, 20 (2), 225–242.

Williams, R. (1961). *Culture and Society 1780–1950*. Harmondsworth: Penguin.

MIKE DANSON

6. Regional and Island Economies of Peripheries and Margins: 'Nordic and Celtic' Comparisons

The northern and western peripheries of Celtic and Nordic Europe, and particularly their highlands and islands, face some of the most difficult geographies and environments in the continent (Danson and de Souza 2012). They share common challenges of marginality, out-migration, demographic imbalances, higher costs and a lack of economies of scale and scope as well as unique environmental assets and concerns. These tend to be exacerbated and intensified for island locations as challenges for transportation, logistics, connectivity of energy and other factors of production and consumption raise costs and reduce choices for residents and enterprises alike (Burnett and Danson 2017). Climate emergencies and related severe weather events are exaggerating some aspects of these negative forces for island economies and societies (Fazey et al. 2018) so that looking at the prospects for these communities on the peripheries and margins has become ever more pressing in recent times. Further, the national and geographical contexts vary across these communities offering different lessons, responses, prospects and potential for learning from strategic and policy interventions.

Social capital and human resources tend to be thinly stretched in isolated locations, and the increasing and broadening demands and opportunities offered over the last century to islanders within wider national and global contexts have encouraged long-established communities to abandon islands in Scotland (Clements and Clements 2019), Faroes (Coull 1967), Ireland (Nic Craith 2019) and elsewhere (Watson 1998). Revealing and understanding the dynamics of the drivers for change and of how the modern world might mitigate distance, whether geographic or psychic, are significant elements in the growth of island studies (Brinklow 2011).

Key to this growth and the underlying development and decline of island communities are the economy and the standards and quality of living it supports. In turn this is determined by the relative enterprise and opportunities, barriers and connections generated by the locality. How the natural and intangible cultural features and factors of these regions are used to create value needs to be explored, therefore, including an appraisal of enterprising activities, and an appreciation of their minority languages, histories and natural heritages. This chapter scopes out these dimensions of life in northern Europe and offers an analysis of their causes and concerns, identifying structures, processes and initiatives that build social capitals and resilience. It seats the analysis in the literature on theories of marginality, peripherality, islandness, economies of scale and scope, extending these to consider how social capital and resilience can support enterprising activity in such remote rural areas. A number of studies are drawn on regarding social and economic features of communities in the periphery but within national, European and global contexts. Specific reference to research on Scotland, Ireland, Norway and the Faroes informs the analysis and provides a range of examples and comparisons while the wider northern European experiences form the backdrop.

Definitions and theories to understand economic challenges for islands and islanders

'Islandness' has been defined and explored as a concept earlier in this volume and, in terms of society and economics, reflects characteristics related to separation, peripherality, marginality, isolation and 'other'. These are all tropes and descriptors with negative connotations which follow from and indeed exacerbate challenges generated by distance, logistics, lack of proximity, and other features and areas of life, community, policy and identity. To understand and examine the lived realities and barriers to promoting and realising sustainable, inclusive and resilient development on islands and archipelagos – which tend to be the aspirations of island communities across the world – it will be helpful to consider the critical defining aspects of marginality and peripherality, of place and space, and of the critical significance of economies of scale and scope and their remoteness counterparts in determining opportunities, threats and potentials for islands and islanders.

For many island and remote communities, even in advanced regional and national economic environments such as the European Union (EU) and Canada, their peripheral geographies are exaggerated by forces of peripheralisation and marginalisation, and this applies both within their own nations and within their own regions (Danson and de Souza 2011). These tendencies are often driven by reorientation of trade following entry to the EU and the completion of the common market in the European context, by globalisation and associated restructuring, and deindustrialisation (Baldacchino 2006a; Danson and Burnett 2015). At all levels in the North Sea and Atlantic Arc macro-regions, for example, the competitiveness agenda has dominated so that cities/city-regions/agglomeration economies are promoted, privileging the core (Krugman 1991; ESPON 2010; Freitas and Kitson 2018). As analyses of the expected impacts of broken supply chains post-Brexit confirm, integrated and metropolitan-centric distribution channels disadvantage communities and producers at the ends of spokes, distanced from the centralised hubs. Therefore, internally and internationally many regions and nations face peculiar difficulties in competing with the firms and communities of the core of the continent (Commission of the European Communities [CEC] 2008; ESPON 2010 for discussion on principles) and so islands with their additional costs, longer times to/from market and smaller market demands have become peripheral and marginal (Danson and de Souza 2011) within their own Member State and in wider continental contexts (Margaras 2016).

In contradistinction to the representation of islands as being typically traditional, backward and lagging, as margins as both 'relic' and 'resolution' to modernity's challenges (Gillis 2004; Burnett and Danson 2016), their reality in the economy contrasts with the revealed spatial preference of the dominant economic development paradigm of recent decades for large metropolitan areas and capital cities. The foundations of this latter core are held to be competitiveness based on agglomeration economies, clusters, connectivity and proximity. The drivers of the private service and financial economy, supplementing state activities, create strong, irresistible centripetal forces attracting resources, power and activity to the centre and core of the economy (Danson and de Souza 2011). This compares with the peripheralisation of remote locations; confounding the higher prices and more limited job and income opportunities for citizens, those establishing and running businesses on islands are especially disadvantaged from operating in areas of high costs, without the benefits of the financial and other drivers of competitiveness present in metropolitan regions (Danson and de Souza 2011; Burnett and Danson 2016).

Against the inherent costs generated by remoteness and limited size, there are some countervailing benefits to entrepreneurs located on islands (Danson and Burnett 2014; Burnett and Danson 2015). As well as the restricted and restricting capacity to gain from local monopoly powers to supply local communities, enterprises on islands may be able to realise opportunities offered by the characteristics of place and space. These latter features of 'otherness' and remoteness can underpin business and economic development as they present potential for added value in the global marketplace, the positive aspects of remoteness can outweigh the negative.

Nevertheless, much of the extensive and growing literature on islands purports to examine them on their own terms (Baldacchino 2006a; Fletcher 2011) but still focuses on their relationship to their respective mainlands, rather than considering islands as separate lands with their own unique strengths and features. As Depraetere (2008: 4) argues, there is a core or 'continental prejudice' where nissology (the study of islands) is 'judged and relegated as some kind of aberration, even by islanders (Edmond and Smith 2003)'. The place of islands in their wider regional and national environments has a degree of ambiguity in this discourse. On the one hand they are progressively marginalised and peripheralised by the dominating economic forces of neoliberalism, criticised and perceived as quintessentially 'backward' and dependent (Burnett 2011). Contemporaneously, islands are spaces and cultural places, offering the essential imagery and often very definition of the nation: their 'otherness' and difference often underpinning the unique selling points of products, services especially in respect of food and drink, tourism and culture (Baum 1996). As playgrounds and retreats, islands are presented as 'pristine' and 'isolated' geographies and environments

(Hennessy and McCleary 2011; Burnett and Danson 2016). This dichotomy in role, purpose and position in the national psyche and economy means islands and islanders continuously face a dilemma in balancing competing aims, objectives and basics of standards of living and quality of life.

Reconciling the additional costs of providing services, supplying goods and maintaining populations especially on smaller islands with the demands from mainland taxpayers and priorities presents challenges for policymakers and practitioners alike. Families and skilled workers and graduates confront similar trade-offs with access to mainstream and 'universal' services, career opportunities and ladders constrained on islands and remote communities. These barriers to maximising utility – in an economic sense – and life chances generally can become self-reinforcing, constraining the island community to a path dependency of relative decline and isolation. Breaking into such downward spirals represents an age-old challenge with 1 in 6 of Scotland's offshore islands being abandoned between 2001 and 2011 although the population on islands increased by 4% in that decade. Between 1851 and 2001, the aggregate population of Scotland's three archipelagos declined by 4% to 91,000, by contrast over that period the Faroe Islands increased by more than five times to over 48,000. These diverging fortunes confirm that the drivers for change need deeper analysis based on data on the economies and societies of different island groups.

Island profiles across continents and seas

There is no consensus over the definition of islands across or within disciplines. However, Depraetere (2008) has offered a consistent set of statistics which offer a record of the numbers of and size of islands across the globe. Adopting the same basic definition, it is estimated there are about 200 islands globally with a population over 100,000.[1] The United Nations

---

1   Although this is taken from Wikipedia, the specific editing protocols offer a reasonable degree of confidence on these totals: <https://en.wikipedia.org/wiki/List_of_islands_by_population> accessed 15 May 2020.

Environment Programme (UNEP) has a directory of islands with a large range of data on each case[2]; however, instances within, for example, the British Isles and Norway are excluded from the detailed databases of their definition of 'significant' islands.

The ESPON Euroislands project was based on an assumption of 362 European islands each with a permanent population of more than 50 inhabitants (ESPON 2011); this identified notable differences between Mediterranean and more northerly island nations and groups. Taking Scotland to illustrate the experiences of islands within a developed economy, at the time of the last Census of Population 103,702 people were living on the 93 inhabited islands, which represented 2% of the national population of Scotland (SIF n.d.). The main islands of each of the three archipelagos (the Outer Hebrides, Shetland and Orkney) and the Isle of Skye each had more than 10,000 residents, with respectively Lewis and Harris (21,031), Mainland of Shetland (18,765), Mainland of Orkney (17,162) and Skye (10,008). Together these four islands accounted for two-thirds (65%) of the total population of all the islands. With populations even in these four islands being sparsely distributed over fairly extensive areas, no location across the Scottish periphery meets the qualification of being any more than a 'small town' (Scottish Government 2019a) so that home markets and economic catchment areas are limited in size and scope.

In aggregate, the population of all Scottish islands rose by 4% (3,963) between 2001 and 2011, and the four largest islands dominated this increase: over the decade increases were 6% for Lewis and Harris, 7% for Mainland of Shetland, 12% for Mainland of Orkney and 8% for the Isle of Skye. Outwith these four, the other islands suffered an aggregate decrease of 3%. Over that decade, there was a mixed record of changes at the local scale; three islands became inhabited again, 50 islands saw an increase in population, 43 islands saw a decrease with 7 becoming uninhabited by 2011, and 7 islands had no apparent change. Although there is no mid-decade census, official estimates (NRS 2018) suggest on a similar coverage of Scottish islands since 2011 numbers have increased slightly (0.5%) from

---

2   <http://islands.unep.ch/Examples.htm#ISLAND> accessed 15 May 2020.

98,234 to 98,712 in 2017. The Outer Hebrides (Eilean Siar) as a whole are believed to have grown by 2.7% over these six years and the Shetland Islands by 0.7%, while the Orkney Islands are expected to have declined by 2.6% and Skye and Lochalsh (the Isle of Skye and its mainland neighbour) by 1.8%. Interestingly, the other islands of the Inner Hebrides and Argyll and of the Firth of Clyde, all closer to the mainland conurbations, have seen recent increases in population 2011–2017 of 2.8% and 3.3% respectively.

A key objective of undertaking forecasting, scenario-building and applying other instruments of predicting the future is to inform policy direction and the opportunity to try and make changes to paths of development or decline. There are many common issues and challenges faced by sparsely populated islands across northern Europe and North America but, as experiences and prospects vary across the different jurisdictions and geographies, so there are potential lessons to be shared to mutual benefit (Danson and de Souza 2011)[3]. Backcasting to 2011 and then forward to 2046 shows 65 more people (an initial rate of almost 5 per 1,000 rising to 12.37 in the early 2020s before progressively falling) settling in the Western Isles each year would achieve this stability. While all parts of the SPAs face similar profiles of required net in-flows of people, the 'Northern Isles consistently has the smallest (relative) net migration requirement, throughout the projection period' (Copus 2018a: 10).[4]

Although the three island groups are expected to increase their proportions of the Scottish SPAs, they are forecast to suffer significant further depopulation over the coming decades, Orkney and Shetland by 19%, the Outer Hebrides by 32% and SPAs overall by 28%. As the population of Scotland has recently risen to record the highest levels in history with

3   And promoted by international networks: European Small Islands Network: <https://europeansmallislands.com/origins-and-aims/>; CPMR Islands Commission:<https://cpmr-islands.org/who-we-are/>; Global Islands Network:<http://www.globalislands.net/about/origin.php> accessed 15 May 2020.

4   For fuller detail see Projected Population of the SPAs and sub regions 2011–2046, <https://www.hutton.ac.uk/sites/default/files/files/RD%203_4_1%20Working%20Paper%203%20O1_2ii%20260218%20-%20published.pdf> accessed 10 May2020.

further national growth and then stabilisation expected, this suggests the further peripheralisation of the remote areas. This is not untypical in the European context of decongestion from conurbations to commuting settlements in or near the core. Copus (2018a) projects that these demographic changes will be uneven with all remote areas, except the Northern Isles, losing more than 30% of their working age population. Those threats confirm the need to ensure that future economic prospects are much improved, with focus on sustainable inclusive growth. His workings suggest that populations could be stabilised and made more sustainable, that is, more balanced, with some fairly modest levels of net in-migration:[5]

> As with many remote rural, mountainous and otherwise marginal locations, the 2011 Euroisland study revealed a set of issues generally facing islands across the continent (ESPON 2011):
> – islands have below average connectivity
> – islands are below the European GDP average
> – economic convergence is slower
> – job and career opportunities are low
> – there is low quality and high cost of services

These barriers to pursuing sustainable development are in harmony with Royle's (2001) conclusions that by definition islands are always affected by a range of constraints, including small scale, size, isolation and resource availability. Further, he argued that peripherality is a permanent, unalterable condition; that approach moves exploration of the challenges facing islands and islanders away from a focus on psychological and cultural factors, on 'otherness', to consideration of economic, social and constructed realities. In their programme of work on 'GEOSPECS – Geographic Specificities and Development Potentials in Europe', ESPON (2012) followed the definitions of Royle (2001) and noted that most of European islands are also 'peripheral regions situated on the EU's external borders'.

---

5   Again, for fuller detail see 'Annual Net Migration required to halt shrinkage in the SPA and Sub-Regions 2016 – 2046', <https://www.hutton.ac.uk/sites/default/files/files/RD%203_4_1%20Working%20Paper%203%20O1_2ii%20260218%20-%20published.pdf> accessed 10 May 2020.

As reported from the seminar organised by the Committee of Regions and Shetland Islands Council

> Insularity has to be considered as a permanent, natural feature that affects negatively, directly and indirectly, islands' attractiveness and subsequently places obstacles to their performance in terms of sustainable development. (Dressler 2016)

To an extent high transportation costs of delivering to islands can still act as a barrier to local entrants where economies of scale of production on the mainland outweigh these costs of logistics. Where island companies are able to compete, the higher costs of production they do face will raise prices and so depress the living standards of the population overall. As noted in 2013

> the budgets required by households to achieve a minimum acceptable standard of living in remote rural Scotland were typically 10–40% higher than elsewhere in the UK. For households in more remote island locations, these additional costs could exceed 40%. (Highlands and Islands Enterprise [HIE] 2016: 1)

HIE updates to these estimates (HIE 2016, Appendix) suggested that falling energy prices had reduced some of these cost penalties from island living, but that proactive policy interventions are required in 'domestic heating costs, the costs of transporting goods, and capitalising on broadband roll-out to create more high-paying jobs' (HIE 2016: 36) and to have significant effects on real standards of living. As that report confirms, and most notably for the Scottish archipelagos, Inner Hebrides and Argyll islands, and mirrored in some other continental fringes such as Norway and eastern Canada, the neighbouring mainland areas are also sparsely populated exacerbating characteristics of remoteness and limiting potential market size. As these also tend to be mountainous, coastal and border regions, there is a multi-layered challenging environment for islanders to survive and compete (de Souza 2017). Critically for the islands of north west Europe and similar geographies in North America are issues of depopulation and ageing, problems of connectivity, high costs of living and lack of opportunities to attract and retain families and young workers.

Adding value: Realising benefits of tangible and intangible assets

Having confirmed that the island communities of the North Atlantic and North Sea must confront natural degrees of isolation due to geography confounded by the forces of underdevelopment generated by neo-liberalism and alternative national priorities, identifying their tangible and intangible assets is necessary for a balanced appreciation of their potential. Dressler (2016) records the implicit ESPON (2012) scorecard of European island characteristics as including features of:

- Appreciable levels of social capital – 'closely knit communities'
- High values of natural capital
- Preserved history and culture, and biodiversity
- Renewable energy potentials (hydropower, offshore wind, wave, tidal energies, biomass, solar energy)
- Goods and services that exhibit significant economic externalities and so do not receive market pricing (air purification, hazard prevention, groundwater recharge, bioremediation of waste and pollutants, recreation)
- Higher vulnerability to climate change (islands – sea level rise, storms, extreme temperatures, flooding)

The first four of these suggest some comparative advantages based on natural and human capital and investments, and of the latent potential offered by engagement with sustainable and inclusive development agendas. The former of these often encapsulates the very essentials of islands and their 'otherness' while the latter hint at a different path than followed hitherto. Both elements, however, can be considered as opening up the possibilities for island communities to adapt to the threats and indeed realise the opportunities of the final two characteristic features revealed by EPSON. All individually and collectively can be recognised as promising to revise the relative fortunes and positions of islands as they have the capacity to alter the core-periphery relationships established over the last two centuries (Burnett 2011). In Scotland, and increasingly elsewhere, underpinning these reappraisals there are moves to incorporate the UN Sustainable Development Goals (SDGs) into national strategies and policies (Scottish Government 2018; United Nations [UN] 2019). Effectively this introduction of the SDGs into global, EU and national aspirations and targets (Scottish Government 2018; CEC 2019; UN 2019) could lead to the determination of the economic position and role of islands returning to their communities. To assess this potential means exploring the assets and resources of islands within their changing contexts and powers.

In briefing Members of the European Parliament, Margaras (2016) recognises the standard challenges facing islands and notes they often offer the iconic images, products and other essential factors of their nations. McHattie, Champion and Broadley (2018: 39) illustrate how literature and research have underexamined 'the value of cultural assets in contributing to the creative economy … and that there is a paucity of understanding of the innovative potential of craft and creative practitioners in the region'. Leask and Rihova (2010) look at the same island group and argue they have extended the existing research to examine 'how the community of Shetland embraces the opportunities afforded by tourism as an alternative to traditional industries', again referencing the assets and resources being applied to improve economic diversity and development. Richardson and Gillespie (1996), however, raise concerns that the reality of many innovations and progressive practices is more likely to arise from 'inward investment – from exogenous firms accessing under-utilised regional attributes such as labour supplies – than through growth in indigenous firms'. In a similar vein of examining ambiguities between promise and outcome, Kelman (2007: 101) notes how many islands must confront development and sustainability challenges, 'but these same characteristics provide significant advantages'; however, while they can support 'sustainable livelihoods from natural heritage', there are dangers of dependency on transient and externally driven incomes, over-exploitation of flora, fauna and traditions, and the import of colonial attitudes by tourists and visitors.

These few examples are but part of a large and expanding literature of action research and reports which explore the assets, resources and contradictions of pursuing sustainable development on islands. In Scotland and elsewhere, islands and islanders have all variously been labelled as 'backward' or lagging (Harvey et al. 2002; Devine 2012;) in terms of economic dependency and culture. Paradoxically, this has fed into promotion of these places for alternative lifestyles and tourism experiences complementing and often dependent on revivals of their traditional cultures as interests in each islands' indigenous 'ways of life', histories and environment are broadcast. Rather than representing the former description of backward, of 'other', there has been a rise of celebrations of 'localness' in enterprise and consumption more generally. Both these tangible and intangible assets facilitate island economies regenerating through applying their assets and comparative advantages to engage with the globalising marketplace for higher value holidays, wildlife experiences and cultural service provision. In turn this animates increased confidence and empowerment of local populations and entrepreneurs.

Facing the penalties of costs of transport and logistics, lack of economies of scale and scope, island enterprises have been progressively unable to compete with mainland suppliers, increasingly further undermining their own and their communities' capacities to survive. Therefore, creating, revealing and realising the value of 'traditional' and artisan imagery can permit incursions into product and service markets characterised by monopolistic competition; that is, in markets where enterprises are small and have products and services differentiated from others by features such as provenance, locality, quality, etc. Ensuring that there is not too much psychic distance from their markets, Wilson and Whitehead (2012) have argued that 'local' product is offered as more global in form. In some circumstances, the authenticity of 'local' can be reduced to be only a relic associated with past localised rural production activities, for example. As in other aspects of island life, to generate sufficient income to support the household and community economy, compromises with the demands of the markets are required with commodification of the culture, traditions and the essence of the place.

Social capital and resilience

To realise the importance of tangible and intangible assets to islands (Baldacchino 2006b; Hull and Sassenberg 2012) an adequate strategy is needed in order to valorise these characteristics within the European context and the global environment. As argued above, this strategy has to make use of the characteristics of insularity and otherness of culture and nature as advantages and opportunities, rather than structural disadvantages and vulnerabilities. Concerning the strengths of the islands, the main comparative advantages are: the quality of life and the quality of their natural and cultural assets; high density of natural and cultural capital; and a strong cultural identity, combined with the fact that islands have 'low nature fragmentation by artificial surfaces'. This advantage is threatened by tourism and residential house sprawl and it is not particularly valorised to create new wealth and employment (cultural professions, environmental management and quality food). Concerning weaknesses, insularity affects directly and permanently some of the most important attractiveness parameters of islands: accessibility, public interest services, private services and networks, economies of scale, market organisation. It is often argued that social capital and local resourcefulness can mitigate the effects of some of the inherent characteristics and costs of island living and economics. 'Enterprising' activities by island communities and individuals are posited as countervailing powers to the negativities of isolation, high costs and limited local markets. In research on the Highlands and Islands, and rural Scotland more generally, the significance and relative importance of the concepts of resilience and enterprise for communities in remote rural and island locations especially have been explored (Danson 2015; Islands Revival 2019).

In their claim that there are 'green shoots' of regeneration in Scottish islands, the partners in Islands Revival (2019) argue that these developments are underpinned by

> the changing perceptions of younger, economically active people, especially out-migrant islanders, who increasingly consider their birthplace as a place to return to, and at an earlier stage in their lives. Connectivity (especially social media) is playing an important role in popularising this attitude. (2019)

Reflecting the characterisation of islands offered by Dressler (2016) and ESPON (2012), they continue by proposing this turnaround is consistent and associated with: an increasing appreciation, particularly by younger people (whether they have stayed, returned or settled), of the cultural wealth, environmental assets, well-being and community-related benefits of island life. [Critically, they continue, this regeneration and revival is focused not on 'growth' but rather on sustainability, renewal, or restored viability, without risk to social, cultural and environmental assets.]

Again this prioritisation hints at these geographies being at the forefront of pursuing the UN SDGs, in contradistinction to their accepted peripheral and remote status and laggard ranking. The factors driving this stabilisation and revival in the prospects of Scotland's islands are expected to include intangible assets associated with community buyouts of land and related assets, increased confidence and cooperation, and evolving enterprising activity and attitudes. As better connectivity is believed to be shrinking relative isolation and improving opportunities and prospects for entrepreneurs, so the positive features of social infrastructure and community well-being on islands supports a diversity of micro and small businesses and promises further improvement in fair work and incomes. This promotion of an upward path of development contrasts with the negativity embedded into the declining population projections reported above. This optimism is attributed to experiences with the moves to community ownership and a 'place-based approach which is holistic, integrated and coherent' (Islands Revival 2019). Where a community lacks coherence, involvement of islanders beyond a limited set of 'leaders' and a positive media presence, then the opportunities for collaborating internally (bonding social capital) and with external partners (bridging and linking social capital) (Baldacchino 2005; Markantoni, Steiner and Meador 2019) becomes critically compromised (McMorran et al. 2013; Simpson 2018).

In a paper exploring community resilience and community empowerment in the Highlands and Islands of Scotland, we have identified the degrees of consensus over these terms and how they could be measured to support interventions to improve the relative economies of islands and raise living standards of islanders (Danson 2015). Specifically with regard to the labour market and enterprise dimensions, this exercise demonstrated the lowly position of islands by applying such proxies as 'average incomes from employment' and 'new firm formation rates'; these tend to show that island communities are relatively less resilient than many of the worst neighbourhoods in urban Scotland (Danson 2015: 13). Despite some of the highest national proportions of school-leavers progressing onto university and apprenticeships, with few graduate level jobs available, levels of productivity

('Gross value added') on islands are well below average. These and related indicators corroborate the low living standards of island communities and their vulnerability and precariousness. Interventions to reduce the relatively high costs of living and doing business would strengthen their economies and help build a more robust base for development and sustainability, as proposed in the recommendations to that report.

Building confidence and resilience through stabilising the economic base, generating new social and private enterprises and raising incomes should contribute to an upward and reinforcing spiral of improvements: *there is a direct link between levels of confidence and levels of economic activity and economic growth* (Roe quoted in DC Research 2014: 29). Agencies such as HIE have strategies and policy interventions to facilitate such objectives, with recognition that

> Placing more value on, and investing in, the native language and cultural traditions of the region will result in fortifying cultural identity and sense of place, increasing confidence and self-esteem. This in turn can lead to population retention, inward migration, greater entrepreneurial activity, business creation and ultimately higher GDP. (Roe quoted in DC Research 2014: 29)

Our own work and review of other studies on workers, enterprises and entrepreneurs in remote rural and island localities (Danson and Burnett 2014, 2015; Burnett and Danson 2016, 2017) has confirmed that the challenges confronting consumers, producers and other economic stakeholders can be addressed by appreciating the potential value in local people's cultures, natural and community heritages. By definition, this means considering the unique selling points of their particular and peculiar circumstances and environments, though knowledge and experiences can be shared across island contexts.

Case studies of islands across northern Europe

Often a crucible for economic and community development initiatives, Scotland has mixed experiences with supporting and appreciating its island and archipelago communities and economies. Most islands are in the north: Orkney and Shetland with their historical Norse links and characteristics, or the west: especially the Inner and Outer Hebrides, with their mixed Norse and Gaelic heritages. Elsewhere we have noted the reliance on the iconography, culture, tangible and intangible assets of the *Gàidhealtachd* – the traditional heartlands of the Gaelic language and culture – for many high value products and services of the industrial core of Scotland (Danson and Burnett 2000) despite the millennium-long tensions between the territories of the Lordship of the Isles and the Kingdom of Scotland. Historically, economic activity in the Hebrides and Shetland is centred on crofting, inshore fishing, land-based activities, public services, the Ministry of Defence and tourism; and the impact of considerable out-migration for work and education is well noted as a contributing factor to economic decline and 'fragility'; Orkney tends to have more small farms and an enterprising culture, though the basics are similar across the three island groups. Land reform has been especially important in addressing the restrictions imposed by landowners on the development and improvement of land-based activities and across the community buy-out areas population stabilisation and subsequent growth, housing improvements and small firm creation have all followed (Danson and Burnett 2020). The activities of the development agency, Highlands and Islands Enterprise, since its establishment in 1965 have been mixed in the islands but overall have been instrumental in raising their profile, resilience and economic stability, sustainability and well-being (Burnett 2011).

While isolation within the Scottish islands and between them and the mainland has been progressively addressed with, albeit contested, transport infrastructure investments and ferry subsidies (Auditor General 2017; Findlay 2017; Copus 2018b), in other island territories across northern Europe there has been a more inclusive approach to protecting and nurturing the periphery. Enshrined in 'Our Vision 2030' (Nordic Council of Ministers 2019), integration, sustainability and mobility are to be promoted and prioritised through 'sustainable energy production and climate neutrality, green transport and investments, the bioeconomy and the circular economy'. Despite most Nordic countries having a dominant capital city, the large size of their respective territories relative to population – and so low density – and strong social welfare models have led to some of the lowest levels of inequalities overall and by location (Kristensen and Lilja 2011). Eurostat analyses on economic and social indicators therefore confirm that islands and remote rural areas fare relatively much better in the Nordic countries than in the UK, Ireland and other perhaps more well-endowed countries closer to the centre of Europe[6]. Quoting Kristensen and Lilja (2011), Wøien, Kristensen and Teräs (2019: 90) highlight that: *The shared geographies and typologies in the Nordic Region, and the corresponding structures building on these natural resource endowments are all part of the 'shared experiences' in Nordic economic history.* Prosperity and sustainable inclusive development into the peripheral island communities are established on these principles, and are enabling and enabled by the collective Nordic pursuit of smart specialisation, innovation and green economics.

Nevertheless, there are tensions and challenges; as reported especially with regard to Iceland but applying elsewhere in the Nordic countries, 'the lack of regional diversity in the economic activities and the small population mean limited expertise, critical mass and funds, as well as a tendency to centralise decision-making' (Wøien et al. 2019). Achieving the successful transition to new foundations for island economies based on their unique tangible and intangible assets of culture, natural and human resources is therefore a goal across northern latitudes. How the structures, processes and philosophies of the respective nation states, wider macro-regional partnerships and the communities themselves align and pursue synergies collaboratively explains where positive outcomes can be attained most readily.

---

6   *Statistics on Rural Areas in the EU*, <https://ec.europa.eu/eurostat/statistics-explained/index.php/Statistics_on_rural_areas_in_the_EU#Risk_of_poverty_and_social_exclusion> accessed 15 May 2020.

Conclusions

This chapter has deliberately focused on the demographics of islands as changes in population size and form are an indicator of the economic health of a location, offer the dimensions of their inherent market size and provide parameters to the pool of resources and skills, while trends demonstrate the direction of travel in enterprise well-being and economic resilience. Although some societies, for example, as applied to the Scottish islands (Burnett 2011), have permitted natural decline to address and facilitate the outcome of market forces, others have actively pursued retention and development as fundamental to cultural and political state building and continuity (Baldacchino 2005; de Souza 2017). Regardless of these differing jurisdictions and philosophical strategies and approaches, there appears to be consensus that the positive characteristics displayed in scorecards by Dressler (2016) and ESPON (2012) of appreciable levels of social capital, high values of natural capital, preserved history and culture, and biodiversity and renewable energy potentials (hydropower, offshore wind, wave, tidal energies, biomass, solar energy) can form the bases for sustainable and inclusive economic development. Applying the advantages inherent in these factors for local production and service activities, trading into a globalised marketplace where these present differentiated offerings, creates the potential for communities to build opportunities for returning young skilled graduates and so resilience for the islanders cooperatively.

Establishing an island economy with an export base to complement a local foundational economy (Foundational Economy Collective 2018) may require new connectivities to be constructed through infrastructure investments in broadband but also tunnels and causeways, internal ferries for archipelagos, and other means to reduce barriers. Experiences from Iceland and the Faroe Islands show how expanding the effective labour supply and local market area can create the conditions to allow lower costs to be delivered through economies of scale and scope. The positive externalities island cultures, products and services present to the nation and globe in an increasingly homogenised world should be recognised within and outwith their localities for the greater benefit. Policymakers and practitioners in reality often need persuaded to appreciate and incorporate these wider considerations into analyses and decision-making, and consultations over the new Islands Bill for Scotland (Scottish Government 2019b) offer a route to embedding such rebalancing into the strategic landscape and to complement community land ownership and empowerment.

Bibliography

Auditor General (2017). *Transport Scotland's Ferry Services*, <https://www.audit-scotland.gov.uk/uploads/docs/report/2017/nr_171019_ferry_services.pdf> accessed 5 April 2019.

Baldacchino, G. (2005). 'The contribution of 'social capital' to economic growth: lessons from island jurisdictions', *The Round Table*, 94 (378), 31–46.

Baldacchino, G. (2006a). 'Innovative development strategies from non-sovereign island jurisdictions? A global review of economic policy and governance practices', *World Development*, 34, 5, 852–867.

Baldacchino, G. (2006b). 'Managing the hinterland beyond: two ideal-type strategies of economic development for small island territories', *Asia Pacific Viewpoint*, 47 (1), 45–60.

Baum, T. (1996). 'The Fascination of Islands: The Tourist Perspective'. In Lockhart, D., and D. Drakakis-Smith (eds), *Island Tourism: Problems and Perspectives*, pp. 21–35. London: Pinter

Brinklow, L. (2011). 'The proliferation of island studies', *Griffith Review*, <https://griffithreview.com/articles/the-proliferation-of-island-studies/> accessed 5 April 2019.

Burnett, J.A. (2011). *The Making of the Modern Scottish Highlands, 1939–1965: Withstanding the 'Colossus of Advancing Materialism'*. Dublin: Four Courts.

Burnett, K., and Danson, M. (2016). 'Sustainability and small enterprises in Scotland's remote rural "margins"', *Local Economy*, 31 (5), 539–553.

Burnett, K., and Danson, M. (2017). 'Enterprise and entrepreneurship on islands and remote rural environments', *International Journal of Entrepreneurship and Innovation*, 18 (1), 25–35.

CEC (2008). 'Report Hearing Paper 1', Hearing on Growth, Institutions and Policy – State of the Art and Territorial Dimension, Brussels, 1–2 July.

CEC (2019). *EU's Implementation of the Sustainable Development Goals (SDGs)*, <https://ec.europa.eu/environment/sustainable-development/SDGs/implementation/index_en.htm> accessed 5 April 2019.

Clements, P. and Clements, D. (2019). 'Abandoned Isles', *Lonely-Isles*, <http://paulmclem.weebly.com/abandoned-isles.html> accessed 5 April 2019.

Coull, J. (1967). 'A comparison of demographic trends in the Faroe and Shetland Islands', *Transactions of the Institute of British Geographers*, 41, 159–166.

Copus, A. (2018a). 'Demographic projections for the Scottish Sparsely Populated Area (SPA) 2011-2046', Working Paper 3. (Objective O1.2ii), *RESAS RD 3.4.1 Demographic change in remote areas*, <http://www.hutton.ac.uk/research/projects/demographic-change-remote-areas> accessed 5 April 2019.

Copus, A. (2018b). 'The wisdom of the fathers? Regional/rural development policy and structures for the Highlands and Islands of Scotland 1965-2015, through the lens of smart specialisation'. In Kristensen, I., Dubois, A., and J. Teras (eds), *Strategic Approaches to Regional Development: Smart Experimentation in Less-favoured Regions*, pp. 86–102. Abingdon: Routledge.

Danson, M. (2015). *Empowered Community-Led Inclusion – Community Resilience*. Edinburgh: Heriot-Watt University.

Danson, M., and Burnett, K. (2000). 'Arts and culture in regional development in Scotland', *Welsh Economic Review*, 12 (2), 38–42.

Danson, M., and Burnett, K. (2014). 'Entrepreneurship and enterprise on islands'. In Henry, C., and G. McElwee (eds), *Exploring Rural Enterprise: New Perspectives on Research, Policy & Practice: Contemporary Issues in Entrepreneurship Research*, vol. 4, Contemporary Issues in Entrepreneurship Research, pp. 151–174. London: Emerald Group Publishing.

Danson, M., and Burnett, K. (2015). 'Enterprise and entrepreneurship on islands and remote rural environments', *The Safeguarding and Promoting of Sea and Island Culture Conference Proceedings*, Viet Nam National Institute of Culture and Arts Studies international conference, Nha Trang City, Vietnam.

Danson, M., and Burnett, K. (2020). 'Current Scottish land reform and reclaiming the Commons: building community resilience', *Progress in Development Studies*, forthcoming.

Danson, M., and de Souza, P. (eds) (2011). *Peripherality, Marginality and Border Issues in Northern Europe*. Abingdon: Routledge.

DCResearch (2014). *Ar Stòras Gàidhlig. The Economic and Social Value of Gaelic as an Asset – Full Report*. Highlands and Islands Enterprise, Inverness.

Depraetere, C. (2008). 'The challenge of nissology: a global outlook on the world archipelago Part I: scene setting the world archipelago', *Island Studies Journal*, 31 (1), 3–16.

De Souza, P. (2017). *The Rural and Peripheral in Regional Development. An Alternative Perspective*. Abingdon: Routledge.

Devine, T. (2012). *The Scottish Nation: A Modern History*. London: Penguin Books.

Dressler, C. (2016). *Overcoming Barriers to Economic Development – A Remote Island Perspective*, <http://www.scottish-islands-federation.co.uk/overcoming-barriers-to-economic-development-a-remote-island-perspective> accessed 12 December 2019.

Edmond, R., and Smith, V. (2003). *Islands in History and Representation*. London: Routledge.

ESPON (2010). *First ESPON 2013 Synthesis Report: Results by Summer 2010: New Evidence on Smart, Sustainable and Inclusive Territories*. Luxembourg.

ESPON (2011). *The Development of the Islands – European Islands and Cohesion Policy (EUROISLANDS). Targeted Analysis 2013/2/2. Final Report*. <https://www.espon.eu/programme/projects/espon-2013/targeted-analyses/euroislands-development-islands-%E2%80%93-european-islands> accessed 12 December 2019.

ESPON (2012). *Final Scientific Report*, GEOSPECS – Geographic Specificities and Development Potentials in Europe, <https://www.espon.eu/programme/projects/espon-2013/applied-research/geospecs-geographic-specificities-and-development> accessed 12 December 2019.

Fazey, I., Moug, P., Allen, S., Beckmann, K., Blackwood, D., Bonaventura, M., Burnett, K., Danson, M., Falconer, R., Gagnon, A., Harkness, R., Hodgson, A., Holm, L., Irvine, K.N., Low, R., Lyon, C., Moss, A., Moran, C., Naylor, L., O'Brien, K., Russell, S., Skerratt, S., Williams, J., and Wolstenholme, R. (2018). 'Transformation in a changing climate: a research agenda', *Climate and Development*, 10 (3), 197–217.

Findlay, J. (2017). *Special Issue: Competitive Tendering and Scottish Lifeline Ferry Services, Fraser of Allander Economic Commentary*, 41 (1) <https://strathprints.strath.ac.uk/view/publications/Fraser_of_Allander_Economic_Commentary.htm> accessed 12 December 2019.

Fletcher, L. (2011). "... some distance to go': a critical survey of Island Studies', *New Literatures Review*, 47–48, 17–34.

Foundational Economy Collective (2018). *Foundational Economy. The Infrastructure of Everyday Life*. Manchester: Manchester University Press.

Freitas, C., and Kitson, M. (2018). 'Perceptions of entrepreneurial ecosystems in remote islands and core regions', *Island Studies Journal*, 13 (1), 267–284.

Gillis, J. (2004). *Islands of the Mind: How the Human Imagination Created the Atlantic World*. Basingstoke: Palgrave.

Harvey, D., Jones, R., McInroy, N., and Milligan, C. (eds) (2002). *Celtic Geographies: Old Cultures, New Times*. London: Routledge.

Hennessy, E., and McCleary, A. (2011). 'Nature's Eden? the production and effects of 'pristine' nature in the Galápagos Islands', *Island Studies Journal*, 6 (2), 131–156.

HIE (2016). *A Minimum Income Standard for Remote Rural Scotland: A Policy Update*. Highlands and Islands Enterprise: Inverness.

Hull, J., and Sassenberg, U. (2012). 'Creating new cultural visitor experiences on islands: challenges and opportunities', *Journal of Tourism Consumption and Practice*, 4 (2), 91–110.

Islands Revival (2019). *The Islands Revival Declaration*, <https://islandsrevival.org/> accessed 12 December 2019.

Kelman, I. (2007). 'Sustainable livelihoods from natural heritage on islands', *Island Studies Journal*, 2 (1), 101–114.

Krugman, P. (1991). 'Increasing returns and economic geography', *Journal of Political Economy*, 99 (3), 483–499.

Leask, A., and Rihova, I. (2010). 'The role of heritage tourism in the Shetland Islands', *International Journal of Culture, Tourism and Hospitality Research*, 4 (2), 118–129.

Margaras, V. (2016). 'Islands of the EU: taking account of their specific needs in EU policy', Briefing, EPRS: European Parliamentary Research Service, <http://www.europarl.europa.eu/RegData/etudes/BRIE/2016/573960/EPRS_BRI(2016)573960_EN.pdf> accessed 12 December 2019.

Markantoni, M., Steiner, A., and Meador, J. (2019.) 'Can community interventions change resilience? Fostering perceptions of individual and community resilience in rural places', *Community Development*, 50 (2), 238–255.

McHattie, L., Champion, K., and Broadley, C. (2018). 'Craft, textiles, and cultural assets in the Northern Isles: innovation from tradition in the Shetland Islands', *Island Studies Journal*, 13 (2), 39–54.

McMorran, R., Scott, A., and Price, M. (2013). 'Reconstructing sustainability; participant experiences of community land tenure in North West Scotland', *Journal of Rural Studies*, 33, 20–31.

NRS (2018). *Local Administrative Units (LAU1) Population Estimates by Sex and Single Year of Age, 2011–2017*. National Records of Scotland, <https://www.nrscotland.gov.uk/statistics-and-data/statistics/statistics-by-theme/population/population-estimates/2011-based-special-area-population-estimates/nuts-population-estimates> accessed 11 November 2019.

Nic Craith, M. (2019). *The Vanishing World of The Islandman: Narrative and Nostalgia*. Basingstoke: Palgrave Macmillan.

Nordic Council of Ministers (2019). *Our Vision 2030*. Nordic Cooperation, <https://www.norden.org/en/declaration/our-vision-2030> accessed 12 December 2019.

Richardson, R., and Gillespie, A. (1996). 'Advanced communications and employment creation in rural and peripheral regions: a case study of the Highlands and Islands of Scotland', *Annals of Regional Science*, 30: 91–110.

Royle, S. (2001). *A Geography of Islands: Small Island Insularity*. London and New York: Routledge.

Scottish Government (2018) *National Performance Framework*. <https://nationalperformance.gov.scot> accessed 12 December 2019.

Scottish Government (2019a). *Scottish Government Urban Rural Classification: Defining Scotland by Rurality*, <https://www2.gov.scot/Topics/Statistics/About/Methodology/UrbanRuralClassification> accessed 12 December 2019.

Scottish Government (2019b). *Consultation on a National Islands Plan and Island Communities Impact Assessment Guidance*, <https://www.gov.scot/publications/national-islands-plan-islands-communities-impact-assessment-guidance-consultation/> accessed 12 December 2019.

SIF (n.d.). *Island Statistics*, Scottish Islands Federation, <http://www.scottish-islands-federation.co.uk/island-statistics> accessed 15 May 2020.

Simpson, A. (2018). 'Uist buy-out fuels bitter row', *The Herald*, 31 May.

United Nations (2019). *Sustainable Development Goals*, <https://www.un.org/sustainabledevelopment> accessed 12 December 2019.

Watson, I. (1998). 'The challenge of maintaining parity for offshore islands', *Middle States Geographer*, 31, 132–137.

Wilson, G., and Whitehead, I. (2012). 'Local rural product as a "relic" spatial strategy in globalised rural spaces: Evidence from County Clare (Ireland)', *Journal of Rural Studies*, 28 (3), 199–207.

Wøien, M., Kristensen, I., and Teräs, J. (2019). 'The status, characteristics and potential of SMART SPECIALISATION in Nordic regions', *NORDREGIO REPORT 2019:3*, <http://norden.diva-portal.org/smash/get/diva2:1295018/FULLTEXT01.pdf> accessed 15 May 2020.

ROSIE ALEXANDER

7. Young People, Out-migration and Scottish Islands: Surveying the Landscape

Concern about youth out-migration from the Scottish islands is longstanding (Highlands and Islands Enterprise [HIE] 2009, 2018). Similar concerns are evident in island communities across the globe, with the need to retain or attract young people understood as key to ensuring population sustainability – both in terms of increasing population numbers and ensuring a strong enough supply of workers to sustain the rest of the ageing population (King and Connell 1999; King 2009; Connell 2018). The risks of not managing to attract or retain enough young people are significant, and in the Scottish imagination the spectre of islands such as St Kilda, Swona, Monachs and other islands that have experienced population collapse loom large.

Despite these concerns, recent evidence shows that island population levels are stabilising and even increasing in the Scottish islands. Whereas there was a 3% decrease in Scottish island population levels between 1991 and 2001, between 2001 to 2011 there was actually a population increase of 4% (National Records of Scotland 2015). There is also anecdotal evidence that young people are increasingly choosing to stay, return or move to island communities (CODEL 2018). This raises the question – how far should youth migration remain a concern in the Scottish islands?

This chapter explores the evidence surrounding youth migration from Scottish island communities, identifying that although Scottish island populations may be generally increasing, patterns of migration are uneven, and some of the smallest and most marginal islands continue to face significant challenges. Exploring the available evidence, this chapter then seeks to address questions of why young people move, and why they stay away or return, as well as issues of who moves and who stays. Considering the diversity of migration experiences, this chapter argues for a contextualised understanding of migration, focusing on how migration experiences are embedded in local contexts and cultures, and in the life course of individual migrants. Considering a more contextualised approach helps to highlight the ecosystem around migration decisions, and as a result the chapter argues that youth migration remains an important area of consideration in the Scottish Islands and that strategies to address migration need to focus on localised ecosystem solutions.

Migration and Scottish islands: The evidence

Despite evidence that the population of the Scottish islands is generally increasing, the evidence shows considerable differences between islands (National Records of Scotland 2015). The most significant population increases have been in islands with populations over 10,000 people, with some increases in islands with populations of 50–499. The four largest islands – mainland Shetland, mainland Orkney, the island of Skye and Lewis and Harris (the largest island the British Isles) – account for nearly two thirds of the total island population, and growth has largely been centred in these islands (*ibid.*). In contrast the smallest islands, with populations of 1–49, and islands with populations between 500–9,999 have actually seen net population *decreases*. Considering population trends by size of island population however potentially overlooks significant differences between islands, including those which 'buck the trend' – for example Barra, Benbecula, South Ronaldsay and Mull are islands with populations between 500–9,999 that have seen increases.

The evidence of different migration experiences in different islands, suggests that the issue of Scottish island population sustainability is far from resolved. Indeed, the Islands (Scotland) Act 2018 specifically identifies an objective for the Scottish islands of increasing population levels. It is also important to note that simply increasing population levels is not sufficient to address issues of population sustainability. In particular island communities show a greater demographic imbalance than other communities in terms of age of residents – with 21% of Scottish island residents in 2011 aged 65 or over (compared to 17% nationally) (National Records of Scotland 2015). Again some islands see a much greater demographic imbalance than others – with 44% aged over 65 in North Ronaldsay (ibid). Although migration can bolster island populations, the appeal of island communities to lifestyle migrants, especially retirees, may exacerbate ageing demographics (King and Connell 1999; Connell 2018). If there are not enough young people in island communities to support an ageing population, island sustainability may still be at risk.

Therefore youth migration patterns remain a significant focus in the policy literature relating to the Scottish islands, and wider Highlands and Islands region (HIE 2009, 2015, 2018). A report in 2009 showed that the region had 25% fewer 15–30 year olds than it would if the population distribution mirrored the rest of Scotland – resulting in a 'population gap' of 18,580 young people (HIE 2009). An updated report in 2018 found that the population of young people in the region fell by two% between 2011 and 2016 (HIE 2018). Concerns around ageing populations is also evident and in 2009, it was reported that over the next twenty-five years the region was likely to see 'the population of people of retired age [...] increase by more than 70 per cent across the region' (HIE 2009: 6).

Again, considering youth migration there is evidently significant diversity in the experiences of different Scottish islands. So, for example, considering the evidence from the 2018 HIE report, Shetland is identified as one of the communities with the highest proportions of young people, and the Outer Hebrides and Skye and Wester Ross as communities with some of the lowest proportions. And in terms of population change, between 2011–2016 the population of 15–30 year olds in Skye and Wester Ross actually saw a 2% increase (compared to the Outer Hebrides where decline was amongst the most significant at 7%). In terms of projected decreases of the 15–30-year-old population Orkney was anticipated to see a 15% decrease, Shetland 18%, Eilean Siar 26% and Argyll and Bute 28% (HIE 2018). The particularly acute challenges of youth out-migration in the Western Isles is clear from these statistics, and has been noted elsewhere (HallAitken 2007; Jamieson and Groves 2008; Royal Society of Edinburgh 2008)

Who moves? Evidence from the literature

Statistical evidence regarding young people and migration can be challenging to interpret because of the difference in definitions of 'young people' used in the literature in terms of the *age* of young people (Crow 2010). A closer reading of the literature actually reveals significant differences between the movements of young people depending on their age. The evidence shows that out-migration is 'particularly concentrated' in the 15–19 age group (HIE 2018: 5) – which corresponds with the ages at which young people leave school and transition to college or higher education (see also Stockdale 2002a). In 2016 in the 20–24 and 25–29 age categories there was net *in*-migration (HIE 2018). In 2009 net in-migration was also reported among those in their 30s (HIE, 2009). The evidence that flows of 'youth migration' are different for different ages of young people and are experienced differently in different islands, is important and yet often over-looked in much public discourse, popular media and some policy discourse, where ideas of 'population decline' and youth out-migration from rural and island communities potentially retain a strong hold (Crow 2010).

The evidence presented here provides valuable context for recent research which has provided anecdotal evidence of changing trends of youth migration in the Western Isles specifically (CODEL 2018). This research was picked up widely by the press as evidence of islands reversing the trend of depopulation. However, it is clear from the statistical evidence presented here that in-migration from older young people to island communities has been extant for some time. Indeed, as the CODEL research defined young people as up to the age of 40, findings around in- and return migration in this group should not be a surprise, as this age group has displayed net in-migration for some time.

Why do people move? Beyond economic/lifestyle binaries

Classically theoretical approaches to explain migration have been drawn from neoclassical economics (Massey et al. 1993; Boyle et al. 1998). Within such perspectives motivations for migration are primarily assumed to be economic, stimulated by an individual's desire for income maximisation. Within these perspectives migration from rural to urban areas is understood to relate to the improved opportunities and earning potential from larger, growing, urban labour markets. At retirement, when income maximisation is less of a concern, migrants may move out of urban areas seeking a better quality of life. Neoclassical models of migration continue to remain very popular with policy makers despite the fact that the evidence shows that the influences on migration are much more complex than these models assume (Massey et al. 1993).

Conceptualising rural and island migrations through a neoclassical economic lens positions rural and island spaces in a particular way. So, where young people are understood to leave for 'better opportunities' and retired or semi-retired people to move in for 'lifestyle' reasons, the underpinning assumption is that islands are places that *lack* opportunities. This potentially ties in with common island stereotypes – which either position islands as idyllic places suitable for rest and relaxation, or 'backward' insular spaces (Baldacchino and Khamis 2018: 370). Within such narratives, islands are places which lack meaningful work, or where opportunities for work may be conceptualised as lower skilled and lower value. These perceptions of islands may also be reinforced through marketing and publicity surrounding islands in the tourist literature (Stalker and Burnett 2016).

The common-sense appeal of neoclassical economic models of migration, and ideas of what island communities 'are' potentially reinforce each other – so that youth out-migration can seem almost inevitable. Further, the evidence from the literature tends to support the importance of economic motivations for rural and island out-migration. Reviewing the literature on rural out-migration in Scotland, Jamieson and Groves note that all of the studies they review: 'Emphasise and to some degree demonstrate an association between migration and the desire for higher education and graduate employment or "good jobs"' (Jamieson and Groves 2008: 3).

However, although employment and education are important, thinking about migration decision-making simply in terms of key motivators or drivers can hide the complexity of migration decision-making, and the ways it is embedded in individual experiences and biographies (Stockdale

2002a; Halfacree and Boyle 1993). Halfacree and Boyle (1993), for example, identify how migration decisions are embedded in a person's biography – embedded in their past experiences and anticipated futures, and subject to multiple, complex factors. In terms of in-migration, research into the Western Isles has shown that despite 'quality of life' being important, more than one in five migrants move for employment (Stockdale 2006). Research into returning migrants in rural areas also shows that although personal factors are important, actual moves are likely to be prompted by economic factors like employment or availability of housing (Ní Laoire 2008).

Scrutinising the data relating to Scottish island out-migration, although economic 'opportunities' are thought of as important in stimulating youth out-migration, the data shows that that movements of young people for education 'dominate' out-migration flows from rural areas (Stockdale 2002b: 357) but is a lot less clear in terms of employment opportunities. Indeed, non-education related migrations typically comprise a complex range of motivations, both economic and other motivations, leading Stockdale to identify 'the multifaceted nature of rural out-migration flows', which are marked by 'the personal negotiation between different influencing factors for different migrant groups' (2002b: 361).

Considering the evidence surrounding out-migration related to educational transition, it is also the case that these migrations are unlikely to simply be related to objectively 'better' opportunities. Instead research from the field of educational sociology has shown that decisions to move away for education may be embedded as part of educational transition in rural communities (Corbett 2007). That is, through the use of national curricula, often taught by teachers who are incomers to rural communities, and histories of out-migration for the pursuit of higher education, young people through engagement with education 'learn to leave' their communities (Corbett 2007). In the Scottish islands, research has supported Corbett's work in Atlantic Canada, and found that academically able young people identify leaving for higher education as 'common sense' (Alexander and Hooley 2018).

Island communities in particular have a strong history of migration and mobility, and this may further reinforce expectations of youth out-migration, so that out-migration is perceived as 'normal' or 'natural' for young people in island communities (Easthope and Gabriel 2008; Alexander 2015b; Hayfield 2017). Research in the Faroe Islands, for example, has demonstrated how there is a strong 'culture of migration', which reinforces youth out-migration (Hayfield 2017). The suggestion that 'cultures of migration' may be particularly important in Higher Education transition has also been evidenced more widely in the UK (Donnelly and Gamsu 2018). A 'culture of migration' potentially provides some explanatory potential for both levels of migration from the islands and destinations for migration – so just as Copenhagen is a favoured destination for Faroese students (Hayfield 2017), the evidence shows that there are similar locational preferences for out-migrants from the Scottish islands. Notably Aberdeen is a favoured destination for many islanders, particularly from the Northern Isles (Alexander 2015a), with Glasgow also a significant destination for those from the Western Isles (Stockdale 2002b; Hall Aitken 2007) and Edinburgh relatively popular with students from the Northern Isles (Lasselle et al. n.d.; Alexander 2015a). These preferences are likely to be in part structured by geographical proximity, with proximity being a key way that students mitigate the risks of moving away for university (Clayton et al. 2009). In the case of islands, proximity is mediated by transport systems that connect communities – meaning that for the Northern Isles the port of Aberdeen is a popular student destination (Alexander 2015a, 2016). The high level of familiarity that students have with proximate cities is also important, with these connections structured socially, historically and culturally – the historic connections with Aberdeen mean that many students in the Northern Isles have family and friends in Aberdeen; many have also developed a 'familiarity' with the city through frequent travel through the city en-route to other destinations and family holidays; and given the popularity of the city, many students have friends who are in the city for higher education already, or intend to be in the future (Alexander 2016). These patterns in youth migration, and the idea of 'cultures of migration' suggests that even if educational opportunities were radically increased in the islands, the desire of young people to move away may never fully stem the out-migration of this group (Crow 2010).

The strength of the 'migration culture' for young islanders accords with evidence that for some young people, the educational course they enrol on is secondary to the desire to leave the islands. Rather than edu-cation being a *motivation* for mobility therefore, education becomes the *means* for allowing mobility. So, for example, Stockdale's (2002) typology of out-migrants from rural Scotland identifies two distinct categories of mover – those who are 'education motivated career aspirers' but also 'es-capees through education' – that is, those who are using educational tran-sition as a means of leaving, where 'leaving' rather than 'opportunity' as such is the main driver.

Conceptualised in this way then, we can see that migration decisions of young people are complex, and not simply motivated by opportunity. This also leads us to consider how the migration motivations of younger people and older people may actually share much in common. So, for ex-ample, young people may move for 'lifestyle' reasons (such as university lifestyle) just as much as older adults. Indeed recent work from Benson and O'Reilly has pointed out that 'the majority of migrants seek a better way of life through their migration' regardless of age (2016: 33). Where 'lifestyle' migration for older migrants may typically involve moving to rural places, for younger people 'lifestyle' migration may involve moving to a large metropolitan area (King 2018). In Scotland, the research litera-ture has typically identified that 'urban lifestyles are more attractive [...] for young people' (Crow 2010: 17)

Leaving: Not always leaving

If it is important to avoid unhelpful binaries of 'opportunity vs lifestyle' and 'young vs old' then it is also important to avoid the assumption that migrations are one-off events: that leavers leave the islands permanently (and indeed that incomers move to the islands permanently). In particular *return* migration is likely to be a significant phenomenon in island com-munities but is potentially less visible and under-researched (Ní Laoire 2008; Crow 2010).

The evidence from rural and island communities around the globe is that 'the myth of return' or a 'homing desire' is strong among emigrant populations (Brah 1996; Ní Laoire 2008). In island communities, which tend to have a strong identity (King 2009) this homing desire may be even stronger than in comparable rural populations. In Scotland, Stockdale (2002a), for example, found that in her research sample 10% from North Lewis had returned, but from the Scottish Borders the level was only 2%. Considering Shetland, Cooke and Petersen identify that 'there is a tradition for most people wanting to return after the completion of their education, provided that the return is able to fulfil people's career and lifestyle needs' (2019: 103). In the Faroe Islands, Hayfield considers that the desire to return is so strong that 'embedded in the culture of migration is a culture of returning' (Hayfield 2017: 9). However, whether these return migration intentions are enacted is another question, with evidence suggesting that a desire to return does not always result in an *actual* return, and that where it does the return move may take place at some point in the future (Stockdale 2006; Hayfield 2017). Two particularly key points in terms of return migration are the period immediately after completing higher education, and the point at which people 'settle down' and have children. The evidence around these two particular points is considered in more depth below.

In terms of return migration immediately after completing higher education, the evidence actually shows that a relatively high proportion of higher education graduates return to the islands. Evidence from the Northern Isles, for example, shows that over one third of higher education graduates are in the islands six months after graduation (Alexander 2015a). However, for some this may be a temporary move before moving away again (Stockdale 2006), and indeed the evidence nationally shows that family homes are important post-graduation destinations for students, partly due to complexity and precarity in graduate transitions (Sage et al. 2013). For other students though, the return home may be part of a planned transition – with rural economies requiring highly trained staff in roles like teaching and nursing, but where student transition into these roles 'might require 'living away' to acquire the necessary credentials'(Cooke and Petersen 2019: 106). In the UK the need to 'go away' to train has potentially been reinforced by the expansion of higher education and specifically the expansion of higher education qualifications in some occupational areas, which traditionally didn't require a degree qualification but increasingly do, becoming classified as 'new' and 'modern' graduate careers

(Elias and Purcell 2003). Evidence in the literature suggests that for some students pathways into careers that they could undertake on the islands is undertaken via specific mobility pathways, so, for example, Stockdale finds that from North Lewis in the Western Isles 'females traditionally embarking on nursing or hairdressing careers complete their training in Inverness (Highlands) following a period of study at Lews Castle College (Stornoway)' (Stockdale 2002b: 52). In this case the structure of the training routes facilitates certain (geographical) pathways out of a community, which may be followed by a return to undertake careers in these roles. In the statistics for Orkney and Shetland, there is some evidence that students are more likely to pursue qualifications in subjects like education, which is a sector with strong graduate employment potential in the islands, and this suggests that students may be engaging in this sector with ideas to later return to the islands (Alexander 2015a). There is also evidence in the international literature of students adopting career and training strategies to facilitate a return to rural communities – with an example of this being Rérat's research in rural Switzerland where he found a high proportion of returners planned to become teachers, as teaching was perceived as a viable career option that is proportionally much more significant than in other parts of the country (with one third of graduates working as teachers compared to one tenth nationally) (Rérat 2014).

Where some students opt to study a course that would allow relatively immediate return (providing a job opportunity were to arise), other students may plan to, or choose to stay away during their early career years in order to build a professional career which would allow for later return to their islands. Staying away to build a career is potentially built into the training routes for some professions, especially those which require an initial training year (post-degree), where students may have limited choice over location (e.g. many medical careers, teaching, law, accountancy and so on). Staying away may also allow individuals the opportunity to capitalise on the 'escalator effect' on their careers offered by urban regions – that is, the way that being able to access a larger pool of employment opportunities allows individuals to 'escalate' their career through multiple job moves. Research in Scotland has shown that Edinburgh, for example, acts as an 'escalator' region (van Ham et al. 2012) – and therefore suggests that Scottish island students may indeed experience some career benefit from staying away from their island communities for the initial parts of their career at least.

Even where out-migration is not part of a planned career trajectory, it may still be part of a young person's move into adulthood. The strength of 'cultures of migration' in which youth out-migration is perceived as normal or natural, and is *particularly* associated with movements for educational progression may result in migration being associated with becoming 'successful' (Easthope and Gabriel 2008; Alexander 2013). The association of mobility, of 'going out and seeing the world' with success is evident in wider cultural narratives in the twenty-first century – for example, in concepts such as 'global careerists' (Reichrath-Smith and Neault 2013) and the 'kinetic elite' (Cresswell 2006). To stay may be to be perceived as a 'failure' (Alexander 2013), and this association may be so strong that as Easthope and Gabriel (2008) found in Tasmania, even students who left the island to pursue education and subsequently withdrew and returned home were perceived positively by the island community. Having experience of 'elsewhere' may therefore act as a kind of career capital in island communities – with the experience of mobility, regardless of what this is, being a mark of 'success'.

Although planned return may involve students returning to the islands immediately after higher education study, it may also involve return at a later point in life. For individuals who grew up in island or rural communities, a particular point when a return may be desired is the point of having children (Ní Laoire 2008; Crow 2010; Hayfield 2017). In the islands of Scotland this pattern of desired return to 'settle down' and have a family is also apparent (Alexander 2016). Being close to extended family and providing children with a similar upbringing to their own is important to many young islanders. The notion of islands as good places to raise a family is also reinforced every year by the well-publicised surveys which suggest the Scottish islands are some of the best places to bring up children (Gander 2015).

Moving 'home' to raise children may classically be understood in terms of seeking a better 'quality of life', however although a better quality of life may encourage mobility, the availability of housing and the availability of work are critical in order to enable these movements. Indeed the desire to return to the region amongst many leavers, and the significance of concerns around housing in relation to this return (as well as job opportunities) is noted in recent work in the Highlands and Islands (HIE 2018). In practice whether a migrant moves is likely to be embedded in their personal lives, relationships and specific contextual circumstances. So if an islander meets and settles down with a partner, then whether or not their partner is happy to move to an island will influence the likelihood of return (Stockdale 2002b). On the other hand, in some contexts divorce and relationship break up have prompted return migration (Ní Laoire 2008) and ageing relatives or family illness may also influence a move back to an island community (Stockdale 2002b).

Island diversity: Socio-economic contexts

So far this chapter has explored the evidence around migration pathways and patterns for islands generally, and has problematised assumptions about straightforward economic and lifestyle motivations. In this section the importance of specific island contexts is explored. Key to thinking about island migration contexts, is understanding migration and mobility as containing multiple forms of mobility, not just permanent migration. In particular, the mobilities turn in the social sciences has raised awareness of the ways that there are many different forms of mobility happening at different scales and for different durations – so commuting for work, tourism, seasonal migration and so on are all forms of mobility which are important to consider alongside migration (Adey 2017). Thinking about island migrations it is important to remember not only that migrations may be temporary, but also that they happen at different scales, and may *not* only be about island-mainland (or rural-urban) migrations but will include intra-island migration – that is, moving to different parts of an island – and inter-island migration – that is, moving to another island (King 2009). The importance of inter-island mobility particularly may be highly significant in the island communities of the Western Isles, Orkney and Shetland, which have all seen a marked centralisation of population to their main towns in recent years (HallAitken 2007, 2009).

An important part of island context includes the economic and education context. At a regional level in the Highlands and Islands, the growth of the University of the Highlands and Islands has been widely recognised for the increased potential it provides for completing higher education in the region, and continuing growth has been recommended to continue to improve the attractiveness of the region (HIE 2018). However, the role of higher education and dynamics of inter-region mobility are less clearly explored and considering how educational opportunities may impact on migration patterns potentially from smaller islands to larger island communities is an area worthy of more exploration.

Where there is evidence in the Western Isles, Orkney and Shetland of centralising populations, it is also notable that the main towns are the main locations for Further and Higher Education, and also the locations of the biggest secondary schools. Here the restricted availability of secondary education in some of the smaller Scottish islands is likely to be important. For some students from these islands daily mobility away from the island to larger settlements may be necessary. Other students may board weekly in hostels, only returning to their smaller island homes at the weekend. These mobilities may provide 'stepping stones' out of their island communities, because of the way that mobility is built into educational progression (Stockdale 2002b: 50). Considering Further and Higher Education, the availability of options primarily in larger island locations may also impact on the migration trajectories of younger people and the wider population dynamics of centralising populations – something which further research could usefully explore.

Considering island economic contexts, it is clear that the larger islands and the larger towns will provide greater job opportunities than some of the smaller islands. Considering the evidence of centralising populations in the Scottish archipelagos, a key factor is the ease of travel between islands. In Orkney, for example, challenges with ferry connectivity to the outer isles means it is not possible to commute on a daily basis from many of the islands to the main town for work. As the Orkney population change study for the islands demonstrated 'the ability to travel to and from work has been a key factor in the drift of population towards Kirkwall' (HallAitken 2009: 2). This highlights how the relative connectivity of islands, their geospatial contexts (particularly whether they are single islands, or part of a wider island archipelago), impact on spatial distributions of population and employment (Grydehøj and Hayward 2014). Specifically the role of bridges (Baldacchino 2007) and different levels and availabilities of inter-island ferries (Grydehoj and Hayward 2014) have been shown to impact on community development. The relative connectivity of an island is therefore important to consider alongside the size of an island as a lack of education or employment opportunities in an island may be compensated for if the island has a high degree of connectivity to locations where economic and education opportunities are more readily available. So, for example, Gear (2014) has explored how the development of a fixed road link from Burra to mainland Shetland enabled a higher degree of commuting to the main town of Lerwick, and impacted on the wider economic development of the island (in terms of the fishing industry). Understanding the role of geospatial contexts and connectivity may go some way to understanding the different migration and population challenges in the Scottish islands. So, for example, one of the mid-size islands which has bucked the trend for depopulation in Scotland is South Ronaldsay, which also has a fixed link to the much larger Orkney mainland.

In terms of economic contexts in island communities it is also important to note that economic conditions can vary considerably between island communities – and that islands do not necessarily have 'poor' employment contexts. As an example, historically Shetland has had some of the highest salary levels in Scotland (due mainly to the fishing and oil and gas industries) with the neighbouring islands of Orkney having salary levels below the national average (HIE 2011a, 2011b). An under-reported concern in island communities is not just economic downturn and feared population collapse, but also potentially population booms, which can put pressure on housing stock and other services, and risk damaging community cohesion and island assets such as the natural environment. In Scotland, consideration of these risks was particularly evident in Shetland in the 1970s oil boom (Johnson et al. 2013).

Interestingly this boom was identified as not significantly impacting on youth migration intentions (which reinforces the findings that young people's decision-making is not simply about 'opportunity') (Seyfrit and Hamilton 1992).

The potential for significant expansion in some industries in the islands of Scotland has been highlighted in the literature, including potential in the marine renewable sector (Johnson et al. 2013). However, one of the key 'booming' industries in the islands of Scotland is tourism. Again the boom in this industry is not equally dispersed through the island communities, with different islands experiencing different challenges and opportunities. Interestingly, of course, tourism is itself a form of mobility, and the movements of tourists to and from the islands creates both employment opportunities in hospitality and tourism (some of this will be seasonal employment, which itself may rely on migrant workers), but also potentially creates a pressure on infrastructure, facilities and accommodation. The impact of tourism has received particular attention recently through the exploration of the role of AirBnB on the availability of housing in communities such as Skye. Second homes too can result in reduced availability of housing in the Scottish islands, again impacting differently in different communities – with 10% of housing in the Scottish Islands classed as second homes overall, but with percentages as high as 43% in Raasay, 42% in Colonsay, 40% in Great Cumbrae and 34% in Tiree (National Records of Scotland 2015).

Despite tourism potentially offering some benefits in terms of availability of employment, there are therefore wider impacts potentially on migration if there is a reduction in availability of housing. Indeed the availability of housing has been identified as a key barrier for in- and return-migration of young people to the Highlands and Islands (HIE 2018). Wider migration dynamics, including in-migration of older migrants, may also impact on rising house prices in rural Scotland – in a process of rural gentrification, something akin to urban gentrification patterns (Stockdale 2010). For young people, particularly those who are seeking rented accommodation, accommodation in shared houses and who are first time buyers may find particular challenges in rural Scottish environments (Hoolachan et al. 2017).

Equalities and inequalities

So far this chapter has considered some of the dynamics behind the migration pathways of individuals, and the role of island context in migration. Understanding these dynamics also raises key questions about equalities and inequalities – both in terms of the differing experiences of island communities and of individual islanders. So, where islands are experiencing population growth or gentrification there can be particular equalities issues for young people who 'often feel that they are continually competing with others with deeper pockets, be they older residents with established careers and smaller mortgage requirements or retirees looking for a rural retreat' (HIE 2009: 7).

Another issue surrounding equality is the evidence surrounding mobility, and particularly the notions of mobility capital or motility (Kaufmann et al. 2004; Corbett 2007) which highlight that the ability to move is not equally available to everyone. So, for example, mainland Orkney, Shetland or the Western Isles may be perceived as relatively well connected to the mainland (via a plane journey of approximately 1 hour), but only for those who have the financial resources to be able to afford the plane fare. Economic resources are important but are only part of the picture surrounding equalities. Particularly important here is the evidence that those young people who move from rural and island communities are more likely to have parents who were incomers to a region (Stockdale et al. 2000) and evidence that movers for higher education are more likely to have degree educated parents (Donnelly and Gamsu 2018). That is, those students from the highest socioeconomic groups are the most likely to move. This is exacerbated by funding mechanisms for higher and further education, and traditional movements for further and higher education, whereby higher education students may feel more able to move than further education students – leading to potential differences between those who feel able to move (and positively inclined to their home communities) and those who, in some cases, would like to move, but feel unable to do so, feeling trapped (Ramage 2019). Indeed in a recent youth migration report evidence was identified that those who stay in their communities often feel less positively about their communities than those who have left (HIE 2009).

Considering the 'island idyll' stereotype it is particularly important to consider here how this idyll is differently available to different individuals. Young people, for example, may find aspects of island or rural life restrictive and boring. Further, the evidence suggests that *some* young people may find rural or island life more restrictive than others, for example, lesbian, gay and bisexual young people are less likely to report that it's 'okay to be different' in the Highlands and Islands (HIE 2018). In some research from very rural communities, there is evidence that young women may also find that their opportunities are more restricted than young men (Bjarnason and Thorlindsson 2006). More widely island returners and incomers may find that the island idyll is more difficult to achieve than they anticipated, resulting in a later move back out of the community. Stalker and Burnett (2016), for example, have explored how for cultural workers coming into the islands material conditions such as difficulties securing housing and work spaces may be important, but under-emphasised in the narratives of islands as 'good' places to work. The literature around 'belonging' in particular has identified how different individuals may 'belong' in different ways to their communities, and that age, social class and other factors impact on this ability to belong (Savage et al. 2005).

Policy implications

Throughout this chapter the complexities surrounding island migrations have been identified, both in terms of the migration motivations of individuals and the migration experiences of island communities. Considering some of the evidence that has been explored, it is possible to draw out some implications for policy makers.

Firstly it is important to consider the focus of youth migration policy. Traditionally there has been a strong focus on 'retain and attract' strategies for young people. However, the evidence considered here and in previous publications suggests that a focus on potential island *returners* may be highly valuable (Crow 2010). Secondly a focus on young people who already choose to *stay* may also be valuable – with evidence that rural stayers have often been over-looked in much of the academic and policy literature (Stockdale and Haartsen 2018). Considering how to support stayers with ongoing training and development to enable them to progress in the labour market may be particularly valuable. Considering evidence that some may feel 'trapped' and the wider evidence about how mobility is widely associated with 'success', identifying ways that short-term or temporary mobilities can be supported may also be valuable – for example, through the facilitation of work experience or exchange programmes, and/ or through addressing the very high costs of transport to the mainland, which may be a particular issue for young people who typically occupy some of the lowest paid employment.

The focus on return migration and helping stayers to also benefit from some forms of mobility ties in with suggestions in the theoretical literature that decisions to 'stay' and 'leave' are not singular decisions taken at one point in time, but are often revisited, and indeed are connected processes. Recent literature has argued that 'staying' and 'leaving' should not be thought of as binary opposites – instead there are different *ways* of staying and leaving. Leaving may involve a later planned return, and frequent trips 'home'. Staying may involve frequent movements 'elsewhere' for holidays or through work and may involve a later migration away from a community. As Stockdale and Haartsen (2018: 4) note 'staying and migration are frequently connected, interrelated, and complimentary within deliberate life strategies […] It is therefore unhelpful to consider mobility and immobility as binary opposites or as dualistic either/ or, which is frequently the case when a migration perspective is adopted.'

The importance of coming and going in Stockdale's research, highlights a further significant point when it comes to island migrations – how even those young people who do not later move back to their island communities may continue to provide benefits to their island locations. So, even where islanders remain away from their island homes, their attachments to their communities may remain beneficial, for themselves, other islanders and ultimately the islands themselves. This identification of migrants with their home communities has been termed 'translocal identity' and King (2009: 62) notes that for islanders particularly the 'usually strong islander identity' means that 'island-origin emigrants' have strong 'translocal identities'. Evidence from the Scottish islands of such identities is clear in, for example, Stockdale's (2002a) identification of how young migrants from the Western Isles often seek to retain connections with their island homes – for example, through joining Gaelic language groups.

Translocal identities can bring economic benefits to islands, especially in the developing world where income in terms of remittances is a very key source of income. 'Remittances' as such may be less significant in the Scottish islands, but regular home visits, supporting hometown initiatives, trading goods and close relationships with family are all also important in translocal identity (King 2009: 62). Networks of other islanders who no longer live in the islands may be a particular resource for those who have returned or move into the islands – allowing local communities to gain from knowledge and connections elsewhere. In practical terms islanders who live away from their islands but retain strong island connections, can be important connections to other islanders – Stockdale (2002a: 62) notes, for example, that young islanders may be 'beneficiaries' of social networks spread through space, and if they settle elsewhere, they may then become a benefactor in these networks.

Considering the importance of migration flows more broadly, Baldacchino (2006) has argued that conceptualising out-migration as a 'loss' for island communities is flawed, representing an unhelpful binary which focuses on fixed notions of space. Considering that migrations may include potential future returns, and how individuals who move may retain connections to island communities, he argues that: 'a cyclical and mul-tiple – rather than a stark, linear, unidirectional – pattern of "intellectual capital" flow may prove beneficial to both sending and receiving destin-ations, as well as to the actual migrants and their families' (Baldacchino 2006: 148). Objecting to the notion of 'brain drain' Baldacchino suggests the use of the alternative terms 'brain rotation' and 'brain diffusion'. These concepts indicate that policy which focuses purely in terms of on-island resources and youth retention may not recognise the full value which can come from migration *flows* between places.

Finally, this chapter has indicated that there are potentially significant considerations for policy makers and island communities in terms of issues of equality and inequality. In particular it is important that *general* trends for the Scottish island population are not understood to apply equally to all islands. Indeed the evidence suggests that some of the smallest and most vulnerable islands continue to experience significant depopulation. Therefore, ideas of 'population revival' in the Scottish islands as a whole need to be challenged, as they potentially overlook issues of inequalities between islands. Strategies and policies therefore need to consider not just 'islands' generally, or 'Orkney' or 'The Western Isles' but need to consider the smaller island communities that make up larger archipelagos and the Scottish islands as a whole.

Further, issues of inequality need to be considered in terms of individual islanders. There are particular issues here with popular narratives of islands as 'idylls' or 'retreats', which may overlook the material conditions that islanders experience (Stalker and Burnett 2016). Notions of island migration which focus on a binary of 'opportunity' vs 'lifestyle' potentially reinforce problematic stereotypes and overlook the commonalities in-migration motivations of individuals. Troubling the problematic binary of migration decision-making is important not just for providing a more accurate picture of migration, but also because the narrative may have material impacts which are unhelpful. So, for example, the 'common sense' assumption of young people that moving away from the island equates to success may negatively impact on some movers (who may have preferred to stay but leave because it is the 'normal' thing to do), and may negatively impact on perceptions (including self-perceptions) of stayers. In addition, challenging notions of islands as places to 'relax' in or 'retreat' to, and also focusing on the economic vibrancy and potential of island communities may support further economic development by increasing the appeal of islands to different potential migrants.

Understanding that beyond lifestyle factors, material factors such as housing availability, house prices, salaries and costs of living are also important for both current island residents and for potential migrants, also opens up potentials for other forms of intervention to address population sustainability. As this chapter has demonstrated, simply 'increasing opportunity' is unlikely to be an effective means of addressing migration. Instead, effectively attracting younger and older people to island communities must involve consideration of issues of infrastructure and connectivity, education and health services, and housing.

Finally, this chapter identifies how island mobilities, including residential migrations of older and younger people, tourism and second-home ownership, and commuting for education and work, have complex interrelations with each other. Increases in tourism, for example, may remove some housing from the market and increases in residential migration of older individuals may lead to a process of island gentrification. Thinking about the wider mobility context and culture of an island is important to be able to realistically address some of the challenges with population sustainability. Therefore, to a certain extent an issue like population sustainability cannot be treated on its own but needs to be considered as part of holistic island development planning. A good example here is how improved island connectivity is likely to impact on tourism, migration and economic development.

Conclusions

This chapter has presented a range of evidence concerning migration, particularly youth migration in the Scottish Islands. This chapter has argued that popular conceptions of migration in terms of a binary between 'opportunity' and 'lifestyle' presents a highly limited perspective on Scottish island migration, arguing instead that it is important to recognise the commonalities between migrants at all life-stages in terms of economic and lifestyle motivations. A more holistic understanding of migration potentially helps to broaden the potential policy focus in terms of population sustainability away from simply improving opportunity to retain and attract young people and helps to focus on other material factors such as housing and accessibility of services.

Further this chapter has argued that a focus on 'retaining and attracting' young people potentially overlooks the potential value of migration flows to and from the islands including importantly the potential value of those young people who leave in terms of the resources that they may provide for an island, and also in terms of the potential value of return migration. Stayers too are often over-looked and finding ways to support stayers is also likely to be important. Considering that stayers may feel 'trapped' potential support for improved opportunities for temporary travel and migration may be valuable.

More broadly the chapter has identified that narratives of migration for 'lifestyle' reasons undervalue the importance of material conditions on islands and addressing some of these materialities is important both for improving the quality of life for current island residents and for potential migrants. Considering material factors such as accommodation availability involves taking a more holistic approach to migration, including under-standing the wider mobility landscape including temporary mobilities such as tourism and commuting. The different contexts that different islands provide goes some way to considering how different islands in different geospatial contexts may have quite different migration patterns. Indeed, calculating data at a Scottish island level, or a local authority level, poten-tially overlooks the evidence that not all islands are seeing an 'island revival' in terms of population, with some of the smallest islands still experiencing significant vulnerability.

Bibliography

Alexander, R., and Hooley, T. (2018). 'The Places of Careers: The Role of Geography in Career Development'. In Cohen-Scali, V., Rossier, J., and L. Nota (eds), *New Perspectives on Career Counseling and Guidance in Europe*, pp. 119–130. Cham, Switzerland: Springer International Publishing.

Baldacchino, G. (ed.) (2007). *Bridging Islands: The Impact of Fixed Links*. Acorn Press.

Baldacchino, G., and Khamis, S. (2018). 'Brands and Branding'. In Baldacchino, G., (ed.), *The Routledge International Handbook of Island Studies*, pp. 368–380. Oxon: Routledge.

Benson, M., and O'Reilly, K. (2016). 'From lifestyle migration to lifestyle *in* migra-tion: Categories, concepts and ways of thinking', *Migration Studies*, 4(1), 20–37.

Bjarnason, T., and Thorlindsson, T. (2006). 'Should I stay or should I go? Migration expectations among youth in Icelandic fishing and farming communities', *Journal of Rural Studies*, 22 (3), 290–300.

Boyle, P. J., Halfacree, K., and Robinson, V. (1998). *Exploring Contemporary Migration*. Harlow: Longman.

Brah, A. (1996). *Cartographies of Diaspora: Contesting Identities*. Oxon: Routledge.

Clayton, J., Crozier, G., and Reay, D. (2009). 'Home and away: risk, familiarity and the multiple geographies of the higher education experience', *International Studies in Sociology of Education*, 19 (3–4), 157–174.

CODEL (2018). *Young Uibhisteach*. CODEL: Community Development Lens. <http://codel.scot/codel-2019/wp-content/uploads//2019/08/Young-Uibhisteach-REPORT-APRIL-2019.pdf> accessed 13 December 2019.

Connell, J. (2018). 'Migration'. In G. Baldacchino (ed.), *The Routledge International Handbook of Island Studies*, pp. 261–278. Oxon: Routledge.

Cooke, G. B., and Petersen, B. K. (2019). 'A typology of the employment-education-location challenges facing rural island youth', *Island Studies Journal*, 14 (1), 101–124.

Corbett, M. (2007). 'Travels in space and place: identity and rural schooling'. *Canadian Journal of Education*, 30 (3), 771–792.

Corbett, M. J. (2007). *Learning to Leave: The Irony of Schooling in a Coastal Community*. Halifax: Fernwood Pub.

Cresswell, T. (2006). *On the Move: Mobility in the Modern Western World*. Oxon: Routledge.

Crow, H. (2010). *Factors Influencing Rural Migration Decisions in Scotland: An Analysis of the Evidence*. Edinburgh: Scottish Government Social Research. <https://www.gov.scot/publications/factors-influencing-rural-migration-decisions-scotland-analysis-evidence/> accessed 24 January 2020.

Easthope, H., and Gabriel, M. (2008). 'Turbulent lives: exploring the cultural meaning of regional youth migration', *Geographical Research*, 46(2), 172–182.

Elias, P., and Purcell, K. (2003). *Measuring Change in the Graduate Labour Market*. Employment Studies Research Unit: University of the West of England / Warwick Institute for Employment Research.

Gander, K (2015). 'Best places to bring up children in the UK: Orkney Islands top list'. *The Independent*, 31 August. <https://my.independent.co.uk/news/uk/home-news/best-places-to-bring-up-children-in-the-uk-orkney-islands-top-list-10479980.html> accessed 20 March 2020.

Gear, R. W. (2014). 'Island paths: Divergent fisheries in the Shetland Islands'. *Shima: The International Journal of Research into Island Cultures*, 8(2), 39–54.

Grydehøj, A., and Hayward, P. (2014). 'Social and economic effects of spatial distribution in island communities: comparing the Isles of Scilly and Isle of Wight, UK'. *Journal of Marine and Island Cultures*, 3 (1), 9–19.

HallAitken. (2007). *Outer Hebrides Migration Study: Final Report*. HallAitken. <https://www.cne-siar.gov.uk/media/5597/ohmsstudy.pdf> accessed 20 March 2019.

HallAitken. (2009). *Orkney Population Change Study: Final Report*. HallAitken.

Hayfield, E. A. (2017). 'Exploring transnational realities in the lives of Faroese youngsters', *Nordic Journal of Migration Research*, 7 (1), 3–11.

HIE (2009). *Young People in the Highlands and Islands: Understanding and Influencing the Migration Choices of Young People to and from the Highlands and Islands of Scotland*. Highlands and Islands Enterprise. <http://www.hie. co.uk/regional-information/economic-reports-and-research/archive/youth-migration.html> accessed 24 January 2020.

HIE (2011a). 'Area profile for Orkney', Highlands and Islands Enterprise, <www. hie.co.uk/regional-information/areainformation/orkney/economic-profile. html> accessed 24 January 2020.

HIE (2011b). 'Area Profile for Shetland', Highlands and Islands Enterprise. <www. hie.co.uk/regional-information/area-information/orkney/economic-profile. html> accessed 24 January 2020.

HIE (2015). *Our Next Generation: Young people and the Highlands and Islands: Attitudes and aspirations. Research report – June 2015*. Highlands and Islands Enterprise. <http://www.hie.co.uk/regional-information/economic-reports-and-research/archive/young-people-and-the-highlands-and-islands--attitudes-and-aspirations-research.html> accessed 24 January 2020.

HIE (2018). *Enabling Our Next Generation: Young People and the Highlands and Islands: Maximising Opportunities*. <http://www.hie.co.uk/regional-information/economic-reports-and-research/archive/young-people-and-the-highlands-and-islands--maximising-opportunities.html> accessed 24 January 2020.

Hoolachan, J., McKee, K., Moore, T., and Soaita, A. M. (2017). '"Generation rent" and the ability to "settle down": economic and geographical variation in young people's housing transitions', *Journal of Youth Studies*, 20 (1), 63–78.

Jamieson, L., and Groves, L. (2008). *Drivers of Youth Out-Migration from Rural Scotland: Key Issues and Annotated Bibliography*. Edinburgh: Scottish Government Social Research.

Johnson, K., Kerr, S., and Side, J. (2013). 'Marine renewables and coastal communities – experiences from the offshore oil industry in the 1970s and their relevance to marine renewables in the 2010s', *Marine Policy*, 38, 491–499.

Kaufmann, V., Bergman, M. M., and Joye, D. (2004). 'Motility: mobility as capital', *International Journal of Urban and Regional Research*, 28 (4), 745–756.

King, R. (2009). 'Geography, islands and migration in an era of global mobility', *Island Studies Journal*, 4 (1), 53–84.

King, R. (2018). 'Theorising new European youth mobilities', *Population, Space and Place*, 24(1), e2117. <https://doi.org/10.1002/psp.2117> accessed 10 March 2020.

King, R., and Connell, J. (1999). 'Island migration in a changing world'. In Connell, J., and R. King (eds), *Small Worlds, Global Lives: Islands and Migration*, pp. 1–26. London: Pinter.

Lasselle, L., Kirby, G., and Macpherson, R. (n.d.). *Access to Higher Education for Rural Communities: An Exploratory Analysis*. University of St Andrews / Scottish Funding Council / Scottish Government.

Massey, D. S., Arango, J., Hugo, G., Kouaouci, A., Pellegrino, A., and Taylor, J. E. (1993). 'Theories of international migration: a review and appraisal'. *Population and Development Review*, 19 (3), 431–466.

National Records of Scotland (2015). *Scotland's Census 2011: Inhabited Islands Report*. National Records of Scotland. <https://www.scotlandscensus.gov.uk/documents/analytical_reports/Inhabited_islands_report.pdf> accessed 20 March 2019.

Ní Laoire, C. (2008). "Settling back'? A biographical and life-course perspective on Ireland's recent return migration', *Irish Geography*, 41 (2), 195–210.

Ramage, E. (2019). 'Career decision making in a rural school', *Journal of the National Institute for Career Education and Counselling*, 42 (1), 26–32.

Reichrath-Smith, C., and Neault, R. A. (2013). 'The global careerist: internal and external supports needed for success', *Journal of the National Institute for Career Education and Counselling*, 31 (1), 51–58.

Rérat, P. (2014). 'Highly qualified rural youth: why do young graduates return to their home region?', *Children's Geographies*, 12 (1), 70–86.

Royal Society of Edinburgh (2008). *Committee of Inquiry into the Future of Scotland's Hills and Islands*. <http://www.rse.org.uk/wp-content/uploads/2016/09/The-Future-of-Scotlands-Hills-and-Islands.pdf> accessed 20 March 2019.

Sage, J., Evandrou, M., and Falkingham, J. (2013). 'Onwards or homewards? Complex graduate migration pathways, well-being, and the 'Parental Safety Net', *Population, Space and Place*, 19 (6), 738–755.

Savage, M., Bagnall, G., and Longhurst, B. (2005). *Globalization and Belonging*. London: SAGE.

Seyfrit, C. L., and Hamilton, L. C. (1992). 'Who will leave? Oil, migration, and Scottish island youth', *Society and Natural Resources*, 5 (3), 263–276.

Stalker, L. H., and Burnett, K. (2016). "Good work? Scottish cultural workers' narratives about working and living on islands', *Island Studies Journal*, 11 (1), 193–208.

Stockdale, A. (2002a). 'Towards a typology of out-migration from peripheral areas: a Scottish case study', *International Journal of Population Geography*, 8 (5), 345–364.

Stockdale, A. (2002b). 'Out-migration from rural Scotland: the importance of family and social networks', *Sociologia Ruralis*, 42 (1), 41–64.

Stockdale, A. (2006). 'Migration: pre-requisite for rural economic regeneration?' *Journal of Rural Studies*, 22 (3), 354–366.

Stockdale, A. (2010). 'The diverse geographies of rural gentrification in Scotland', *Journal of Rural Studies*, 26(1), 31–40.

Stockdale, A., and Haartsen, T. (2018). 'Editorial introduction: putting rural stayers in the spotlight'. *Population, Space and Place*, 24 (4).

van Ham, M., Findlay, A., Manley, D., and Feijten, P. (2012). 'Migration, occupational mobility, and regional escalators in Scotland', *Urban Studies Research*, 1–15.

CALUM MACLEOD

8. Community Land Ownership and Sustaining Scotland's Islands: Lessons from the Western Isles

In recent years land reform has re-established itself as a mainstream issue on Scotland's public policy agenda. Much of the impetus for that re-emergence lies in Scotland's unusually concentrated pattern of private rural land ownership, of which 67% is calculated as being owned by 0.025% of the population (Warren 2009). That pattern of concentrated land ownership is said to act as a structural barrier to local sustainable development as a consequence of its negative monopolistic effects on the distribution and exercise of economic and social power within communities experiencing such ownership monopolies (Danson 2019; Glenn et al. 2019).

A distinctive feature of Scotland's land reform journey has been the emergence of community land ownership as an alternative model to private or state ownership to further sustainable development. In turn, Scotland's islands have provided a focal point for that expansion in community ownership from the buyouts of Eigg and Gigha in the 1990s and mid-2000s (Hunter and MacLean 2012) to the more recent community buyout of the Isle of Ulva in 2018 (*Guardian* 2018). The Western Isles have proved especially fertile ground for the expansion of this new ownership model, given that these islands collectively contain around two thirds of the 209,810 hectares of Scotland's land currently in community ownership (Scottish Government 2019).

This chapter analyses the emergence of community land ownership as a means for delivering sustainable development in the Western Isles, set against the wider trajectory of land reform as a Scottish public policy issue since re-establishment of the Scottish Parliament in 1999. It draws on primary research conducted with representatives of community landowning

Trusts in the Western Isles[1] to identify factors that explain why this model of ownership has been mainstreamed so comprehensively there. The applicability of lessons from the Western Isles experience of community ownership for other Scottish islands and Scotland as a whole are evaluated and conclusions drawn.

Scottish land reform in context

It is essential to root any discussion on community land ownership within the wider conceptual context of land reform as it relates to Scotland's framework of land tenure. That framework consists of three main elements: property laws governing land ownership; regulatory laws governing land use; and non-statutory public sector measures to influence how land is owned and used in the public interest (Land Reform Review Group 2014). Land reform can broadly be defined as 'measures that modify or change the arrangements governing the possession and use of land in Scotland in the public interest' (Land Reform Review Group 2014: 20). A tension between the private and public interest regarding the distribution of property rights[2] lies at the heart of the often deeply contentious land reform debate within Scotland. Much of that debate has centred on the relationship between land ownership and use. Specifically, whether land ownership is a determining factor in inhibiting or encouraging land use that reflects wider, shared societal objectives associated with the common good.

1   The research was part of a wider study titled *Re-writing the Rulebook of Landownership: Analysing and Assessing the Economics of Community Landownership*, funded by the Scottish Universities Insight Institute (SUII) and conducted in partnership with Community Land Scotland.
2   The array of property rights is wide-ranging but can be broadly classified as use rights, control rights and transfer rights (Food and Agricultural Organization of the United Nations 2002).

Opponents of land reform in Scotland argue that it is the way in which land is used rather than who owns it that matters in achieving sustainable development outcomes. In contrast, proponents of land reform contend that Scotland's extraordinarily concentrated pattern of private land ownership acts as a significant barrier to sustainable development, itself a highly contested concept (Hopwood et al. 2005). From this perspective the dominant exercise of monopoly power (*economic, political, social*) derived from large-scale and concentrated land ownership enables these predominantly private landowners to shape, control and benefit from land-based developments in ways that can run contrary to the wider public interest (Danson 2019). Scotland's land reformers have therefore long supported a democratisation of property rights through co-ordinated application of a range of legislative and fiscal policy measures that redistribute these rights whilst recognising interdependencies between public and private interests. Rather than seeking to abolish private property rights, land reformers thus advocate redistribution of these rights more widely within the context of an increasingly diverse, transparent and democratic pattern of land ownership in Scotland in support of sustainable development.

Set against that background, community land ownership has captured the political imagination in Scotland to the extent of defining and dominating much of the land reform agenda's evolution in the post-devolution era. The idea that geographically defined communities should have a say in shaping the development of the places where they live is neither new nor unique. Community involvement has long been a staple of natural resource management and local development (Bryden and Geisler 2007). The emphasis placed upon it can be seen as part of a paradigm shift in rural development in which competitiveness is driven by local assets and resources, broadly based rural economies, investment rather than subsidy, and the involvement of local stakeholders in governance arrangements (OECD 2006). More generally, the emphasis on community 'empowerment' as a goal of public policy has been linked to a neo-liberal strategy of 'governing through community' (Mackinnon 2002) because of what Rose (1996) terms 'the death of the social': a consequence of the State's retreat from welfarism and the erosion of mutual obligations and responsibilities connecting individuals and political authorities within national, regional and local spaces.

In Scotland the 'land question' is also laden with historic significance as a consequence of the Highland Clearances of the eighteenth and nineteenth centuries, involving the often forceable removal by landlords of their tenantry to make way for more economically profitable sheep and deer farming on their estates (Richards 2008). The highly concentrated structural pattern of land ownership in the region, inextricably bound to the politics and social injustices of landlordism, has helped facilitate the social, cultural and political conditions for communal ownership of land to gain traction in the Highlands, and Islands. A long legacy of government intervention to resolve the so-called 'Highland problem', shorthand for the region's perceived socio-economic 'backwardness' (Perchard and Mackenzie 2013), has also indirectly played its part.

As long ago as 1936, the Highland Development League – its name derived from the Highland Land League of years earlier, set up to agitate for land reform – was established to involve the British government in stimulating economic activity in the Highlands and Islands (Hunter 1999). In 1965 the Highland Development League was replaced by the Highlands and Islands Development Board (HIDB), a new and altogether more ambitiously equipped organisation in terms of the extent of its powers to intervene to expand and diversify the Highland economy. Beyond the new agency's capacity to offer financial assistance in the form of grants, loans and equity, it could also 'set up businesses on its own account, acquire land, build factories, equip and service those, produce promotional material, assist with the construction of community facilities and market the Highlands and Islands as a tourist destination' (Hunter 2000: 355–356). An explicit social development element was added to the remit of HIDB's successor body, Highlands and Islands Enterprise (HIE), when it was formed in 1991. The establishment of HIE was to have a significant influence in shaping subsequent government support for community land ownership, as the next section explains.

Community land ownership before and after devolution

The antecedents of community land ownership in Scotland can be traced back to 1923 when the Stornoway Trust in the Isle of Lewis was created to own and manage a 69,000 acre estate gifted by Lord Levehulme (Hutchinson 2003) in and around the 'Long Island's' largest settlement. In contrast, the origins of contemporary community ownership lie in the purchase of the North Lochinver Estate for £300,000 in 1993 by the Assynt Crofters' Trust (MacAskill 1999). That purchase generated widespread media attention and acted as a catalyst for further high-profile community buyouts of the Isle of Eigg in the Inner Hebrides in 1997 and the 17,500 acres Knoydart Estate in the West Highlands in 1999.

These early pioneers of community land ownership's 'first wave' sought to use their ownership of the land to redress the balance between landed power and communities in favour of meeting the social and economic needs of the latter. The radically different approach to the purposes of community land ownership in comparison to the traditional rural model of the large-scale private estate is summarised as follows:

> community ownership is intended not only to encourage the development of resources that private investors might otherwise ignore; but also to enable local communities to guide the development process. Whereas unfettered, market-driven entrepreneurship might generate increased wealth, but not necessarily benefit the local community, community ownership aims to make sure that wealth generated from the land remains within the community; that the benefits of development are evenly spread; that needed services are provided; that the population is maintained; and that resources are managed for the long-term benefit of the community. In this way the Scottish land reform represents a shift (or rather a broadening) of emphasis, from a focus on wealth creation to a recognition of the importance of effective local democratic governance. (Hoffman 2013: 289)

Some of the early political momentum for the shift of emphasis towards local democratic governance through community ownership was underway by the mid-1990s, initiated by the UK's Conservative Government of the time. Ministers had been supportive of the Assynt Crofters' Trust receiving financial support from both HIE and Scottish

Natural Heritage (SNH) in aid of their buyout of the North Lochinver
Estate. Following a visit to Assynt in 1995 the then Secretary of State for
Scotland, Michael Forsyth, introduced the Transfer of Crofting Estates
(Scotland) Act that received Royal Assent in 1997 shortly before the
new Labour Government assumed office under the leadership of Tony
Blair (Hunter 2009). A series of measures that were to profoundly alter
the course of land reform generally and community ownership in particular quickly followed in the wake of the incoming Labour administration. In 1997 the Scottish Office Minister, Brian Wilson, instructed
HIE to create a Community Land Unit to provide advice and financial
support to communities looking to emulate the examples of Assynt and
Eigg by taking ownership of the land on which they lived into their own
hands. That same year the Labour Government created a Land Reform
Policy Group (LRPG) to identify and assess proposals for land reform
in rural Scotland, thereby acting as an important institutional sponsor of
an agenda for action by the Scottish Parliament following devolution in
1999 (Lloyd and Danson 2000).

The re-establishment of the Parliament has undoubtedly been central to land reform's continuing evolution as an issue of public policy in
Scotland, reflecting the intrinsically political nature of the 'land question'
alluded to earlier in this discussion. As much was reflected by the then
Secretary of State for Scotland, Donald Dewar, in his 1998 McEwen Lecture
on 'Land Reform for the 21st Century':

> there is undoubtedly a powerful symbolism – which attracts me greatly – of land
> reform being amongst the first actions of our new Scottish Parliament.

Much of that symbolism was evident in the Land Reform (Scotland)
Act 2003, legislation introduced by the Labour-Liberal Democrat co-
alition Government during the Scottish Parliament's first term. The Act
included a Community Right to Buy land and other eligible assets for
geographically defined rural communities of under 10,000 people where
there is a willing seller. It also introduced a Crofting Community Right
to Buy where there is an unwilling seller, subject to a public interest test
being met. The 2003 Act was widely seen as flagship legislation for the

new Parliament and a powerful signal that land reform would be an important feature of public policy following devolution.

Things did not initially work out that way. There were some high-profile estate buyouts in the first decade of the twenty-first century, notably in North Harris in 2004 and in Galson in Lewis in 2007. Yet despite the introduction of the new community rights to buy, continuing support from HIE's Community Land Unit, and a Scottish Land Fund that provided £3 million annually to support community buyouts between 2001 and 2005, there was a sense that much of the political momentum for further land reform had drained away by 2009 at which point the Scottish National Party (SNP) was midway through its first term in Government. That was certainly the sense amongst land reform's supporters, prompting creation of Community Land Scotland in 2010 to act as the representative, campaigning voice of the community land movement (Hunter 2009).

The SNP Government's decision to establish an independent Land Reform Review Group (LRRG) in July 2012 with a remit to develop 'innovative and radical' proposals indicated that land reform's policy hiatus might soon be coming to an end. So it proved. The LRRG's final report, *The Land of Scotland and the Common Good*, was published in 2014. Crucially it confirmed the close relationship between land ownership and land use, stating

> Ownership is the key determinant of how land is used, and the concentration of private ownership in rural Scotland can often stifle entrepreneurial ambition, local aspirations and the ability to address identified community need. The concentrated ownership of private land in rural communities places considerable power in the hands of relatively few individuals, which can in turn have a huge impact on the lives of local people and jars with the idea of Scotland being a modern democracy. (2014:165)

The LRRG's report was similarly uncompromising in its assessment that land reform measures since 2003 were

> specific responses to particular issues, rather than part of any wider land reform strategy or programme. Many of the measures were not generally seen as 'land reform' as such. This has resulted in a sense of loss of momentum in taking forward the type of broad, modernising land reform agenda covered by the LRPG's recommendations. (2014: 25)

The LRRG's advocacy of a coherent framework for land reform based on the common good and the public interest was an unambiguous call for land reform to be placed at the centre of Scotland's public policy agenda. One that was reinforced by the report's recommendations for a National Land Policy with new institutions (Scottish Land and Property Commission, Community Land Agency, Housing Land Corporation) and adequate resources and strengthened legislation to support community acquisitions. The LRRG's report also proposed devolving the Crown Estate's powers, investigating scope for introducing a Land Value Tax, capping the size of privately owned estates, modifying inheritance laws and removing business rates exemptions for rural landowners.

Many of the proposals contained in the LRRG's report were considered radical, at least within the Scottish context. Several, including introducing a Land Value Tax and capping the size of privately owned estates have not been introduced as land reform policy by Government, as yet. Nevertheless, *The Land of Scotland and the Common Good* was influential in shaping the content of the Community Empowerment (Scotland) Act 2015 and, especially, the Land Reform (Scotland) Act 2016.

The Community Empowerment Act simplified existing Community and Crofting Community Rights to Buy land first introduced in the Land Reform (Scotland) Act 2003 and extended the Community Right to Buy to cover urban as well as rural areas. It also introduced a new Community Right to Buy land which is abandoned, neglected, or detrimental to the environmental well-being of local communities without the necessity of a willing seller. The Act included a new right for communities to make requests to Scottish Ministers, local authorities and a range of other public bodies to own, lease or otherwise use land or buildings they could make better use of.

The Land Reform (Scotland) Act 2016 represented another important step forward in Scotland's land reform journey. Amongst other things it made provision for the following: a Land Rights and Responsibilities Statement to help inform policy and practice around land issues in Scotland; a register of controlling interests in land; guidance on engaging communities in decisions relating to land which may affect them; a new Community Right to Buy land to further sustainable development, again without the need for a willing seller; and creation of a Scottish Land Commission (SLC) to review the effectiveness and impact of any law or policy relating to land matters and to make recommendations accordingly, as well as commissioning research and providing information and guidance on relevant issues. The SLC's creation was particularly noteworthy given its important role in ensuring that land reform remains on the public policy agenda in Scotland.

Community land ownership in the Western Isles

Both the long lineage of Scotland's 'land question' and the episodic evolution of land reform policy development since devolution belie the fact that community land ownership is a young and still maturing phenomenon. Data published by the Scottish Government indicates that, as of December 2018, there were 209,810 hectares of land in community ownership (Scottish Government, 2019). Figure 1 illustrates the relative increase in community land ownership since 1990.

The amount of land in community ownership is still a very small part of the overall structure of land ownership in Scotland. However, as the data show, it has grown significantly since 1990, a year that predates the first wave of community buyouts in Assynt, Eigg and elsewhere. As Figure 1 also shows, there are clear spatial patterns in relation to the geographical distribution of community ownership in Scotland. Virtually, all of that community-owned land (96%) is located in the Highlands and Islands. Further disaggregation of those figures reveals that over two thirds (68%) of the Scotland's community-owned land is located in the Western Isles (na h-Eileanan Siar). The Scottish Government's data also show that the four largest land assets (above 20,000 acres) are all located within the Western Isles. Against that background, the remainder of this section considers why the community variant has become such a significant component of the land ownership pattern in the Western Isles and provides a case-study example of some of the benefits delivered through community ownership in practice.

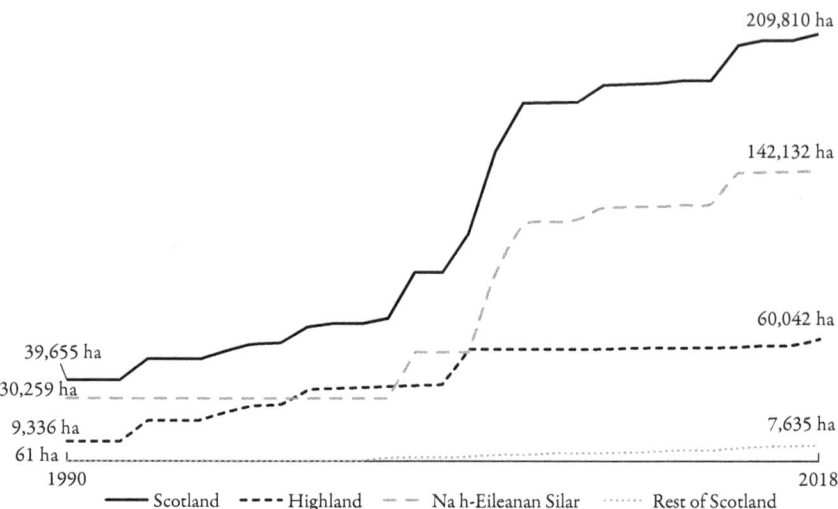

Figure 1: Land in Community Ownership between 1990 and 2018. (Source: Scottish
Government (2019), 'Community Ownership in Scotland 2018'. Rural and
Environmental Science and Analytical Services: Edinburgh)

Many rural areas within the Highlands and Islands share characteristics
linked to their geographical features. Some of these characteristics – such
as remoteness from major markets, low population densities and physical
constraints – act as a drag on development. Others, most notably out-
standing natural and cultural heritage, can and do drive key industries and
sectors in particular locations. These characteristics are well known and
have framed public policy responses to encourage the sustainable development of the Highlands and Islands – in economic, social and environmental terms – over decades.

A central challenge to the sustainability of many communities in
the Highlands and Islands as a whole relates to negative demographic
change within their resident populations. The existential threat posed to
many rural communities by that demographic challenge was confirmed
by Scottish Government commissioned research undertaken by the James
Hutton Institute in 2018. It projected that Scotland's sparsely populated
area (SPA) – covering almost half of Scotland's land area but containing

less than 3% of the nation's population – faces losing more than a quarter of its population by 2046 if current demographic trends are left unchecked. Along with Argyll and Bute, and the Southern Uplands, the Western Isles were identified as one of the worst affected sub-regions of the SPA, being forecast to lose more than 30% of its 2011 population by 2046, with the working age population projected to decrease by 33% in that period (Copus and Hopkins 2018).

As noted earlier, a key argument in favour of community land ownership is that it enables development to be done differently, unshackled from the negative monopoly effects of landed power through concentration of private ownership and free to distribute development benefits more evenly and justly within communities for the common good (Mackenzie 2010; Hoffman 2013; LRRG 2014). In the Western Isles that ambition for a different development model was stimulated both by structural barriers of geography referred to above and the mostly private crofting estates blanketing the islands prior to the twenty-first century. An ambition that the increasingly favourable policy environment for community ownership in the first decade of the twenty-first century did little to dampen.

Many of these crofting estates had served as trophy assets for mostly absentee private landowners unwilling or unable to invest in the sustainable development of the land – and, by extension, the communities – that they controlled from afar, even when the estates in question have substantial potential or actual revenue generating capacity. At best, there appears to have been the passive exercise of monopoly power on the part of landowners, leading to a relationship with their estates that one roundtable participant in the *Re-writing the Rulebook of Landownership* research study described as consisting of "benign neglect". Another participant elaborated on that perceived lack of engagement with their estates and by extension the communities that lived on them:

> [The previous owners] weren't a malevolent presence. It would be wrong to say that, but they were totally anonymous to the extent that people didn't know who they were. But they never did anything so they never upset anybody but they never helped anybody either. (A1)

The idea that community landowners in the Western Isles are pursuing a different development path and approach from these traditional private landowners came through clearly from roundtable participants. One noted

> We are more approachable and we're not in it solely for the money. We're in it for the benefit it can bring to a community, that's really the bottom line. But I think that's recognised with people when they come to us, it's recognised with the agencies, we have these people on-side for the most part. [B]

Another participant agreed that their Trust had an overarching social remit in serving their community while also highlighting increased community engagement as an important success factor:

> I see the Trust as a business working for the best interests of the community and [...] a measurement of success is that people are seeing the benefit of land community ownership and the fact that you get people willing to put themselves forward to take up these positions on these boards is also a measure of success .....[T]he fact that people are willing to see that a) that they have the ability and b) that they have the commitment and the interest, it's a measurement of success. (C)

The extent to which ownership of land has enabled communities to play a more proactive role in development activities was also noted by participants. One stated

> I think as far as the Local Authority is concerned, it's quite interesting that they've come out to talk to us and say almost ... 'the community seems to be kind of running itself, in some respects, these days. Perhaps we can work together on it'. [It is] quite interesting that they say that to us. But within the Western Isles there is so much land now under community ownership, it's not something they are just noticing here, it's Harris and it's just more and more areas so the people are all at different stages. (A2)

Another participant noted

> Almost invariably, apart from one or two who see things differently, virtually every community landowner turns into mini development agencies on their own. And once they are able to prove they can run something, do something, build something and generate more money to be reinvested in their community, the agencies

are beginning to trust. Whether it's SNH or the John Muir Trust or the Còmhairle or anybody: they want to be associated with success as well. (D)

The issue of public investment in landowners to provide community and wider public benefits was also highlighted in the roundtable discussions. One participant suggested that public support for Community Trusts enabled the delivery of services that would otherwise normally be delivered by the State in remote, rural areas:

> Public investment in the projects that the community are doing. When, principally, a lot of those projects are providing facilities, providing services, in many cases, which the State says it should be providing but is unable to do so in remote, rural, areas. So therefore that [...] tranche of money is completely defendable and justifiable in terms of delivering public policy and it's not the individual company that's making the benefit; it's the whole community. (E)

Local institutional support is also recognised as having been an important driver for helping to normalise community ownership in the Western Isles:

> The local authority here is very supportive, both in terms of making the right political statements but also in very practical assistance to community groups and they, themselves, because they didn't have the resources to deliver services and facilities that people would deliver elsewhere, they already had a track record of putting it in to the voluntary sector. (E)

The institutional recognition of the importance of community land ownership as a means for delivering sustainable outcomes is also evident in the Outer Hebrides Community Planning Partnership's (OHCPP) economic development strategy to 2020, *Creating Communities of the Future*. It identifies community land ownership and community facilities as key strengths in relation to the economic situation in the Western Isles. Similarly, land resources and community enterprises are listed as opportunities for further economic development on the islands. The document articulates 'working closely with the community landowners to support their development aspirations' as an area of strategic action (OHCPP, undated).

Case study: The West Harris Trust

The West Harris Trust provides an illuminating case study of how community ownership is addressing issues of land monopoly and unsustainable development in practice. In 2010 the West Harris community bought the crofting estates of Scarista, Borve and Luskentyre, totalling 7225 hectares, on which they lived from the Scottish Government using the Transfer of Crofting Estates (Scotland) Act 1997, that had been Michael Forsyth's brainchild. Prior to the community buyout, West Harris had been subject to the same corrosive demographic trends, absence of affordable housing and employment opportunities experienced elsewhere in the Highlands and Islands. The community's resident population had fallen to 119 with only 1 child under pre-school age. 35% of houses were either holiday homes or self-catering cottages and there were no social or private rented houses in the community. The area had no business units or community facilities within its geographical boundary.

Set against the above stark metrics, the West Harris Trust was established to own and manage the three estates on behalf of the community. Its aims included 'creating housing and employment opportunities, providing renewable energy and educating the community about the culture, heritage and history of the area have made West Harris a more sustainable place to live' (Armstrong 2019). Changing the demography of the area was a key priority. Therefore, the Trust set a target of having 130 people resident in West Harris by 2015, including an increase in the working age population (16–64 years) from 46% to 50%. It also sought a reduction in the economically inactive population from 42% to 37%.

Speaking at the time of the buyout in 2010, Murdo Mackay, the Trust's Chair, outlined the vision for West Harris under community ownership (*The Scotsman*, 25 January 2010):

> We want to promote Harris as a great place to live and work and we hope to get more families into the area and create new crofts and bring currently under-used land into production. We are very excited about the fact that control of our own land will breathe new life into the community and encourage people to set up homes and raise families.

Substantial progress has been made in transforming that vision for West Harris into reality under community ownership at the time of writing (2019). The resident population had increased by 20% to 151 people. Crucially the number of pre-school aged children living in the area has increased from 1 to 7 and there are 22 people aged under 18 years living in West Harris. That represents substantial progress given the baseline from which the community was working. It has been achieved by generating economic development opportunities leading to employment creation and through provision of affordable housing. Talla na Marra is a multi-functional facility built by the Trust in 2017 to provide business units, office accommodation and a restaurant which supports up to jobs in the area. The former primary school in Seilebost and a marine shorebase, created by the Trust, are leased to local businesses. Business units supporting two local enterprises have been built. As part of the Talla na Marra development 6 affordable houses have been constructed in collaboration with Hebridean Housing Partnership. Various housing plots have also been made available for new residents at substantially below market value. Renewable energy generation has also featured as part of the Trust's strategy for sustainability. A 100 kw hydro scheme has been developed which is forecast to generate £100,000 in income when borrowing is repaid after years. The West Harris Trust has also installed two wind turbines on the estate which generate further income for the community.

These are all transformational initiatives for the future of the West Harris community that would not have been possible under the continued state ownership of the land as conventional crofting estates.

Conclusions

Community land ownership has come to occupy an increasingly central place on Scotland's land reform agenda in the post-devolution period. Its main purposes can be traced to the motivations behind the pioneering 'first wave' of buyouts in the 1990s in Assynt, Eigg and elsewhere. The community ownership model seeks to recalibrate relationships of power and control by democratising decision-making at the local level regarding land and asset use. Within its rural context, such recalibration is designed to overcome barriers to sustainable development associated with dominant interests inherent in concentrated patterns of mainly private large-scale land ownership. As such, community land ownership offers a reimagining of local development; one in which a diverse range of economic, social and environmental benefits are retained within and experienced by the geographical communities in the places where they are generated as a consequence of their ownership of the land.

Scotland's islands have proven particularly attuned to this ostensibly radical model of development; nowhere more so than the Western Isles, the vanguard of the quiet revolution that community land ownership represents. Much of the explanation for that lies in historical factors that have shaped the longstanding enclosure of land within large-scale crofting estates, held primarily but not exclusively in concentrated private ownership. Consequently, Hebridean communities have increasingly mobilised to bring the land on which they live under their control as an antidote to monopolistic land ownership that has slowed or prevented development that can arrest negative demographic trends and help secure these communities' sustainability.

The increasingly 'community-centric' dimension of land reform policy outlined earlier has been vital in enabling that mobilisation to occur, especially in the post-devolution era. Financial support for the capital costs of buyouts from the Scottish Land Fund has been especially important in that respect. Legislation in the form of the Community and Crofting Community Rights to Buy contained in the Land Reform (Scotland) Act 2003, although hardly used in practice in the Western Isles, has helped create the conditions to enable a succession of negotiated buyouts to occur. Institutional support at the national and regional levels from Scottish Government and its agencies has also made a significant contribution to facilitating a policy culture conducive to community land ownership as a means to help achieve local sustainable development. Arguably that institutional factor has been particularly important at the local level in the Western Isles given the formal recognition by Comhairle nan Eilean Siar, and the wider Community Planning Partnership, of community ownership as a means for delivering sustainable development outcomes.

In essence the normalisation of community land ownership in the Western Isles is ultimately an assertion of these communities' fundamental right to 'be' (Bryden and Gielser 2007). Several overarching and inter-linked themes of broader significance may be discerned within that asser-tion. One concerns the relationship between people and the land and the balance between the public and private interest; essentially a recalibration of rights and responsibilities in relation to land ownership and use to better serve the public interest. Another relates to the characteristics of governance structures in society and the extent to which power in decision-making is devolved to the local level to genuinely empower people; essentially an issue of democracy and civic engagement. Still another relates to the rela-tionship between the State and 'community' in achieving outcomes that add to rather than subtract from the sustainability of Scotland's islands communities and the nation as a whole.

The normalising of community ownership in the Western Isles may therefore be viewed as a response to these overarching themes within a specifically islands context. It illustrates the importance of building a socio-political culture that positions community ownership of land and assets at the centre of the local development process rather than consigned to its margins. As developments in West Harris illustrate, that normalisation of community ownership in the Western Isles is delivering tangible benefits to communities' everyday lives. Continuing to equip Scotland's commu-nities with appropriate legislative, financial and institutional support is essential if the Western Isles' experience of community ownership is to be replicated and enhanced elsewhere in support of Scotland's common good.

Bibliography

Armstrong, L. (2019). 'Community Enterprise and Population Turnaround in West Harris'. *Islands Revival*. <https://islandsrevival.org/page/2/> accessed 6 January 2020.

Bryden, J. M., and Geisler, C. (2007). 'Community-based land reform: lessons from Scotland', *Land Use Policy*, 24 (1), 24–34.

Copus, A., and Hopkins, J. (2018). *Demographic Change in the Sparsely Populated Areas of Scotland (1991–2016)*. Aberdeen: The James Hutton Institute.

Danson, M. W. (2019). 'Scoping the classic effects of monopolies within concentrated patterns of land ownership'. A discussion paper for Community Land Scotland.

Dewar, D. (1998). 'Land Reform for the 21st Century'. The 1998 McEwen Lecture. *Caledonia Centre for Social Development*. <http://www.caledonia.org.uk/land/dewar.htm> accessed 6 January 2020.

Food and Agricultural Organisation of the United Nations (2002). *Land Tenure and Rural Development*. Rome: FAO.

Glenn, S., MacKessack-Leitch, J., Pollard, K., Glass, J., and McMorran, R. (2019). *Investigation into the Issues Associated with Large Scale and Concentrated Landownership in Scotland*. Inverness: Scottish Land Commission.

Guardian (2018). '"We are in Love": The Scottish Islanders Rebuilding a Community'. 1 June 2018, <https://www.theguardian.com/uk-news/2018/jun/01/we-are-in-love-the-scottish-islanders-rebuilding-a-community> accessed 6 January 2020.

Hoffman, M. (2013). 'Why community ownership?: understanding land reform in Scotland', *Land Use Policy*, 31, 289–297.

Hopwood, B., Mellor, M., and O'Brien, G. (2005). 'Sustainable development: mapping different approaches', *Sustainable Development*, 13.

Hunter, J. (2000). *Last of the Free: A History of the Highlands and Islands of Scotland*. Edinburgh: Mainstream Publishing.

Hunter, J. (2009). 'Getting Community Ownership Back On Track', Keynote Address: Community Land Conference, Isle of Harris, 29 September 2009.

Hunter, J., and MacLean, C. (2012). *From the Low Tide of the Sea to the Highest Mountain Tops: Community Ownership of Land in the Highlands and Islands*. Stornoway: The Islands Book Trust.

Hutchinson, R. (2003). *The Soap Man: Lewis, Harris and Lord Leverhume*. Edinburgh: Birlinn Ltd.

Lloyd, M.G., and Danson, M.W. (2000). 'The Land Reform Group in Scotland: institutional sponsorship for land reform?', *Local Economy: The Journal of the Local Economy Policy Unit*, 15 (3), 214–224.

LRRG (2014). *The Land of Scotland and the Common Good*. Edinburgh: The Scottish Government.

MacAskill, J. (1999). *We Have Won the Land: The Story of the Purchase by the Assynt Crofters' Trust of the North Lochinver Estate*. Stornoway: Acair.

MacKenzie, F.D. (2010). 'A common claim: community land ownership in the Outer Hebrides, Scotland', *International Journal of the Commons*, 4 (1), 319–344.

Mackinnon, D. (2002). 'Rural governance and local involvement: assessing state-community relations in the Scottish highlands', *Journal of Rural Studies*, 18, 307–324.

Organisation for Economic Co-operation and Development (2006). *The New Rural Paradigm: Policies and Governance*. Paris: OECD Publishing.

Outer Hebrides Community Planning Partnership (undated), 'Economic Regeneration Strategy to 2020'. <https://www.cne-siar.gov.uk/media/5768/economic-regeneration-strategy.pdf> accessed 6 January 2020.

Perchard, A., and MacKenzie, N. (2013). ' "Too much on the Highlands?": recasting the economic history of the highlands and islands', *Northern Scotland*, 4, 3–22.

Richards, E. (2008). *The Highland Clearances*. Edinburgh: Birlinn.

Rose, N. (1996). 'The death of the social: refiguring the territory of government', *Economy and Society*, 25, 327–356.

The Scotsman (25 January 2010). 'Historic Sale of Estate to Community Set to Rejuvenate Life on Isle of Harris'. <https://www.scotsman.com/news/historic-sale-estate-community-set-rejuvenate-life-isle-harris-1736619> accessed 6 January 2020.

Scottish Government (2019). *Community Ownership in Scotland 2018*. Edinburgh: Rural & Environmental Science and Analytical Services. <https://www.gov.scot/publications/community-ownership-scotland-2018/> accessed 6 January 2020.

Warren, C. (2009). *Managing Scotland's Environment*. Edinburgh: Edinburgh University Press.

MIKE DANSON AND KATHRYN A. BURNETT

9. Margins of Resilience, Sustainability and Success: Island Enterprise and Entrepreneurship

'Survival' and a fragility of development are much associated with the economic history of Scotland's geographical periphery and margins, most notably the Highlands and Islands. The shift over recent decades towards a greater emphasis on both local enterprise and an enhanced sustainability agenda has firmly impacted on the nature of production and consumption economies within all of Scotland's rural spaces (Anderson 2000) but it has increasingly informed policy and opportunity within more remote rural regions, most especially in the spaces of contemporary and complex 'margin' – Scotland's offshore islands. Our previous work on enterprises in island and remote rural areas (Danson and Burnett 2014; Burnett and Danson 2016, 2017) has demonstrated the need to avoid a simple transfer of sectoral and national strategies and policies to what are defined as local and sub-national peripheral and marginal regions. Furthermore, research and debate on the nature of behaviours and attitudes to island enterprise and entrepreneurship have been an important focus of research in island studies more generally (see especially Baldacchino 2005, 2010, 2015, 2019) and local and national context case studies offer useful insight to comparative experience elsewhere. Our interest lies in Scotland and the 'offshore' economy of its small island communities.

The popular and default narrative of small offshore islands of the British Isles (and indeed for Scottish reference also, those especially of our neighbouring nation, Ireland) is one consistent with the idea that small islands lying offshore the mainland (not withstanding any idea of an 'island nation') are marginal spaces embedded in 'peripheral regions' that are somehow limited – behind the curve – in terms of innovation and entrepreneurial activity. Yet such narratives are somewhat challenged with the fuller realisation that all peripheral regions are complexly embedded into a global capitalist system. Specifically, and by way of example, the economies of regions such as the Highlands and Islands of Scotland are dominated by multi-national companies in leading sectors such as food and drink (particularly whisky), marine harvest in terms of seafood, and energy production both extraction/generation and distribution. Servicing national, UK and international customers, there nonetheless exists a *competitive fringe* to these oligopolistic producers consisting of island-based SMEs (i.e. 'small and medium enterprises') delivering across regional and – in certain circumstances – global markets. These SMEs are integral to the longer-term sustainability of Scotland's island economies but also to the social, cultural and ecological resilience of each island and their inter-connected island, remote and broader coastal economies and synergies futures.

Within these competitive fringes there is much evidence of entrepreneurial activity in terms of SMEs, of self-employment and of home-working. Although there are limited rigorous statistics on entrepreneurship and enterprise on Scotland's islands, official records on remote and other rural areas offer a reasonable proxy. In the private sector in Remote Rural areas, 68% of employees are in businesses with fewer than fifty people, whilst in Accessible Rural areas 54% of employees work in these small businesses. In the rest of Scotland only 34% of private sector employment is in small businesses whereas 54% is in businesses with 250 or more employees (Scottish Government 2018a). Disaggregating these data further reveals 87% of Accessible Rural and 81% of Remote Rural SMEs are micro-businesses of 1–9 employees; this compares with 18% in Remote Rural Scotland and 11% of SMEs in Accessible Rural areas being small businesses with 10–49 employees (Scottish Government 2018a). In terms of self-employment, there are greater numbers in both Remote Rural Areas, 28%, and Accessible Rural, 22%, than in the rest of Scotland, 14% (Scottish Government 2018a). With regard to home-based businesses, there is a similar pattern: 43% in Accessible Rural, 40% in Remote Rural and 17% in the rest of Scotland (Scottish Government 2018b). While islands do not cover all 'Remote Rural' Scotland, there is a good deal of congruence between the two areas, and so these official statistics offer a very good indicator of the relative shares of SMEs and self-employment in Scottish island communities.

Alongside this evidence of entrepreneurial activity within the rural economy a further issue worth highlighting is the varying extent of churn amongst businesses, that is, the relative differences between start-up and closure rates of businesses. Figures suggest a lower degree of churn within Remote Rural and Accessible Rural areas compared with the rest of Scotland, this might be due to a lack of a competitive environment or to a greater resilience within these communities (SRUC 2016). Crucially, small businesses are deemed to be important for the delivery of local services, creating local employment opportunities (Eachus 2014). This is especially argued to hold in the retail, hospitality and tourism sectors leading to the survival of rural communities but also developing the opportunities for community development (Steiner and Atterton 2014, 2015). In other words, local enterprise and entrepreneurship assist in the establishment and maintenance of resilience in rural communities. Yet, whilst resilience is a multi-disciplinary concept frequently used to describe the ability to absorb social, environmental and economic disturbances while retaining the same functions (Folke 2006), it is in danger of becoming a vulgate word, taking on multiple meanings (Bourdieu and Wacquant 2001; Cooper and Johnston 2012). Economic instability, whether at a micro or macro level, will impact on a community's resilience through generating effects which have consequences beyond the immediate economic elements and if communities are to survive they need to be able to respond (Danson 2015; Fazey et al. 2018). It is better to limit negative disturbances in the first place by adapting to reduce potential risks, however and this requires community-based enterprise to be proactive (Steiner and Markantoni 2014).

Community resilience therefore not only embodies maintaining the status quo and the current equilibrium, it also requires initiatives to reduce risk and to promote a sense of sustained community well-being. An integral part of this community resilience concept is the ability to learn from past negative events to prepare for similar situations in the future through being active and proactive, flexible and adaptable, and shaping, adjusting and enhancing their circumstances. In the case of small businesses this entails maintaining their entrepreneurial flair responding to the changing demands of their customers, actively pursuing an innovation strategy and being aware of future risk. Any decisions affecting this adaptability and change should not be considered in silos (Steiner and Farmer 2017). Instead, in order to avoid the 'resilience trap' of 'adopting short-term strategies, re-badging existing strategies and widening governance networks that obfuscate sub-national mobilization around adaptation' (Kythreotis and Bristow 2017: 1530), community stakeholders, such as small businesses, should carefully consider wider and long-term impacts of their own and others' decisions. The Scottish islands are more vulnerable to adverse environmental and economic drivers and so the need to build resilience is crucial in promoting sustainability through enterprising activity.

Narratives of sustainability: Island and rural enterprise in context

It is useful to consider Scotland's island enterprise by first commenting on the very idea of rurality and the countering of a widespread and institutionalised view that 'modern times, it seems, have no place for rurality' (Halfacree 2012: 387). Despite a tendency for the rural to be continually positioned as 'other' (i.e. 'lesser') within academia itself, (as well the enduring complexity of what might be construed as an 'Anglo-British' culture's continued love affair with particular kinds of rural) rurality remains a concept worth thinking about; albeit, as Halfacree (2012) notes, it is a complex and shifting category. Rural, remote and island experiences undoubtedly vary yet it is important that research and policy highlight, counter and co-operate *across* competing rural, remote and island enterprise drivers, agenda and narratives in Scotland, and beyond. Simply, it would be difficult to position Scotland's islands as something other than rural if – as some geographers claim – we are 'beyond' the rural. It is difficult to imagine such rhetoric – that 'rural' is no more – gaining any serious traction in the living rooms, pubs, churches and crofts of the island communities of Scotland, however.

Such enterprise and entrepreneurship of and from rural and remote communities and spaces, in 'the margins' and 'of the periphery', is increasingly celebrated and championed in just these terms. The very ruralness celebrated widely in produce promotion and across enterprise policy accounts serves to reinforce the category of remote rural as alive and well in Scotland, not least in the islands. The broader enterprise discourses of rural success are key to countering what might be termed outmoded accounts of certain geographies' 'marginal' status, classification and experiences of the periphery and margin (Danson and Burnett 2014). Nonetheless, continuing to acknowledge the particularities that small island and remote rural contexts experience and contend with – the economic growth and social structural resilience of small island places should not be taken for granted – and consequently the 'fragility' and the particularity of local conditions, complexities and ambitions should continue as a key underpinning of research ambitions of island scholarship, and this includes retaining a longer view of economic history, development and labour policies that have shaped and defined Scotland's island economies today.

Enterprise theory, harnessing and exploitation of 'resources'

Much has been sought and achieved to embrace a broader sustainability ethos in and for Scotland and key targets and ambitions both underpin and inspire broader and deeper relations between people, the land and natural resources. In 2011 the Scottish Government consultation on *Our Rural Future* set out the main priorities needed to make rural Scotland 'even more successful'. The priorities are infrastructure, land use, community participation, community enterprise and business and skills. Scotland's National Performance Framework (Scottish Government 2018c) established key aims such as: to reduce inequalities and give equal importance to economic, environmental and social progress; to create 'a more successful country'; to give opportunities and to increase the wellbeing of all people living in Scotland; and to create sustainable and inclusive growth. These outcomes of the national framework are aligned with the United Nations Sustainable Development Goals (SDGs) and Scotland has 'led the way' on this within a UK context.

Within the sorts of rural contexts being analysed here, enterprises face a challenging economic environment of small home markets, high costs and all the difficulties of being at the end of long supply chains. Internalising externalities is one way of reducing some of these limitations in a Coasian manner (Whittam and Danson 2001) through forward and backward integration within working estates, for instance. Much work in these 'vulnerable' areas has focused on not-for-profit businesses which necessarily and inherently have access to local resources. In particular, both private and community organisations in 'peripheral' or 'marginal' locations have the potential to build social capital in three forms: bonding – by encouraging and protecting the bonds that exist between families and communities in terms of shared values and norms; bridging – by strengthening the linkages between different communities, which may be communities of interest as well as location; and linking – promoting relationships between people from markedly different power or economic structures (Birch and Whittam 2009; Granqvist 2012). As will be demonstrated below, many private enterprises in these marginal economic environments display the characteristics of social enterprises, relying on and building social capital in pursuit of sustainability in both economic and ecological terms. Analysis based on the Scottish Index of Multiple Deprivation (SIMD) and using Fragile Area socio-economic indicators (for the Highlands and Islands region) confirms that many areas of rural Scotland have difficult social and economic issues to address including: (1) remoteness and permanent geographical barriers; (2) a high dependency on micro-businesses, self-employment and public sector employment (the latter of which has substantially contracted); and (3) falling employment in some primary sectors.

The obstacles for social enterprise in remote rural areas and islands are critically reflected upon in the wider enterprise and entrepreneurship literatures of micro and small enterprises more generally in these environments (North and Smallbone 2006; Danson and Whittam 2008; Bosworth 2012; Henry and McElwee 2014). Furthermore, the establishment of social and community enterprises in these locations can be explained in terms of the failures of markets to service such places effectively and at costs that are sustainable for islanders and others. To an extent, then, social enterprises and private networked enterprises exist and are able to compete because they embrace externalities – offering social benefits which are greater than the private rewards available to private businesses and able to reduce direct costs by accessing resources which are not traded through the marketplace such as volunteer labour, and other social capital. With regard to such externalities, community buyouts of land and estates have led to locally derived strategies which emphasise longer time horizons and sustainable social and economic development in contrast with the traditional private ownership model of the lairds (Callaghan et al. 2012).

The exploitation and harnessing of natural resources and the USPs (i.e. Unique Selling Point, or sometimes Proposition) of remote rural areas, whether through community or private enterprises, may well depend on a greater range and more intensive use of social capital than their urban counterparts. This complements the consensual research on rural entrepreneurs which has suggested that motivations of business owners are less oriented to growth in rural areas than elsewhere (Galloway and Levie 2001; Deakins and Freel 2009; Galloway et al. 2011). These studies and others (Culkin and Smith 2000; Reynolds et al. 2003) have identified positive relationships between business orientations and ambitions towards growth on the one hand and experiences of success on the other, with those purchasing enterprises as likely to have such motivations as start-up entrepreneurs, and there are cases of entrepreneurs pursuing *high-growth* within the broader cultural accounts of island enterprise. Nevertheless, the overall rhetoric is 'small', niche, often 'crafted', and 'local'. The causes for such restricted ambitions and outcomes may be the limited local markets of island enterprises. Otherwise, these commentators put weight on the common tendency for island-based enterprises to be 'lifestyle businesses' where priority is given to quality-of-life factors (sustainability, low impact presence, work-life balance) rather than more singular profit and expansion motifs. Tension – dissonance – exists between different understandings of the attitudes, motives and ambitions of the sorts of enterprises that succeed in island and remote rural contexts, not least in terms of an appreciation of the complex nature of drivers of those who pursue more sustainable, and place-work-life balanced, operations.

Scottish key sectors: An island focus

Underpinning and framing development in all parts of Scotland is the *Scottish Economic Strategy*, which has been constructed to be consistent with the UN's SDGs and with the aim of pursuing sustainable inclusive growth (Scottish Government 2015, 2018c). Analysis and the economic strategy have identified six key sectors where 'Scotland has a distinctive comparative advantage' (Scottish Government 2015, 42): Food and Drink, Financial and Business Services, Life Sciences, Energy, Tourism and Creative Industries. These sectors do reveal some locational bias but all are represented in the island economies to greater or lesser extent. Since the deindustrialisation of the 1970s and 1980s, the structure of national and regional economies now shows diversity and degrees of functional specialism that contrast with former levels of local dependencies. With the development of underdevelopment (Danson 1991) of local and regional economies through mergers, takeovers, concentration and centralisation of activities and processes, the reduced capacity of remote rural communities to sustain some higher order occupations and functions is only partially countered by the extension of supply chains and specialised economic offerings into all areas of local, regional, national and global economies. Therefore, while Food and Drink, Tourism and Creative Industries can be readily considered as important for the economies of island and remote rural areas, particular elements of the other sectors which tend to cluster in the core: Financial and Business Services, Life Sciences and Energy can also be recognised as offering significant opportunities for small firms and enterprises in these geographies.

Financial and business services

Although this sector employs over 3,000 across the Highlands and Islands of Scotland, closer consideration of the sorts of jobs and their roles demonstrates an emphasis on 'contact centre, non-voice business services and knowledge-based processes' and 'services delivered for the Telecommunications and ICT sector dominates employment in the sector' (Highlands and Islands Enterprise [HIE] 2019a). While some of the commercial factors attractive to international investors would also encourage and support SMEs and entrepreneurs, for example, a local skill and talent pool and very low staff turnover rates, pioneering home-working opportunities and robust telecommunications and digital infrastructure (SDI 2015), there is a dearth of information to suggest that this is a priority for home grown enterprise to be established (HIE 2019a). Beyond call and contact centre work, potential appears to be around workers who are returning to work after a career break, have caring responsibilities, have a disability, have taken early retirement, want to improve their work/life balance or have greater flexibility in work patterns. Nowadays, entrepreneurs seeking to set up on an island will have concerns over connectivity, especially in terms of IT for accessing markets whether tourism, business services or otherwise. Unfortunately, the published 'case studies' promised for the islands are not available (HIE 2019a) but those promoting business development based on the next generation broadband wireless network connecting businesses, teleworkers and others in the Hebrides (Connected Communities n.d.) offer encouraging examples of successful start-ups and developments. This latter site argues that 'broadband is essential to the economic development of the Western Isles to allow businesses in the most rural communities to compete in world markets. Due to the wide distribution of the population across a number of islands, more traditional methods of providing broadband are impractical and would leave those at great distances from their exchanges without a service' (Hebrides.net n.d.). Critically, this recognition of the need to address the barriers to communication for island-based enterprises offers no further comparative advantages for such activities rather just a closing of the connectivity gaps (Munro 2016; Townsend et al. 2017).

Life sciences

Scotland has the UK's second largest Life Sciences cluster and one of the most sizeable in Europe and the rich and varied natural resources in Scotland, and its islands in particular, offer the elements for both envisioning and developing traditional and innovative products and services (Life Sciences Scotland 2011). Collaboration between the key players in a classic triple helix: university/research laboratory-industry-government is encouraged as part of the national strategy, and HIE is taking a leading role for promoting the islands especially (HIE 2019b). Although most of the economic activity in the region is on the mainland, focused around the Inner Moray Firth, there is evidence of enterprise establishment, growth and development in the Northern and Western Isles. Strong performances have been recorded in the health sector: especially in digital healthcare, medical technologies and devices, and diagnostics where remoteness is a key driver for pursuing new solutions to deliver improved care; in marine and natural products, particularly in macro and micro algae, where Scotland's massive offshore territories and extensive land mass present very significant potentials; and in animal health and aquaculture activities, again built around university-industry-regional development agency support (HIE 2019b).

Initiatives in health care and diagnostics are being driven to meet the needs of the 100,000 Scots 'living on 93 inhabited islands', with 'projects and services that are being delivered in remote and rural communities' (Fiona Laing, 2017, quoting James Cameron, head of health and life sciences at HIE), with ongoing recognition of innovative and award-winning practice and product development (HIE 2018a; WHFP 2019). Businesses across the islands and coastal rim are increasingly demonstrating the innovation capacity of the rich natural and marine resources to underpin an economy diversifying away from primary production of agriculture and fishing alone. Seaweed is an excellent example of a native resource that has been exploited in different ways over the centuries, and it is back on the Scottish enterprise map (Burrows et al. 2010; HIE 2018b). It has re-emerged as an opportunity for 'sustainable' business in Scotland's remote rural places buoyed up by a broader media headlining of its celebrity endorsement and 'superfood' credentials. The seaweed business success narrative is to champion a sustainable rural enterprise sphere tied in with ideas of 'local community' knowledge built on historic (often narrativised in media and promotional accounts as 'ancient') practice and the rich potential of 'unspoiled' shorelines and in-shore waters. The sector has the potential to thrive and develop to support a range of business that have identified uses for seaweed products (HIE 2018b) (discussed in Burnett and Danson 2016). Seaweed enterprise is an example of the continuing trend to monetise 'margin' resources variously as sustainable but also as pedigree, luxury and ethical brands and engage consumers accordingly. It is a good current example of successful cross-sector collaboration in Scotland not least between public research (higher education) and private enterprise. Telling this story through quality media formats (journalism, broadcast, advertising and social media) to a wider audience of both consumers and politicians has become a key focus for research centres and commercial enterprises alike, not least to ensure a broader platform of debate and critical accountability regarding island enterprise sustainability credentials more generally.

Food and drink

Another sector that has perhaps 'told its story' to successfully engage consumers more widely is that of Scotland's island food and drink enterprise. The Scottish Food and Drink sector (SF&D) – with its horizontal linkages across the industry and with the Scottish Government and its vertical linkages with suppliers and consumers, not only with selling the final product but also through educational programmes – demonstrates all the characteristics of a classic industry cluster. This collaboration, orchestrated through the trade body Scottish Food and Drink, has resulted in the industry growing to a £14 billion sector with the objective of growing to £30 billion by 2030. SF&D is now Scotland's largest manufacturing sector accounting for 29% of total manufacturing turnover and generating gross value of £3.8 billion, almost a third of Scotland's manufacturing gross value added (Scotland Food and Drink Partnership 2018). This growth has been driven by iconic products such as salmon and

whisky, which often emphasise an apparent dependency on island and
remote rural provenances (Burnett and Danson 2004), displaying their
strength as the UK's top food and drink exports, and these have provided
a platform for a global identity for world class produce in the sector more
broadly. The impact of Brexit and tariff barriers imposed by the US on
products such as Scotch Whisky at the time of writing, are still unknown;
however, some of these impacts can be offset by increasing sales in emerging markets such as India, which in 2018 saw a 14% increase in sales of
Scotch.

SF&D is also becoming a valuable draw for tourists interested in
learning about the heritage of Scotland. For example, in 2016, a record
1.7 million people visited over whisky distillery visitor centres across
Scotland, with one in five tourists visiting a whisky distillery during their
stay, spending on average £31. The increasing number of Whisky tourists
is a boon for the wider Scottish economy as hotels, pubs and restaurants
reap the benefits of the increased investment in customer experience by the
distillers. Notably, although salmon and shellfish and whisky have significant presence in the islands, their ownership is typically non-Scottish and
so the benefits of incomes, profits and further processing are often furth
of the island communities and Scotland. This set of disconnects suggests a
potential for improvement to the advantage of island economies, entrepreneurs and communities. By way of partly addressing this, the competitive
fringe of the drinks industry is being populated by craft producers led by
gin and whisky distillers with a complementary significant increase in small
craft breweries also (Danson et al. 2015). As proposed in the early 2000s
(Whittam and Danson 2001), these producers are realising the potential of
their locations and so providing much needed economic activity in island
and rural areas. As members of SF&D, Scottish Craft Distillers Association
(SCDA) are facing similar issues as the Scotch Whisky Association in
terms of protecting brands, image and ensuring that any business utilising
SCDA materials does indeed produce and bottle in Scotland. There were
over 60 gin distilleries in Scotland employing over 7,000 people in 2018
and that number continues to increase (SPICE 2018); this compares with
128 malt and blended whisky distilleries at that time and again numbers
are increasing. The spirits industry as a whole, accounts for approximately

3% of Scottish GDP. Paralleling this growth is the brewing industry which currently consists of 115 plants, the majority of which are microbreweries (SPICE 2018) and have a much more balanced distribution across the country. Furthermore, new craft distilleries continue to establish themselves throughout the islands, each promising relatively significant numbers of skilled, well-paid jobs for locals, maintaining people and incomes within the local economies. How sustainable this can be, not least if the related tourism visitor markets are impacted, for example, with Covid-19, as is the case in 2020, is an issue for the islands craft drink economies to contend with. What becomes clear from the analyses of the broader food and drink sector in Scotland is that most jobs, supply chain activities and benefits are all concentrated well away from the islands despite their respective critical contributions to primary production and images. Distance and lack of proximity to consumer markets, and to large labour pools for processing and packaging facilities, means that island food and drink enterprises face constraints in retaining and capturing value added locally. Moves into niche markets alone curtail the potential for further growth without significant investment in capital, people and supply chains to expand and embed production for national and international markets, as achieved by the fish processing sector of the Faroes, for example (see Holm, O'Rourke and Danson 2019).

Energy

In recent years with falling output from the North Sea Oil and Gas Sector and increasing awareness of the global emergency, there has been an increase in demand, support and focus on the renewables sector. In the Energy Strategy, the Scottish Government published ambitious targets to reduce carbon emissions by 50% by 2030 and be carbon neutral by 2050 (Scottish Government 2017), subsequently tightened further. Nevertheless the 'big 6' currently supplying over 50 million homes across the UK will continue to dominate the market for the foreseeable future as they are heavily involved in renewable energy production. However, there is a growing competitive fringe particularly around renewables, many located in remote rural communities. Included in the Energy Strategy, the development of 'innovative local energy systems' was set as one of six strategic priorities with the aim of 1 GW worth of renewable energy to be produced by community and locally owned projects by 2020 and 2 GW by 2030. The Community and Renewable Energy Scheme (CARES) supported hundreds of local community groups and other eligible organisations to develop, own and/or take a stake in local renewable energy projects across Scotland, including the islands where poor access to and high costs of energy for consumers is particularly problematic meaning fuel poverty is especially acute. To facilitate community energy enterprises, Community Energy Scotland (CES) was initially established as a subsidiary of HIE before becoming a Scotland-wide registered charity that provides practical help for communities on green energy development and energy conservation.

CES has promoted almost 300 community renewable energy projects (Scottish Renewables 2019: 10) and developed the 'Local Energy Economies' concept in Scotland based around a series of principles: use renewable energy near to where it is sourced, retain its financial value in the local economy, minimise transmission losses or shipping costs, displace carbon-based transport and heating fuels as much as possible. CES and a number of other funding and support schemes have been aiming to empower communities 'through the enterprise and responsibility of taking ownership of their energy resources' (CES 2019a). Projects and programmes to create new local smart hubs and grids based on innovative technologies offer opportunities for island and remote communities with examples of initiatives captured from across Scotland (CES 2019b) demonstrating the potential being realised in rural and urban locations. Scotland has appreciable shares of Europe's renewable energy potential: 5% of Europe's entire offshore wind power resources, 25% of Europe's tidal energy resources and 10% of wave potential complementing existing onshore wind, hydro and other renewables. Scotland will soon be meeting the equivalent of 100% of its electricity needs from renewable sources. Many of these initiatives and projects are located on or near to islands and other remote places. As 'offshore wind is now almost as cheap as onshore wind and solar PV, and around half the price of new nuclear power' (Scottish Renewables 2019: 4), there are economic benefits for both community producers and consumers from involvement in this sector.

However, just as with food and drink and other key sectors, much of the technology, manufacturing and so employment and income generation is developed and reserved for mainland and central regions, reducing the potential impacts in the periphery. Despite this, there are still examples of significant effects on such islands as Gigha (where four turbines have a combined capacity approaching 1 GW and produce electricity worth well over £100,000 each year which is reinvested into community activities through the Isle of Gigha Heritage Trust), Eigg (which has developed its own off-grid electricity system through Eigg Electric, a community-owned company which provides electricity for all island residents – 95% of which is produced renewably, from wind, water and solar) and Fair Isle (located halfway between Orkney and Shetland, which also established its own off-grid system using a combination of three wind turbines, a ground-mounted solar PV system and battery storage) (Scottish Renewables 2019). Some larger schemes based on a range of energy sources feature as important components of the economies from South Uist and North Uist to Unst (Shetland) and Westray (Orkney) and many have been offering higher returns to their respective local communities. The European Marine Energy Centre – a world-leading test and research centre focusing on wave and tidal power development, based in the Orkney Islands has initiated the creation of 250 direct jobs in the marine energy sector locally and continues to attract further energy-based enterprises to the islands confirming its role globally in developing new technologies and enterprises (European Marine Energy Centre [EMEC] 2019). As with the comparable key sectors discussed above, there is massive potential in and for the islands but local capital and human resources are constrained in their capacity to enter and compete with multi-national enterprises.

Tourism

Tourism has a long relationship with islands: often it is through tourism that many non-islanders will experience an island place, product, experience or 'adventure'. Tourism is not a one-way process, however, and the tourism sector in Scotland increasingly acknowledges that the exchange of ideas and values between 'hosts' and 'visitors' is valuable and necessary for longer-term success and sustainability. Tourists are themselves 'agents of change' (Everett 2012) who facilitate wider discussion and narratives of island tourism expectations, ambitions and realisations. Tourism is a wide-ranging set of enterprises, and island economies have diversified to both respond to broader trends such as screen tourism (film and television), adventure tourism, and food tourism (e.g. Arran's Taste of Arran campaign was a trend setter and the recent 'Food Tourism Scotland Action Plan' was launched in 2018 on Arran by way of tribute to its success). Whisky tourism is well established (on Islay in particular) but all island regions are making increasing efforts to attract visitors via drink (Scotland's island hospitality *is* legend) whether it be whisky, gin or craft beer. Expansion across food and drink tourism has been spearheaded by a number of island-based companies and collectives drawing on both local food cultures and natural environments as well as innovative stimulation of future tastes and consumption. As VisitScotland (2016: 5) notes: the rural island context of tourism is particular, where development opportunities need to be approached in a different and distinct way 'as dependency on a more limited seasonal market and need for greater business diversification are key issues for businesses serving the rural and island markets.'

History and heritage tourism relating to the Scottish island diaspora are globally known and further enhanced by a national tourism policy targeting genealogy and ancestral tourism growth including digital archive enterprise and 'homecoming' events (Jolliffe and Smith 2001; Basu 2007) and by marketing toolkit advice for businesses seeking to tap into this reliable, repeat and global market. In conjunction with the mosaic of rich island history, arts and cultural heritage appeal, it is arguably the islands' natural and scenic environments that increasingly unite all of Scotland's island tourism marketability. The special attraction narratives of island tourism enterprise as 'isolation' 'remoteness, 'wildness' – with key draws such as bird watching and marine wildlife, mountain, moor, coast and beach adventure focused activity – are all framed by the very physicality of having to cross to an island over the sea. This journeying remains a narrative of pilgrimage, of distinction and of enchantment and underpinning much of Scotland's 'cold-water' island tourism offer (Baum et al. 2000). Too much entrepreneurial innovation and 'success' has brought its own challenges, however with pressures emerging within islands of 'too many' tourists, spending 'too little' money in 'too few' concentrated arenas. Questions on the resilience of both culture and nature in the face of (an over-reliant economy) on high volume tourist consumption of the islands are justified and complex, not least in the Covid crisis and related tourism/visitor pressures ranging from no tourists (economic collapse) to 'too many/ unwanted' (social, environmental and *well-being* pressures) that emerged during the spring-summer season of 2020. Resilience in this regard offers both entrepreneurial opportunity and complex challenges as to who/what and where *sustainable well-being* is being best considered.

Culture offers solace and enrichment and across island communities, small enterprises harness a wider interest in the past – history, archaeology and heritage – through the provision of accommodation, tours, cultural events, museum and archive focused services. Museum and heritage services underpinned by local (and national) governance are key to island tourism policy and its success more generally. The interface with arts policy is largely self-evident but worth noting all the same. The arts, not least enhanced by the interface with local education provision (with the University of the Highlands and Islands playing an expanding and crucial role), is a strong island economic growth success story. Festivals and eventing have been particularly key to this success; it is a rich and varied offering from jazz to stone-skimming, to traditional highland games and adventure and extreme sport events. A variety of pressures, including over-success but also climate change, and global and local health concerns all impact on business policy regarding event sustainability. Such pressures nevertheless stimulate business solutions and *island proofing* the entrepreneurial responses to shifting cultural and environmental policy and good practice are increasingly key *reflexive* references for SME business success. Cultural critiques play an essential role in showcasing debates and issues more generally, as well as offering informed 'emplaced' solutions.

Stimulation of island tourism demand is unrelenting although still patchy, with certain islands and sites drawing more 'heat' and growth than others. Concerns have been raised recently over the more damaging aspects of unregulated visitor flows into the islands and unsustainable 'honeypot' pressures and problems at particular sites, most notably on Skye. The national body for tourism, VisitScotland highlights Scotland's ferry services and related infrastructure as being key to supporting business and employment opportunities generally as well as underpinning the visitor economy. Notably in Scotland the RET (Road Equivalent Tariff) price reduction on some routes is a considerable *enhancement* for tourist access and has stimulated considerable demand on certain ferry routes. However, VisitScotland has also reflected concerns that RET has impacted on car deck space availability on 'some of the more popular islands' and that this could have a negative impact on the visitor potential of coach tour and/or independent tourist travellers to the islands. The limited car space issue may well be of concern to both tourists and tourism businesses, but with advance booking a general feature of such travel, the real issue surely remains one of the limited ferry space available for all resident island–based businesses and travellers during tourist peak season where there is no resident status priority booking policy? All these challenges have been exacerbated during the staycation Covid-19 summer season of 2020 with capacity constraints and a lack of facilities revealed and highlighted across the highlands and islands. The broader theme for remote rural tourism generally, including Scotland's islands, to develop the season more fully, especially to extend the shoulder months, not least to dissipate pressure from the summer months as well as to diversify the tourism offer across different sites and time frames, remains a goal but it is not without challenges not least weather impacted travel and demands for competitive cost-margins.

Creative industries

Across the islands the arts, creativity and culture have provided a sound basis upon which industry and enterprise have flourished. In recent decades an enhanced policy focus, not least from HIE as well as other national bodies, has sought to support and harness local creativity as well as introduce new forms of creative and cultural enterprise within the region, albeit under the banner of sustainable local partnership. Digital technologies have unquestionably informed the growth and success of a range of creative and cultural industries including creative writing, journalism, filmmaking, music production, graphic design, publishing, journalism and broadcasting. The broader sweep of arts, creative and cultural employment and industry has expanded and innovated across the islands in recent decades as demand for island-based creative products and services, whether it be locally, nationally or internationally, has grown within rural and remote economies, often complementing urban and metropolitan interests (Scottish Government 2019). The potential for further growth and innovation in island and remote regions is noted as McKerrell and Hornabrook (2018) have evidenced for Argyll and Bute in regards of traditional music, and film-maker Chris Young has championed in regard of the global potential of creative screen hubs in 'world-ranking' island environments such as Skye. The creative industries nationally are estimated to support around £9 billion of activity within the wider Scottish economy and contribute around £5.5 billion to Scottish GDP representing about 4% of total Scottish GDP. Recently the Scottish Government (2019) reiterated its narrative of success as underpinned by 'strong identity, authenticity, tradition, distinct languages such as Gaelic and Scots, and a spirit of innovation contribute to their success. Taking advantage of Scotland's scale and strong connections, successful creative businesses are innovative, resourceful, agile, and open'.

Island creative industries involve the making, promotion and consumption of both 'material' and digital artefacts, and services, and both are responsive to the island place, people and physical environment from which they emerge be it creative writing, photography, radio, film or fashion. Digital broadcasting most especially in Gaelic is an expanding success story that required considerable vision and policy support to engender a platform for growth (crucially the £9.6 million Gaelic Television Fund made available following the 1990 Gaelic Broadcasting Act provided necessary funding for independent production companies to take forward a range of new programming genre and formats). The precariousness of minority languages such as Gaelic was recognised at national level and this has incubated and innovated a range of talent that serves both Gaelic and non-Gaelic speakers alike, not just as different consumers and audiences but also as employers, entrepreneurs and island industry advocates. Minority language (old and new) including the island Scots dialects in Shetland and Orkney, and nuanced language use across the island communities more widely, and related cultural heritage, is an enriching driver for creative industries and cultural enterprise across Scotland's islands, often drawing on and informing of wider European experience. Rather than emphasising competition, the synergy across the creative and cultural industries sector is crucial for island and remote rural success. Cultural industries interface with other key sectors, notably tourism but also the heritage, museums, archives and the arts economies (Munro 2016; Burnett 2017). They also interface with manufacturing such as crafts, fashion and textiles, and food and drink where 'craft', creativity, narrative and the visuality and sensory nature of consumption and experience are key. Finally in this section, we note that educational provision at all levels (nursery, schools, college and university) all operate in a connected realm of island knowledge sharing, skills development and research that each contribute to the expanding sense of a broader island creative knowledge economy as a shared space of expertise, innovation, validation and celebration.

Conclusions

There are complex relations and discourses in remote rural and island economies which impact on entrepreneurs and enterprises nevertheless the landscapes of enterprise and sustainability continue to evolve and refine. Previously, we have highlighted how issues facing SMEs and new start-ups of rural areas generally are further compounded in the offshore island setting where enterprises on islands and particularly remote coastal localities face different, additional and exaggerated problems. Small and isolated local markets, restricted access to business services and skills, and located at the beginning and end of lengthy supply chains means they face higher costs and export charges, and a status of lower power in contracts and markets. Brexit may only compound this further. Provenance and reference to environmentally and economically sustainable practices in their marketing do nonetheless allow dynamic island enterprises to capture higher value in the marketplace and so overcome some of the higher prices they must impose in their monopolistic consumer markets. On the supply side, without internal and external agglomeration economies of scale and scope, they either crucially call upon social capital emanating from and inherent to their communities or they internalise the sourcing of certain resource inputs through backward and forward integration in a Coasian sense. These two sides of measures and characteristics of island and remote enterprises can be mutually reinforcing, as revealed in examples from the seaweed and micro-distilling and brewing sectors but increasingly too from the creative industries. Post-Covid-19 realities may yet impact further on ideas and practices of 'remoteness' and pressures to relocate to 'physical remoteness' yet retaining enhanced digital and well-being assurances are emerging as key rural 'plus points'. Scotland's islands increasingly offer an attractive and 'good option' for resituating one's business, work and health security if one has sufficient economic and cultural capital to successfully realise such relocation. For most others, Scotland's islands continue as 'home' secured and disrupted through the contingent nature of economic labour markets (including seasonality and shifting sectoral policy).

Sustainability wholly underpins Scotland's 'remote rural' policy and much practice. Its varied, changing and sometimes contradictory aspects interface with the lived-reality of island business and the nature of 'economic' but also socio-cultural and ecological resilience offers rich interdisciplinary opportunity for ongoing critique. Such focus will provide a fuller appreciation of enterprise in and of the 'margin', the 'peripheral' and the 'edge' realms of Scotland's offshore island economies where such location is both contingent and expressive of the elemental, dynamic, challenging and rewarding aspects of enterprise and sustainability practice more broadly.

Bibliography

Anderson, A. R. (2000). 'Paradox in the periphery: an entrepreneurial reconstruction?', *Entrepreneurship and Regional Development*, 12, 91–109.

Atterton, J. (2017). 'Successful policy and delivery for rural Scotland: learning from elsewhere', *Rural Policy Briefing August 2017* (RPC RB 2017/02). Edinburgh: Scottish Rural University College.

Baldacchino, G. (2005). 'Island entrepreneurs: insights from exceptionally successful knowledge-driven SMEs from five European island territories', *Journal of Enterprising Culture*, 13, 145–170.

Baldacchino, G. (2010). 'Island brands and 'the Island' as a brand: insights from immigrant entrepreneurs on Prince Edward Island', *International Journal of Entrepreneurship and Small Business*, 9, 378–393.

Baldacchino, G. (ed.) (2015). *Entrepreneurship in Small Island States and Territories*. London: Routledge.

Baldacchino, G. (ed.) (2016). *Archipelago Tourism: Policies and Practices*. London: Routledge.

Baldacchino, G. (2019). 'How far can one go? How distance matters in island development', [Ahead of Print]. *Island Studies Journal*, doi: 10.24043/isj.70.

Basu, P. (2007). *Highland Homecomings: Genealogy and Heritage Tourism in the Scottish Diaspora*. London: Routledge.

Baum, T. G., Hagen-Grant, L., Jolliffe, L., Lambert, S., and Sigurjonsson, B. (2000). 'Tourism and cold water islands in the North Atlantic'. In Baldacchino, G., and D. Milne (eds), *Lessons from the Political Economy of Small Islands*, pp. 214–229. London: Palgrave Macmillan.

Birch, K., and Whittam, G. (2008). 'The third sector and the regional development of social capital', *Regional Studies*, 42, 437–450.

Bosworth, G. (2012). 'Characterising rural businesses: tales from the paperman', *Journal of Rural Studies*, 28, 499–506.

Bourdieu, P., and Wacquant, L. (2001). 'Notes on the new planetary vulgate', *Radical Philosophy*, 105, 2–5.

Burnett, K. A., and Danson, M. (2004). 'Adding or subtracting value? Constructions of rurality and Scottish quality food promotion', *International Journal of Entrepreneurial Behavior and Research*, 10, 384–403.

Burnett, K. A., and Danson, M. (2016). Sustainability and small enterprises in Scotland's remote rural 'margins', *Local Economy*, 31, 539–553.

Burnett, K. A., and Danson, M. (2017). 'Enterprise and entrepreneurship on islands and remote rural environments', *International Journal of Entrepreneurship and Innovation*, 18, 25–35.

Burrows, M. T., Macleod, M., and Orr, K. (2010). 'Mapping the intertidal seaweed resources of the Outer Hebrides', *Scottish Association for Marine Science Internal Report No. 269*, Scottish Association for Marine Science Hebridean Seaweed Company Co-funded by Highlands and Islands Enterprise.

Callaghan, G., Danson, M., and Whittam, G. (2012). 'Economic and enterprise development in community buy-outs'. In Danson, M., and P. de Souza (eds), *Regional Development in Northern Europe: Peripherality, Marginality and Border Issues*, pp. 196–211. Abingdon: Routledge.

Cooper, C., and Johnston, J. (2012). 'Vulgate accountability – insights from the field of football', *Auditing and Accountability Journal*, 25, 602–634.

Culkin, N., and Smith, D. (2000). 'An emotional business: a guide to understanding the motivations of small business decision makers', *Qualitative Market Research: An International Journal*, 3, 145–157.

Danson, M. (1991). 'The Scottish economy: the development of underdevelopment?', *Planning Outlook*, 34, 89–95.

Danson, M. (2015). 'Empowered community-led inclusion – community resilience', report to Highlands and Islands Enterprise, Edinburgh: Heriot-Watt University.

Danson, M., and Burnett, K. (2014). 'Enterprise and entrepreneurship on islands'. In Henry, C., and G. McElwee (eds), *Exploring Rural Enterprise: New Perspectives on Research, Policy and Practice (Contemporary Issues in Entrepreneurship Research, Volume 4)*, pp. 151–174. Bingley: Emerald Group Publishing Limited.

Danson, M., Galloway, L., Cabras, I., and Beatty, C. (2015). 'Microbrewing and entrepreneurship: the origins, development and integration of real ale breweries in Britain', *International Journal of Entrepreneurship and Innovation*, 16, 135–144.

Deakins, D., and Freel, M. (2009). *Entrepreneurship and Small Firms*. Fifth Edition. Maidenhead: McGraw-Hill.

Eachus, P. (2014). 'Community resilience: is it greater than the sum of the parts of individual resilience?', *Procedia Economics and Finance*, 18, 345–351.

EMEC (2019). <http://www.emec.org.uk/> accessed 3 July 2019.

Fazey, I., Moug, P., Allen, S., Beckmann, K., Blackwood, D., Bonaventura, M., Burnett, K., Danson, M., Falconer, R., Gagnon, A., Harkness, R., Hodgson, A., Holm, L., Irvine, K.N., Low, R., Lyon, C., Moss, A., Moran, C., Naylor, L., O'Brien, K., Russell, S., Skerratt, S., Williams, J., and Wolstenholme, R. (2018). 'Transformation in a changing climate: a research agenda', *Climate and Development*, 10, 197–217.

Folke, C. (2006). 'Resilience: the emergence of a perspective for social–ecological systems analyses', *Global Environmental Change*, 16, 253–267.

Galloway, L., and Levie, J. (2001). *Global Entrepreneurship Monitor: Scotland.* University of Strathclyde, Glasgow.

Galloway, L., Sanders, J., and Deakins, D. (2011). 'Rural small firms' use of the internet: from global to local', *Journal of Rural Studies*, 27, 254–262.

Granqvist, M. (2012). 'The political entrepreneur as an unconventional problem solver in a Northern Periphery'. In Danson, M., and P. de Souza (eds), *Regional Development in Northern Europe: Peripherality, Marginality and Border Issues*, pp. 232–246. Abingdon: Routledge.

Halfacree, K. (2012). 'Diverse ruralities in the 21st Century: from effacement to (re) invention'. In Kulcsar, L. J., and K. J. Curtis (eds), *International Handbook of Rural Demography, International Handbooks of Population 3*, pp. 387–400. Dordrecht Hiedelberg London New York: Springer.

Hebrides.net (n.d.). 'HEBRIDES.NET – bringing broadband to the Western Isles', <http://www.hebrides.net/index.htm> accessed 5 February 2020.

Henry, C., and McElwee, G. (eds) (2014). *Exploring Rural Enterprise: New Perspectives on Research, Policy and Practice (Contemporary Issues in Entrepreneurship Research, Volume 4)*. Bingley: Emerald.

HIE (2018a). 'Highlands and Islands firms triumph in life science awards', Highlands and Islands Enterprise, <http://news.hie.co.uk/all-news/highlands-and-islands-firms-triumph-in-life-science-awards/> accessed 3 July 2018.

HIE (2018b). 'Wild seaweed harvesting as a diversification opportunity for fishermen', HIE Report, Inverness.

HIE (2019a). 'Global business services', Highlands and Islands Enterprise, <https://www.hie.co.uk/our-region/our-growth-sectors/finance-and-business-services/> accessed 5 February 2020.

HIE (2019b). 'Growth sectors: life sciences', Highlands and Islands Enterprise, <https://www.hie.co.uk/our-region/our-growth-sectors/life-sciences/> accessed 5 February 2020.

Holm, A., O'Rourke, B., and Danson, M. (2019). ' "Employers could use us, but they don't": voices from blue-collar workplaces in a northern periphery', *Language Policy*, 19, 389–416.

Kythreotis, A., and Bristow, G. (2017). 'The 'resilience trap': exploring the practical utility of resilience for climate change adaptation in UK city-regions', *Regional Studies*, 51, 1530–1541.

Laing, F. (2017) 'How digital health takes away patients' boundaries', *The Scotsman*, 30 November, <https://www.scotsman.com/business/companies/tech/how-digital-health-takes-away-patients-boundaries-1-4613800> accessed 3 July 2019.

McKerrell, S., and Hornabrook J. (2018). *Traditional Music and the Rural Creative Economy in Argyll & Bute*, Mapping Report. Newcastle upon Tyne: Newcastle University.

McQuatters-Gollop, A. (2012). 'Challenges for implementing the Marine Strategy Framework Directive in a climate of macroecological change', *Philosophical Transactions A*, 370, 1980. doi: 10.1098/rsta.2012.0401, <http://rsta.royalsocietypublishing.org/content/370/1980/5636> accessed 3 July 2019.

Munro, E. (2016). 'Developing the rural creative economy 'from below': exploring practices of market-building amongst creative entrepreneurs in rural and remote Scotland', *Media Culture*, 19 (3), <https://www.storre.stir.ac.uk/bit-stream/1893/26741/1/Munro.pdf> accessed 3 July 2019.

North, D., and Smallbone, D. (2006). 'Developing entrepreneurship and enterprise in Europe's peripheral rural areas: some issues facing policy-makers', *European Planning Studies*, 14, 41–60.

Reynolds, P. D., Bygrave, W. D., and Autio, E. (2003). *Global Entrepreneurship Monitor: Executive Report*. Kansas City, MO: Kauffman Center for Entrepreneurial Leadership.

Royal Society of Edinburgh (2008). *Report of the RSE Committee of Inquiry into the Future of Scotland's Hills and Islands*. Edinburgh: Royal Society of Edinburgh.

Scotland Food and Drink Partnership (2018). *Scotland Food and Drink Industry Performance Review* <https://scotlandfoodanddrink.blob.core.windows.net//media/1466/sfd-2018_web.pdf> accessed 3 July 2019.

Scottish Development International (2015). *Global Business Services in the Highlands and Islands*. SDI and HIE, Inverness.

Scottish Executive (2004). *Harnessing Scotland's Marine Energy Potential*. Edinburgh: Scottish Executive.

Scottish Government (2015). *Scotland's Economic Strategy*, <https://www.gov.scot/publications/scotlands-economic-strategy> accessed 12 October 2019.

Scottish Government (2017). *The Future of Energy in Scotland: Scottish Energy Strategy*, <https://www.gov.scot/publications/scottish-energy-strategy-future-energy-scotland-9781788515276/pages/2/> accessed 12 October 2019.

Scottish Government (2018a). *Understanding the Rural Economy*, <https://www.gov.scot/publications/understanding-scottish-rural-economy/pages/5/> accessed 12 October 2019.

Scottish Government (2018b). *Rural Scotland the Key Facts*, <https://www.gov.scot/publications/rural-scotland-key-facts-2018/> accessed 12 October 2019.

Scottish Government (2018c). *National Performance Framework*, <https://nationalperformance.gov.scot/> accessed 12 October 2019.

Scottish Government (2019). Creative Industries Policy Statement, Scottish Government: Edinburgh, <https://www.gov.scot/publications/policy-statement-creative-industries/> accessed 12 October 2019.

SRUC (2016). *Rural Scotland in Focus*. Edinburgh.

Steiner, A., and Atterton, J. (2014). 'The contribution of rural businesses to community resilience', *Local Economy*, 29, 228–244.

Steiner, A., and Atterton, J. (2015). 'Exploring the contribution of rural enterprises to local resilience', *Journal of Rural Studies*, 40, 30–45.

Steiner, A., and Farmer, J. (2017). 'Engage, participate, empower: modelling power transfer in disadvantaged rural communities', *Environment and Planning C: Politics and Space*, 36, 118–138.

Steiner, A., and Markantoni, M. (2014). 'Unpacking community resilience through capacity for change', *Community Development Journal*, 49, 407–425.

Townsend, L., Wallace, C., Fairhurst, G., and Anderson, A. (2017). 'Broadband and the creative industries in rural Scotland', *Journal of Rural Studies*, 54, 451–458.

VisitScotland (2016). Tourism Development Framework for Scotland: Role of the planning system in delivering the visitor economy (Refresh 2016), Visit Scotland, Edinburgh, <https://www.visitscotland.org/binaries/content/assets/dot-org/pdf/policies/tourism-development-framework-dec16.pdf> accessed 12 October 2019.

WHFP (2019). 'Isle of Skye tech company launches recruitment drive after record year of growth', *West Highland Free Press*, 21 June, <https://www.whfp.com/2019/06/21/isle-of-skye-tech-company-launches-recruitment-drive-after-record-year-of-growth/> accessed 12 October 2019.

Whittam, G., and Danson, M. (2001). 'Power and the spirit of clustering', *European Planning Studies*, 9, 949–963.

ZeroWasteScotland (2015). Sector study on beer, whisky and fish, circular economy report for the Scottish Government, <https://www.zerowastescotland.org> accessed 12 October 2019.

FRANCESCO SINDICO AND NICOLA CROOK[1]

10. The Islands (Scotland) Act: Island Proofing through Legislation

This chapter will provide an account of the *Islands (Scotland) Act* (2018) (the Act) and the emerging themes stemming from the consultation carried out to inform the National Islands Plan (Scottish Government 2019). The Act was adopted by the Scottish Parliament in June 2018, but its roots go back to the *Our Islands Our Future Strategy*[2] in 2014. The chapter will highlight the process and the key moments leading to the adoption of the Act. It will then highlight the main sections of the Act, with an emphasis on the concept of island proofing, which is at the heart of the Act. The second part of the chapter will discuss the consultation that has been carried out in 2019 to inform both the National Islands Plan and the guidance and regulations related to island communities' impact assessment. The consultation highlighted four key values that capture the interests of island communities across Scotland: fairness, sustainability, environmental protection and inclusiveness. Each one will be analysed in the chapter clarifying how future island centred policies underpinned by such values have the potential to deliver effective island proofing as promised by the Act itself.

1   Francesco Sindico is the Co-director of the Strathclyde Centre for Environmental Law and Governance (SCELG) and Nicola Crook is a PhD researcher at SCELG. Both Francesco and Nicola provided technical assistance to Scottish Government in the development of the National Islands Plan and in work around island communities impact assessment. This chapter reflects their personal opinions and does not reflect in any way the position of Scottish Government.

2   Our Islands Our Future (n.d.). 'Constitutional change in Scotland – opportunities for island areas', <http://www.orkney.gov.uk/Files/Council/Consultations/Our-Islands-Our-Future/Joint_Position_Statement.pdf> accessed 24 October 2019.

Scotland has inhabited islands that stretch from the Isle of Arran in the south west of Scotland up to Unst in the Shetlands (National Records of Scotland 2015). Scottish islands, hence, cover a wide stretch of sea and are part and parcel of Scotland and its cultural and historical identity. At the same time, each island is unique with its own history, culture and socio-economic realities. Even two islands that are very close to one another, like Islay and Jura, or Tiree and Coll, are very different both in terms of geography and economic opportunities and challenges. Additionally, communities on the same island can also be extremely different in their needs and wants; the distinctions between 'urban' and 'rural' living are still very much present within many of Scotland's islands. Take Lewis, for example, where those living in Stornoway, which has a population of approximately 8,000 making it the largest town in the Hebrides, are living a much more 'urban' lifestyle than those in the village of Flesherin, which has a population of around 100. However, other aspects do bring groupings of islands together. Language, for example, is one of these aspects, with Gaelic being spoken across a range of islands including, but not limited to, the Western Isles (McLeod 2020). Moving up to Orkney and Shetland, it is their historical connections with Norway that bring these islands together (Walters 2014). The uniqueness of each island was routinely stressed by participants throughout the consultation exercise. The consultation analysis report includes several quotes on the issue, including: 'Listen to the people in EACH community. No two island communities are the same, even within the same island group. We often have the best solution to our unique problems, but we MUST have legislation and funding to allow us to help ourselves' (Sanday, Orkney).[3]

According to the 2011 census 103,700 people live on Scottish islands (National Records of Scotland 2015). Lewis and Harris is the most populated, with 19,918 inhabitants, while at the other end of the spectrum there are some islands with fewer than 20 people living on them, such as Canna, Erraid and Gometra. Inhabited islands in Scotland fall under the

---

3   Scottish Government, 'National Islands Plan and Island Communities Impact Assessments: Analysis of responses to the public consultation exercise' (publication pending).

jurisdiction of six local authorities: Shetland, Orkney, Comhairle nan Eilean Siar, Highlands and Islands, Argyll and Bute, and North Ayrshire. The first three are solely 'island' Local Authorities and the latter three are not, having the largest percentage of their population living on the mainland. Furthermore, political decisions affecting islands in Scotland will often be taken centrally in Scotland (Edinburgh), in the United Kingdom (London) and, in some cases (at least until BREXIT happens, at the time of writing in June 2020) in the European Union (Brussels). This continued central decision-making has resulted in many island communities contesting that decisions are taken by those who do not understand the realities of island life, and therefore fail to take into account the interests of the island communities in Scotland.[4] This theme was prevalent throughout the consultation exercise, with respondents asking Scottish Government to:

- Devolve power and funding to local communities. (Mull)
- To increase local decision making and accountability. (Lewis)
- Talk to the islands and let them have more 'power'. As most public services like to use statistics, or percentage of population, when you live in a remote community, then your voice is seldom taken seriously. (Mull)[5]

Against this background, this chapter shows how Scotland has reversed this trend and put the interest of island communities in statutory language through the Islands (Scotland) Act 2018. The chapter highlights how the Islands (Scotland) Act, through the preparation of the National Islands Plan, can be seen as being an example of a piece of legislation that is underpinned by a strong requirement of public participation. The

---

4   Our Islands Our Future (n.d.). 'Constitutional change in Scotland – opportunities for island areas', <http://www.orkney.gov.uk/Files/Council/Consultations/Our-Islands-Our-Future/Joint_Position_Statement.pdf> accessed, 24 October 2019 and Reid-Howie Associates Ltd. (2016). 'Consultation on provisions for a Future Islands Bill – analysis of responses', <https://www.gov.scot/binaries/content/documents/govscot/publications/research-and-analysis/2016/03/consultation-provisions-future-islands-bill-analysis-responses/documents/00496550-pdf/00496550-pdf/govscot%3Adocument/00496550.pdf> accessed 25 October 2019.
5   Scottish Government, 'National Islands Plan and Island Communities Impact Assessments: Analysis of responses to the public consultation exercise' (publication pending).

chapter will take the reader through the journey that has led to the adoption of the Islands (Scotland) Act 2018. It will then clarify how island proofing implements the need to take into account the interests of island communities in law and policy and where it can be found in the Islands (Scotland) Act 2018. The chapter then moves on to the consultation that has led to the National Islands Plan, as provided for in the Islands (Scotland) Act 2018, explaining how it engaged with critical aspects of the consultation process which has previously led to scepticism and 'consultation fatigue' throughout island communities. It will then highlight some emerging themes stemming from the consultation itself and how such themes have the potential to drive the implementation of the National Islands Plan. The chapter concludes with some further thoughts about island proofing and the good practices stemming from Scotland when it comes to consultation exercises.

From the *Our Islands Our Future Strategy* to the Islands (Scotland) Act 2018

In June 2013, Comhairle nan Eilean Siar, Orkney Islands Council and Shetland Islands Council launched the *Our Islands – Our Future* campaign, with the aim of ensuring that the needs and status of island areas in Scotland were clearly recognised.[6] As a result, the Scottish Government went on to form the Island Areas Ministerial Working Group, which, upon its conclusion in June 2014, published the *Empowering Scotland's Island Communities* prospectus,[7] presented as a coherent package of

---

6   Our Islands Our Future (n.d.). 'Constitutional change in Scotland – opportunities for island areas', <http://www.orkney.gov.uk/Files/Council/Consultations/Our-Islands-Our-Future/Joint_Position_Statement.pdf> accessed 24 October 2019.

7   Scottish Government (2014). 'Empowering Scotland's Island Communities', <https://www.gov.scot/publications/empowering-scotlands-island-communities/pages/3/> accessed 22 October 2019.

measures that developed a set of proposals based on three underpinning objectives:

- Promoting the voice of island communities;
- Harnessing island resources; and
- Enhancing the wellbeing of island communities.

Following from this, the Scottish Government adopted a *Framework for the Islands* where it developed 'island proofing' as a principle whereby policy and legislation must take into account islands' circumstances.[8] A consultation process was then undertaken on the provisions for a future Islands Bill, a key focus of which was the aspect of 'island-proofing', and its inclusion as a principle within any future Island Bills to formalise the approach in legislation. As a result, the *Islands (Scotland) Bill 2018* received Royal Assent on 6 July 2018. The first Commencement Regulations for the Island Act were laid on 20 September 2018 and came into force on 4 October 2018. The Islands (Scotland) Act 2018 aims to provide a normative space for islands and island communities within the Scottish legal system, in an effort to rectify the previous exclusion that Scottish island communities have too often felt when it comes to law and policy.[9] It does so by providing the foundations to allow island communities to have their concerns heard and interests fully taken into account.

---

8   UK Government and the Three Scottish Island Councils (2014). 'A framework for the Islands', <https://www.gov.uk/government/uploads/system/uploads/attachment_data/file/344446/UKG_ISLANDS_FRAMEWORK_-_15_August.pdf> accessed 22 October 2019.

9   Our Islands Our Future (n.d.). 'Constitutional change in Scotland – opportunities for island areas', <http://www.orkney.gov.uk/Files/Council/Consultations/Our-Islands-Our-Future/Joint_Position_Statement.pdf> accessed 24 October 2019; and Reid-Howie Associates Ltd. (2016) 'Consultation on provisions for a Future Islands Bill – analysis of responses', <https://www.gov.scot/binaries/content/documents/govscot/publications/research-and-analysis/2016/03/consultation-provisions-future-islands-bill-analysis-responses/documents/00496550-pdf/00496550-pdf/govscot%3Adocument/00496550.pdf> accessed 25 October 2019.

Island Proofing through the Islands (Scotland) Act

One of the drivers that led to the *Islands (Scotland) Act* has been the perception that, for far too long, island communities have felt disconnected from the mainland[10]; there was more than just a stretch of water between Scottish island communities and the shore. Instead, there was a sea of misunderstanding, whereby decisions taken on the mainland did not truly reflect the interests and desires of island communities. This was reflected throughout the consultation process, with online submissions including the likes of:

- Ensure that the government does not make 'a one-size-fits- all policy which is to the detriment of islands or rural areas' (Shetland), and that rather, it must 'Consult [...] and listen [...] to the island community. Enabl[e] island communities to develop/ shape their own future' (Mull).[11]
- Island proofing has been hailed as a clear way to navigate such choppy waters.[12]

As previously mentioned, this concept was first introduced by a *Framework for the Islands* in the journey from *Our Islands Our Future Strategy* to the *Islands (Scotland) Act* and it referred to the desire of bridging the gap between island communities and centralised decision makers when it came to legislation, policies and strategies that affect

10   Our Islands Our Future (n.d.). 'Our islands: our future: submission to The Smith Commission' Proposal 8.3, <https://www.cne-siar.gov.uk/media/7963/oiof-submission-to-smith-commission.pdf> accessed 25 October 2019.

11   Scottish Government, 'National Islands Plan and Island Communities Impact Assessments: Analysis of responses to the public consultation exercise' (publication pending).

12   The Waste (Scotland) Regulations 2012 are a prime example of mainland policy not being adapted to take into consideration the uniqueness of islands. These regulations introduced new measures to help Scotland become one of the most resource efficient nations in Europe. However, although the new Regulations clearly recognise the differences between rural and urban areas, they do not acknowledge that island communities will face significantly higher challenges if they are to meet the aims of this legislation. Where increased Landfill Tax rates have made recycling services financially sustainable in mainland locations, the cost of haulage of recyclable materials to the mainland, combined with processing charges, is often still in excess of the landfill tax savings when dealing with island wastes.

island and their communities.[13] In other words, island proofing was and is about recalibrating discourse between islands and the mainland. The *Islands (Scotland) Act* is very much based on the concept of island proofing. The latter can be seen as central to several provisions within the *Islands (Scotland) Act*. The first is the provision laying out the duty to prepare a National Islands Plan, according to which: 'The purpose of preparing a national islands plan is to set out the main objectives and strategy of the Scottish Ministers in relation to improving outcomes for island communities that result from, or are contributed to by, the carrying out of functions of a public nature.'[14] The mere fact that the Act provides for a National Islands Plan implies that island proofing is at the heart of its development and future implementation. Additionally, it is evident that island proofing is absolutely crucial to 'improving outcomes for island communities' and must underpin all objectives, functions and strategies of the Scottish Ministers.

A second crucial provision is the duty to have regard to island communities. This stems from section 7 of the Act that maintains that: 'A relevant authority must have regard to island communities in carrying out its functions'. One of the ways to have regard to island communities is by undertaking an island communities impact assessment.[15] A third important provision that embodies island proofing is the scheme for requests by local authorities for devolution of functions, according to which regulations need to be developed in order to 'establish a scheme for the making by a local authority listed in the schedule of a request to them to promote legislation devolving a function to the authority'.[16] A fourth important provision refers to the review of wards in certain local government areas, which will allow that in relation to an electoral ward consisting wholly or partly of one or more inhabited islands 'an order made under section 17

---

13 UK Government and the Three Scottish Island Councils (2014). 'A framework for the Islands', p. 3. <https://www.gov.uk/government/uploads/system/uploads/attachment_data/file/344446/UKG_ISLANDS_FRAMEWORK_-_15_August. pdf> accessed 22 October 2019.

14 Island (Scotland) Act (2018) [ISA], section 3(2).

15 ISA, section 15(1).

16 ISA, section 15(1).

of the 1973 Act may determine that the number of councillors to be returned is either one or two.'[17] A fifth provision that is closely linked to the
concept of island proofing is the section of the Act relating to additional
requests. Regulations are being developed to implement schemes aimed
at enabling a 'process by which a local authority listed in the schedule (a
"relevant local authority") may request that additional functions, duties
or responsibilities are transferred to the authority'.[18] A final section that
brings island proofing to the fore relates to the Scottish island marine area
where attempts to limit and regulate development activities in the waters
surrounding Scottish islands is highlighted:

> The Scottish Ministers may by regulations establish a scheme by virtue of which a
> person must not, except in accordance with a licence granted by a local authority,
> carry on a development activity within such part of the Scottish island marine area as
> is designated in the regulations as a part in which such a licence is required to carry
> on a development activity (in this Part an 'island licensing area').[19]

As for so many other parts of Scottish society and policy, BREXIT and
how a future relationship with the European Union will be framed, will
have a strong impact on the Scottish island marine area. In conclusion,
throughout the *Islands (Scotland) Act* the concept of island proofing permeates efforts to recalibrate island policy in Scotland so that island communities can have a stronger role and voice. In the next section we will explain how the island communities' voice has informed the development
of the National Islands Plan.

National Islands Plan consultation

The obligation to consult the public in the development of public policies
is an 'essential and important aspect of Scottish Government working

17   ISA, section 19(1).
18   ISA, section 21(2)(a).
19   ISA, section 24(1).

methods'.[20] The principle of public participation is accepted internationally and a strong formulation thereof in the field of environment and development international public policy can be found in Principle 10 of the Rio Declaration on Environment and Development (United Nations 1992), according to which

> Environmental issues are *best handled with the participation of all concerned citizens, at the relevant level* [our emphasis]. At the national level, each individual shall have appropriate access to information concerning the environment that is held by public authorities, including information on hazardous materials and activities in their communities, and the opportunity to participate in decision-making processes. States shall facilitate and encourage public awareness and participation by making information widely available. Effective access to judicial and administrative proceedings, including redress and remedy, shall be provided. (1992)

Public participation has been developed further at an international and regional level with the 1998 UNECE Aarhus Convention,[21] the 2010 Bali Guidelines[22] – 'putting the Rio Principle 10 into action' – and the 2018 Escazu Agreement.[23] However, in our view public participation has become a victim of its own success in many countries. Scotland is no exception. Since public consultation has become a general practice, people are now increasingly exposed to it. While this may appear to be a positive development, it is positive only if those who have been consulted perceive that their voice has 'really' been heard and that their ideas have 'really' shaped public policy. If those consulted do not perceive this, then consultation fatigue kicks in (Clark 2008). Consultation fatigue and overall scepticism were prevalent in the consultation process that the Scottish

20 Scottish Government, 'About the consultation process', <https://www2.gov.scot/Consultations/About> accessed 12 May 2020.

21 Convention on Access to Information, Public Participation in Decision-Making and Access to Justice in Environmental Matters ('Aarhus Convention') (1998).

22 Guidelines for the Development of National Legislation on Access to Information, Public Participation in Decision-making and Access to Justice in Environmental Matters' (The 'Bali Guidelines') (2010).

23 Regional Agreement on Access to Information, Public Participation and Justice in Environmental Matters in Latin America and the Caribbean ('Escazu Agreement') (2018).

Government undertook to inform the National Islands Plan. In order to tackle these challenges, the consultation sought to address key challenges, and through the adopted methodology three questions were posed:

- Who is the island community that will be consulted?
- How do we prevent one voice from representing an entire island community?
- How do we include the island communities involved in the consultation in shaping the Plan and its future implementation once the consultation has finished?

Who is the island community?

Starting with the first question, it is evident that consultations often target specific sectors of society or, in this case, of an island community. For example, a consultation process may want to engage with those more closely linked to the transport sector or the health system. The nature of the National Islands Plan itself prevented this narrow approach from being taken. The goal of the Plan, as stated in the Act, is: 'To set out the main objectives and Strategy of the Scottish Ministers in relation to improving outcomes for island communities that result from, or are contributed to by, the carrying out of functions of a public nature'.[24] In addition, the Act already provided a rather long list of key areas that needed to be improved in the Plan, which can be found in section 3(3).[25] With this in mind, it is evident that the Plan is not about improving a specific aspect of island life, but rather embraces all aspects of society. With such a

---

24   ISA, section 3(2).
25   ISA, section 3(3).
        (3) improving outcomes for island communities includes
          (a) increasing population levels
          (b) improving and promoting
            (i) sustainable economic development
            (ii) environmental well-being
            (iii) health and well-being, and
            (iv) community empowerment
          (c) improving transport services
          (d) improving digital connectivity
          (e) reducing fuel poverty

wide scope, it was never going to be possible to have a narrow approach to a consultation. This led to the question of how to adequately engage with an island community and consequently, who are the people on an island that represent the interests of the island community? These are not just rhetorical questions, but rather issues that the Act itself needed an answer for. In fact, the consultation that informed the National Islands Plan was required by the Act and island communities were included as consultees in the following way: 'In preparing the national islands plan, the Scottish Ministers must consult such *other persons* as they consider *represent the interests of island communities*.'[26]

So, who represents the interests of island communities in the context of something as broad as the Plan? The answer we provided was a very simple one: everybody! Every single person on an island represents the interests of an island community. One of the themes that emerged from the consultation process is the fact that, as you would imagine, all aspects on an island are integrated. If every factor on an island is related to other factors, it is nonsensical to focus solely on one group of people on an island (following GDPR (i.e. General Data Protection Regulation), no quotes from individuals are offered here). By opening up the consultation to anybody living and present on an island, the consultation was effectively open to all sectors of the island community. The Act itself has a definition of an island community, which we believe supports our decision to open the doors of the consultation to everybody:

> 'island community' means a community which – (a) consists of two or more individuals, all of whom permanently inhabit an island (whether or not the same island), and (b) is based on common interest, identity or geography (including in relation to any uninhabited island whose natural environment and terrestrial, marine and associated ecosystems contribute to the natural or cultural heritage or economy of an inhabited island).[27]

(f) ensuring effective management of the Scottish Crown Estate (i.e. the property, rights and interests to which section 90 B (5) of the Scotland Act 1998 applies)

(g) enhancing biosecurity (including protecting islands from the impact of invasive non-native species).

26   ISA, section 4(1)(a)(ii). Emphasis added.

27   ISA, section 2.

We therefore reached out to the island communities as a whole and found ways to ensure that everybody had the opportunity to engage with the consultation process. This is where promotion and networks become crucial. A combination of traditional channels, such as posters in shops and ferries, and local newspapers and social media were used to boost interest in the events. Consultation events usually took place in community halls and we tried to have them at a time of the day that worked for most people on the island. Somewhat predictably, and largely due to logistics and the differences in schedules of those living on the island, this was not always possible. However, it became apparent that the key resource when trying to reach out to the entire island community is to have a local connection. This could be in the form of community council or a local development trust, of which there are many in Scotland.[28]

Allowing all voices to be heard

The National Islands Plan consultation process targeted everyone on the islands where events took place. On those islands that the team was unable to visit physically, Scottish Government offered to pay the travel expenses for residents of geographically close islands who wished to attend the events and encouraged those unable to attend to participate in the online consultation format and get in touch directly with any queries and/or feedback. Some events were very well attended, others slightly less, but in all there was the risk, as in all consultation processes, that one attendee ends up dominating the entire event and not necessarily offering the community's view. Not only is this not desirable, since the goal of public participation is to gauge the voice of the public and not the voice of just one person, but it can also be disruptive, as consultation events can become tense if attendees feel that they cannot share their own insights.

---

28   The consultation process has benefited from the support of the Scottish Islands Federation who arranged local contacts and provided logistical assistance throughout.

The National Islands Plan consultation process engaged with this challenge and sought to give all participants the opportunity to share their ideas and their thoughts.[29] This was done by using the well-established World Café methodology combined with an Open Space Technology format that enabled participants to engage in a wide discussion about what 'works well' on their island and what 'needs to be improved'.[30] The consultation saw more in-depth discussion on several aspects important for island participants at the events.[31] Rather than taking the reader through step by step on how the consultation was carried out,[32] let us sketch some of the key moments from a typical event.

A first important moment was to provide the necessary context to the consultation. Many people arrived at the event unaware of what the *Islands (Scotland) Act* entailed, and most did not know what the Plan was or the role it would play going forward in island policy in Scotland. Add to this the above-mentioned consultation scepticism and fatigue and, perhaps predictably, the initial reception at consultation events was not always warm. Hence, it was important to explain to the participants why the team leading the consultation was on the island and what was expected from the attendees to the consultation. However, rather than a long, lengthy, technical and slide-heavy presentation, the team decided to provide a brief, passionate talk that not only provided the necessary legal and policy context,[33] but also gave the attendees a sense of how this consultation differed from the more

---

29   Observation based on feedback from participants such as: 'I did not think I would be able to contribute as much as I did' and 'I came to the event with very low expectations. I am much more optimistic now'.

30   Methodologies used in the consultation <http://www.theworldcafe.com/> and <https://openspaceworld.org/wp2/what-is/> accessed 20 May 2020.

31   Reports from all the islands visited are available here: <https://www.strath.ac.uk/ research/strathclydecentreenvironmentallawgovernance/ourwork/research/ labsincubators/eilean/islandsscotlandact/consultations/> accessed 20 May 2020.

32   The consultation process was designed by Sandy Brunton, Convenor of the Mull and Iona Community Trust and Chair of DTAS.

33   We initially conducted a trial consultation event on Grimsay (Uist) and slightly changed the original format based on feedback from the participants to the trial.

traditional consultation methods they may have previously been used to[34] and highlighted the uniqueness and importance of the process for both the Plan and the Act.[35]

A second factor in the consultation process was that attendees were asked to work in groups and participate actively in the format of the event. In other words, this was not an event that followed a somewhat traditional 'consultation' format where a presentation was made and then people reacted to it. It is also useful to highlight that the team endeavoured to ensure that the events themselves conveyed an informal atmosphere in order to encourage engagement between participants and the event facilitators. The National Islands Plan consultation events were an opportunity for members of the island community (who participated) to work in small groups to, firstly, identify together what worked very well and made their island a great place to live and work on. Members were then asked to sit in different tables with different members of the community and come up collectively with the challenges that the island community was facing. In all these discussions there were not more than four or five people in each group and throughout the evening one could see how participants felt more comfortable in sharing their ideas with a smaller group, rather than with the entire community hall.

A third and final factor in ensuring diversity of views were aired and recorded was that the only moment in the event when the discussion was brought back in a plenary mode (i.e. involving everybody in the room) was at the very end. By then, the atmosphere in the hall was often more relaxed than at the beginning and people generally felt more comfortable sharing with everybody else any further comment, idea or concern that they may have had on the specific challenge that was being discussed.

---

34   The main difference lies in how we tried to answer the last question: 'How do we include the island communities involved in the consultation in shaping the Plan and in its future implementation once the consultation has finished?'

35   Scotland is one of very few countries in the world with a place-based piece of legislation which focuses solely on islands.

Meaningful action from consultations

The title of this sub-section was written by a participant on a post-it note in one of the consultation events.[36] It was a reminder of our approach to avoid the consultation fatigue and overall scepticism that was addressed at the beginning of each event. In order to have meaningful action from consultations the key question is the following: 'How do we include the island communities involved in the consultation in shaping the Plan and in its future implementation once the consultation has finished?'

The National Islands Plan consultation process took time to reflect upon this question and embedded in its procedure a means to enter into an immediate relationship with the participants in the events. Often, people deliver a consultation event to only a small section of a community, and in some instances such an event can be tense. Additionally, it is often common practice that those who have organised the consultation do not remain in contact with the participants. We tried to break this cycle and build an element of trust and confidence between the attendees and those delivering the consultation. The main way we aimed to achieve this was through the development of a feedback loop. Once the event was concluded, the organisers inputted into pre-determined tables the information gathered by the attendees. The tables were determined by the categories present in section 3(3) of the Islands (Scotland) Act. As soon as possible after the events on a specific island, the team drafted a report that had the same headings and the same format for each island, highlighting what worked really well, what were the challenges and a more qualitative assessment of some of the key challenges as discussed by specific groups at the events and in the plenaries. At the beginning of each event, participants were asked to provide us with their emails or other contact details. Once the above-mentioned report had been produced, the team then sent it to the consultation attendees and gave them a two-week time frame to respond with any comments and feedback. We are pleased to say that we received enough responses to see the value in such feedback from the participants as it allowed us to fine tune the reports and to better report on the discussions that took place at

36   This was a contribution to the event held on Whalsay.

the consultation events. Therefore, participants from the island community have been integral to producing the reports, which have been instrumental in informing the content of the National Islands Plan.[37]

However, the question that we have posed has a second element to it, which is 'How do we include the island communities involved in the consultation in its future implementation once the consultation has finished?' As we write, Scottish Government is planning the process that will lead to the implementation strategy of the National Islands Plan. It will be crucial to build on the good practices that have arisen in the consultation process. At the same time, one has to be realistic and realise that for the development of indicators the methodology will need to be tweaked and it is likely that it will not be possible to undertake such a thorough consultation as has been done for the preparation of the Plan. In fact, it is worth mentioning that, during the consultation, the Scottish Government's Islands Team (consisting of two Strathclyde researchers, two Government officials and one independent consultant who specialises in consultation methodology) visited 41 islands and organised 61 events which allowed them to engage face-to-face with almost 1,000 people.[38] The live events were complemented by an online consultation where participants could provide their views electronically,[39] for which 411 online responses were received. In addition, young people were invited to attend specific events that allowed them to share their input to the development of the National Islands Plan. This was an unprecedented exercise of public participation in the context of Scottish islands and one that has not only informed the content of the National Islands Plan, but has also forged relationships between those that

37   Reports available at: <https://www.strath.ac.uk/research/strathclydecentr eenvironmentallawgovernance/ourwork/research/labsincubators/eilean/ islandsscotlandact/consultations/> accessed 20 May 2020.

38   Islands visited: Arran, Mainland Orkney (Kirkwall and Stromness), Barra, Mainland Shetland (Lerwick), Benbecula, Muck, Brae, Mull, Bute, North Ronaldsay, Canna, North Uist, Coll, Raasay, Colonsay, Rum, Cumbrae, Sanday, Easdale, Seil, Eigg, Skye, Gigha, South Uist, Harris, Stronsay, Hoy, Tiree, Iona, Ulva, Islay, Unst, Jura, Vatersay, Kerrera, Westray, Lewis, Whalsay, Lismore, Yell and Luing.

39   Online consultation available at: <https://consult.gov.scot/agriculture-and-rural- communities/national-islands-plan/> accessed 20 May 2020.

have drafted the Plan and will be tasked with its implementation and the island communities that stand to benefit from a successful implementation of the Plan. Direct positive feedback from participants included the following: 'I applaud the work of the Islands Team to date, the consultation process has been very engaging and I look forward to seeing the outcomes in due course' (Mull).[40] The chapter now moves to sketch the emerging themes that have arisen from the consultation and how they will underpin the Plan and its implementation.

Emerging themes

The methodology undertaken during the consultation events included a democratic voting phase which enabled participants to indicate which topics they wished to spend more time on to provide more details about specific challenges. Figure 1 depicts a graph as replicated in the Scottish Islands Plan (2019), detailing how many times participants discussed in more depth specific areas of concern.

It is evident that there are several issues that came to the forefront during this exercise, including transport, economic development and depopulation to name the most frequent three.

Issues with regard to transport were mostly frequently mentioned by participants to the online consultation in response to the question regarding the specific challenges of living on the islands:

- Ferry disruptions and limited options for ferry connections in evenings. (Arran)
- The major stress for living in Shetland is the cost and difficulty in travelling to and from the mainland. It means separation from friends and family. It means the cost of a holiday for people on low or median incomes is very difficult. (Shetland)[41]

40   Reports available at: <https://www.strath.ac.uk/research/strathclydecentr eenvironmentallawgovernance/ourwork/research/labsincubators/eilean/ islandsscotlandact/consultations> accessed 20 May 2020.

41   Scottish Government, 'National Islands Plan and Island Communities Impact Assessments: Analysis of responses to the public consultation exercise' (publication pending).

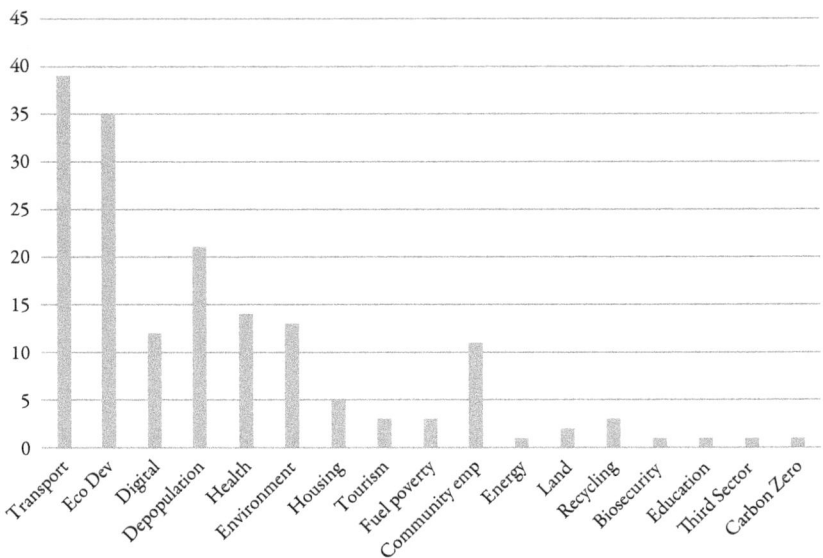

Figure 1: Thematic Responses: Consultation for The National Plan for Scotland's
Islands. (Scottish Government 2019: 8)

Respondents also emphasised the unique economic challenges of each
island, and the need to target and support particular opportunities for
economic growth in each and every case:

- The islands of Scotland are important to the economy of Scotland. (Islay)
- All islands should have facilities to support main industries. (Orkney)[42]

The issue of reversing the depopulation trend was also prevalent, including
calls to:

- Ensure there are jobs and career paths that keep/prevent islanders from leaving
  the islands. (Lewis)[43]

42 Scottish Government, 'National Islands Plan and Island Communities Impact
    Assessments: Analysis of responses to the public consultation exercise' (publica-
    tion pending).
43 Scottish Government, 'National Islands Plan and Island Communities Impact
    Assessments: Analysis of responses to the public consultation exercise' (publica-
    tion pending).

However, it is essential to stress that, whilst some challenges may appear more prominent, every community, on every island, at every single event, emphasised that none of these issues can be approached in silos. Every sector on an island is integrated and no single aspect, regardless of its prominence, operates in isolation. This view was stated repeatedly in our interactions with island communities and features prominently in the reports from the consultation.[44] Consequently, whilst the Plan takes into account all of the issues highlighted by island communities, it does so based on four principles which have emerged as overarching themes during the consultation process. The Plan is therefore based on a number of key principles, namely that it is *fair*, *integrated*, *Green* and *inclusive*. The remainder of this section will explore in more detail each of these themes, and how the Plan will incorporate them to the benefit of island communities.

Fair

The principle of fairness recognises that every member of society has a right to live with dignity and to enjoy high quality public services wherever they live (Scottish Government 2019: 13). The Plan aims to ensure that this principle is applied to Scottish Islands and that island communities are not deprived of services due to the geographical nature of the islands themselves. As previously mentioned, many island communities have felt unfairly disadvantaged and neglected by central based governance systems. Although the Islands (Scotland) Act was the first step in remedying this, the Plan goes further by following a place-based human rights approach. The Plan itself states that: 'The geographic, demographic, socio-economic, cultural and other particularities of the Scottish islands mean that many issues of significance to island communities are of such a fundamental nature that they are likely to interact with a range

---

44   Reports available at: <https://www.strath.ac.uk/research/strathclydecentr eenvironmentallawgovernance/ourwork/research/labsincubators/eilean/ islandsscotlandact/consultations> accessed 20 May 2020.

of human rights' (Scottish Government 2019: 11). A focus on a human rights approach within the Plan also aligns with ongoing policy developments in Scotland[45] and has the potential to support island communities by encouraging community empowerment across the public sector and in relation to private sector provision of services of a public or quasi-public nature.

Integrated

The principle of integration aims to ensure that, going forward, law and policy embraces an integrated approach and moves away from governing in silos. This reflects the feedback gathered during the consultation process, which indicated that all sectors of island society were reliant on one another, and that there has historically been a lack of communication between policy and legislation which relates to these sectors; often to the detriment of island communities.[46] The Scottish Government has already adopted the Place Principle,[47] which enables a more joined-up

45   The First Minister's Advisory Group on Human Rights Leadership reported in December 2018 and recommended, inter alia, the development of a new statutory human rights framework for Scotland. This proposed legislation would bring internationally recognised human rights into domestic law – including economic, social, cultural and environmental rights covering areas such as education, health, housing, food and cultural rights. The Advisory Group's report can be found here: <https://humanrightsleadership.scot/wp-content/uploads/2018/12/First-Ministers-Advisory-Group-on-Human-RightsLeadership-Final-report-for-publication.pdf> accessed 20 May 2020. In June 2019, the Scottish Government announced that the Advisory Group's recommendations will be taken forward by a new national task force.

46   *The Scotsman*, 'Scottish islands want more powers devolved from Holyrood' (2019), <https://www.scotsman.com/news/politics/scottish-islands-want-more-powers-devolved-holyrood-1429051>, and Our Islands Our Future (n.d.) 'Our Islands: Our Future: Submission to The Smith Commission', Proposal 8.3, <https://www.cne-siar.gov.uk/media/7963/oiof-submission-to-smith-commission.pdf> accessed 14 May 2020.

47   More information available at: <https://www.gov.scot/publications/place-principle-introduction/> accessed 20 May 2020.

and collaborative approach to services, land and building to maximise the impact of collective energy and resources to deliver the outcomes of the National Performance Framework.[48] The Plan aims to align with this strategy and promotes joined-up services based on an integrated and holistic approach to policy that captures economic, social and environmental considerations.[49]

Green

The inclusion of an overarching green principle aims to highlight the vulnerability of Scottish islands to the effects of climate change and should underpin future efforts stemming from islands to mitigate and adapt to climate change, whilst simultaneously protecting the incredible biodiversity of Scottish islands and demonstrating the potential such islands have to become hubs of innovation, for example, when it comes to renewables and electricity generation. The Plan (Scottish Government 2019: 13) itself states that: 'A green Plan is about focusing not only on the challenges, but also on the opportunities that Scotland's islands have because of their environment and natural resources and assets.' The participants to the consultation routinely highlighted that the concept of a green Plan was extremely important to island communities, and that they were particularly aware of the threats that climate changed posed to them and their current way of life. Additionally, a green Plan aligns with Scotland as a global leader in its wider efforts to tackle climate change, especially with the Government's Climate Change ambition to achieve net-zero greenhouse gas emissions by 2045.[50]

48　More information available at: <https://nationalperformance.gov.scot/> accessed 20 May 2020.

49　A focus on sustainability throughout the Plan also aligns with Scotland's global leadership when it comes to the implementation of the Sustainable Development Goals.

50　Climate Change Secretary Roseanna Cunningham's statement to the Scottish Parliament on 14 May 2019. <https://www.gov.scot/publications/global-climate-emergency-scotlands-response-climate-change-secretary-roseanna-cunninghams-statement/> accessed 22 October 2019.

Inclusive

It was evident from the consultation process that islanders feel that decisions which directly affect them are often taken by institutions that do
not fully understand the reality of life on the island. This indicates the
need for an inclusive Plan, which allows avenues for island communities
to have their say in decisions that directly affect them. The aim of the
principle is to encourage genuine community empowerment of island
communities, to ensure that their needs are fully taken into account
during any decision-making process and as close as possible to where the
effects of such decisions will be felt. The presence of inclusivity as an integral pillar of the Plan also aligns with current Scottish Government
policy, including the implementation of the Community Empowerment
(Scotland) Act 2015[51] and the ongoing Local Governance Review,[52] which
strive to ensure a more even distribution of power, responsibilities and resources between national and local government, and with communities.

Conclusion

The introduction of the Islands (Scotland) Act 2018 has ensured that
Scotland is at the forefront of island law and policy at international level.
The concept of island proofing, which permeates both the Act and the
National Islands Plan, aims to recalibrate Scottish island policy to rectify
the previous perceived marginalisation of Scottish island communities,
and ensure that the voice of such communities can be heard and influence
decision-making going forward.[53] The consultation process undertaken

---

51   Community Empowerment (Scotland) Act (2015).
52   More information available at: <https://www.gov.scot/policies/improving-public-
     services/local-governance-review/> accessed 20 May 2020.
53   *The Scotsman* 'Scottish islands want more powers devolved from Holyrood' (2019)
     <https://www.scotsman.com/news/politics/scottish-islands-want-more-powers-
     devolved-holyrood-1429051> accessed 14 May 2020.

to produce the National Islands Plan can be heralded as good practice in three key areas: the broad level of engagement with all members of island communities, the methodology of the events defusing tension and allowing for detailed group outputs, and the continued relationship with participants through the initial introduction of the feedback loop. Although it is perhaps unfeasible to assume that such a wide-ranging consultation process can be undertaken at every stage of the policy process, the lessons learned from this exercise can be beneficial across all policy areas, and should be used to ensure a high level of public participation in other consultations undertaken by the Scottish Government. This exercise should also be viewed in the context of the Citizens' Assembly of Scotland, which is one strand of the Scottish Government's three-pronged approach to determine constitutional and governance change. Genuine public participation, as demonstrated by the consultation process undertaken for the National Islands Plan, supports this vision and should be regarded as good practice for similar exercises going forward.

Four key themes and principles emerged from the consultation: the Plan is to be fair, integrated, green and inclusive. These overarching themes underline every section of the Plan itself, and aim to ensure that the Plan aligns with and can be used in conjunction with other current Government policy. However, despite the largely positive process of the National Islands Plan so far, the real test will be whether it results in concrete changes to the lives of those living on Scottish islands. At present, the Islands Team within Scottish Government is devising an Implementation Strategy that will detail the actions and indicators that will allow progress to be measured against the outcomes and commitments provided in the Plan. It is crucial that the relationships formed with island communities during the consultation process are nurtured and extended, to ensure that they continue to have a say in the formulation of island law and policy that affects them so directly. The Plan has a duration of years with a requirement for annual reports on progress and a review at the end of the -year period. Although the concept of island proofing and the Plan itself provide a life-raft to sail the 'choppy waters' between islands communities and law and policy developed on the mainland, the real test of the boat and the crew will be to ensure that communities continue to actively participate in the process throughout and beyond the duration of the initial Plan. Only then, will a safe harbour have the possibility of being reached.

Bibliography

Clark, T. (2008). 'We're over-researched here!': exploring accounts of research fatigue within qualitative research engagements. *Sociology*, 42 (5), 953–970.

McLeod, W. (2020). The national 'securing Gaelic in the Western Isles and beyond', 31 January 2020, <https://www.thenational.scot/news/18200196.securing-gaelic-western-isles-beyond/> accessed 12 May 2020.

National Records of Scotland (2015). 'Scotland's Census 2011: inhabited islands report', 24 September 2015, <https://www.scotlandscensus.gov.uk/news/inhabited-islands-analytical-report> accessed 22 October 2019.

Scottish Government (2019). The National Islands Plan Plana Nàiseanta nan Eilean, December 2019. Edinburgh: The Scottish Government, <https://www.gov.scot/publications/national-plan-scotlands-islands> accessed 14 May 2020.

United Nations (1992). Report of the United Nations Conference on Environment and Development, 12 August 1992, <https://www.un.org/en/development/desa/population/migration/generalassembly/docs/globalcompact/A_CONF.151_26_Vol.I_Declaration.pdf> accessed 14 May 2020.

Walters, G. (2014). The Telegraph 'British Isles where Viking blood still flows', 01 September 2014, <https://www.telegraph.co.uk/news/uknews/scottish-independence/11066878/British-isles-where-Viking-blood-still-flows.html> accessed 14 May 2020.

JAMES OLIVER[1]

11. Islandness: Articulating and Emplacing Relationality

It is 2020. There is a global pandemic and the Shetland Islands are formally exploring measures for enhanced 'self-determination'.[2] This statement immediately prompts images of social and political disruption that might be thought of as scene-setting for a new season of the eponymous BBC TV drama series 'Shetland'. Or perhaps for a novel in the emerging genre of Decolonial Speculative Fiction and Fantasy (DSFF). In fact, the statement reflects a real situation and news headline in Scotland in 2020. What is obscured behind the image-making headlines of the media, of course, is the deeper complexity and nuance of lived experiences and situational imaginaries of islandness. Islandness (as with any place) is an intersection of the plurality of life. What seems less plausible is that a sympathetic researcher, in an island studies journal, will still premise their discussion of one of Scotland's archipelagos (a different one) as 'remote' (Lane 2016). The trope is strong, a mode of reification that limits relationality.

In times past, almost all of Scotland's islands (northern and western, Norse and Gaelic) were in a direct relationship with the seagoing empire of the Norse, along with the Isle of Man, at the southern reaches of the Norse-Gael routes, and Iceland at the northernmost. Across Scotland this is reflected in the large legacy of place-based and family-based names of Norse origin

---

1   *Is mise Seumas Chatriona nigh'n Dhomhnuill Aonghais Bhig mac Dhomhnuill mhic Pheadar mhic Mhurchaidh.*

2   *Shetland News*, 10 September 2020, 'Self-determination motion a "first small step towards a brighter future"', writer, Chris Cope: <https://www.shetnews.co.uk/2020/09/10/self-determination-motion-a-first-small-step-towards-a-brighter-future/> accessed 10 September 2020.

and relation, especially throughout the islands. Further south, an interesting legacy in the Isle of Man is that its parliament is still called Tynwald (meaning the assembly field; incidentally, this is the same name as Dingwall in the Highlands). Further north in Iceland, their parliament is called the Althing (meaning whole assembly). The words *tyn, ding, thing* here all mean the same: assembly. In fact, it is the exact same origin word for that everyday utilitarian word in English: thing (an assemblage): a bringing into relation.

Islands are demonstrably 'things' in the world; islandness emphasises that 'thingness'.

*

That an island is land is axiomatic and ontological, also axiological and relational. Islands are also ideas; this is part of their islandness, through the social and material configurations of the human imaginary (like with a nation: Anderson 1991), including in relation to land and water. If an island is land, then islandness emphasises and opens up the relationality of its land-ness. Whilst islands might be located within or even congruent with political geographies such as a regions, nations or even empires, their habitation is situational and therefore differentiated and mediated by the intersections, entanglements and ecologies of lived experience as emplace-ment (Pink 2015); as experience 'on the ground' and 'in the mind' (see Pahl 2005).[3]

Islands are just that: plural. They are not homogenous or uniform, not within their own entities nor within archipelagos. Nevertheless, configur-ations and interrelations of lived experience do emerge as expressions and formations of social and cultural cohesion but also of change and diver-gence. As the editors of this volume note in their introduction, island studies is an inter-disciplinary area of research. This collection purposefully reflects that, with particular reference to Scotland's inhabited islands. The range of enquiry includes: island economies (Danson; Burnett and Danson); community land (MacLeod); island protections and policy (Sindico and

---

3   Ray Pahl (2005) discusses 'communities of the mind' and critiques the privileging of conceptions of community 'on the ground' as objectively real and therefore experience-near over equally real subjective, socially cohesive relations and experi-ences of personal communities.

Crook); identity and work (Burnett and Stalker); island youth (Alexander); cultural histories and languages, through literatures (Jennings) and ethnology (Cheape); and deep historical relations (Burnett, R.).

In this contextual diversity on Scotland's inhabited islands – which I interpret as (in)habitations and (inter)actions with place and environment – this chapter is devised as a personal and conceptual reflection on islandness: reflexive and progressive. My basic premise is that islandness presents us with a double ontology: the relationality of place and the relationality of emplacement. This engages an interaction of dialogues and dialect(ics) that iterate and evolve between islandness 'on the ground' and islandness 'in the mind', where islandness articulates more than just traditional, located social cohesion experiences but also personal communities of practice, such as writing this book on islandness (Wenger 1998; Kohn 2002).

*

Scotland's islands are not just plural but marked by multiplicity. Marine Scotland (an agency of the Scottish Government), measures Scotland's coastline at a length of over 18,000 km. There are various methodologies and purposes for measuring coastlines; nevertheless, for a so-called 'small country', Scotland has an extraordinary coastline, in no small part comprising its islands. According to Marine Scotland, there are more than 900 offshore islands; the vast majority of these are uninhabited, and many not deemed habitable by humans, although historically many more were inhabited; but 118 are still inhabited.[4] Most of these islands are situated off the western and northern coasts of mainland Scotland, the 'mainland' being a portion of an island too. In the majority, these islands are also situated within the three dominant archipelagos of the Hebrides, the Orkney Islands and the Shetland Islands. The geological movements and the social and political geographies that produce and inhabit these islands are rich and varied, and not unrelated, but are differently mobile: in their ecologies, impacts and perturbations in relation to place, both inhabited and environmental, from deep 'Lewis Gneiss' time to the Anthropocene.

---

4   <http://marine.gov.scot/data/facts-and-figures-about-scotlands-sea-area-coastline-length-sea-area-sq-kms> accessed 10 September 2020.

As indicated above, islandness should not be misapprehended as homogenous and bounded or closed and complete, including socially (culturally or politically), but as future-oriented and progressive. As such, the inhabited complex of multiplicity, as relational and emplacing, is (re) producing island relationships and islandness. It should also be clear that in this situation of simultaneous multiplicity (Massey 2005) there are still distinctions between the relationships of things, otherwise relationality (and ethics) would not enact. Therefore, multiplicity is not inevitably or necessarily a situation of singularity where the density of it matters exponentially: otherwise, the relationality would become isotropic and flattened (uniform and then commodified?); or worse, entropic and eliminated (social collapse?). Instead, spaces emerge for relational encounter, as boundaries of dialogue and negotiation; not as sites of singularity but spaces for plural ethical relationships.

To summarise, islandness 'on the ground' and islandness 'in the mind' become emplaced encounters with ethics and futures – axiological and ontological – engaging the critical (more-than-just-human) challenge of our time: how to re-centre ethical relations between people, place and environment.

*

Islandness in Scotland is about inter-island as well as intra-island relationships and relationality. Islandness is therefore a modality of imagining with islands, that is, one 'thinks *with* them' (Gillis 2004: 1). As Pugh (2013) also elaborates, we can further our enquiry by thinking 'with the archipelago':

> The concept of archipelago deeply challenges how we think about the world and our relation to it. On this point, Stratford et al. (2011), effectively argue for a double de-stabilization that dislocates and de-territorializes static island tropes of particularity, so that they are instead conceived of as fluid island-island inter-relations rather than the binaries of mainland/island or sea/island. (2013: 11)

An archipelago of island relations can reveal the macro, even (often!) at intersections with the micro, and islandness becomes an open abstracting of possibility. If you are familiar with island studies, you will likely be familiar with Oceanian theorist and poet Epeli Hau'ofa. One legacy of his work is his memorable critique of the external perspective and objectifying gaze and language of 'the Pacific Islands', His appropriate articulation being, 'Our Sea of Islands' (Hau'ofa 1994), to challenge and counter the paternalistic colonial gaze by recentring the agency and structure within and between islands – connected across the sea not separated by it. As Nadarajah and Grydehøj (2016: 443) note, the 'challenge for island studies is to address the full range of island perspectives, to approach island decolonization in a manner that is both progressive and reflexive'. They also comment

> Knowledge in the West is often conceived of as separate from the sociality and intimacy in which it is embedded. It is often defined as acquiring a certain control, which inevitably leads to the authority of those who pose the questions over those who answer them; those who observe over those who are observed. In this cycle of hegemony, coloniality lurks, ever present. (2016: 440)

It is a relatively straightforward extension to think of our whole world in such archipelagic terms, as being connected by one ocean but ideologies and political practices can also limit this as a sphere of ethical relations and undermine understanding. Certainly, it is all too convenient for the discourse and practice from within some sites of power and privilege to misapprehend or obviate the inter-island intersections that have sustained social and cultural power and privilege. These same intersections also reveal control and coloniality and all their legacies beyond empire. As my colleague Yoko Akama (forthcoming) indicates

> The plurality of archipelagos means that many worlds exist simultaneously and often in close proximity. If being entangled is already our pre-existing condition, it compels one to act within an obligation, responsiveness and responsibility.

Growing up in a north-western corner of a 'north-western' island in the middle of an archipelago, my islandness is intricately informed by the littoral horizon, its interpolations of relationality manifested between and within the proximities and communities of islands. This is both 'on the ground' and 'in the mind' islandness. From a young age I have been explicitly conscious of and ontologically oriented by islandness (situational-relational), not just as an islander (nominal-relational). As a Hebridean

in Scotland I grew up in our own 'sea of islands', visiting family regularly
between the islands of Skye, Lewis and Harris. I have also been aware
from a young age (although not necessarily understanding) of the study
of islands as emplaced cultures, communities and histories. At around
the age of eight (in the early 1980s), I distinctly remember being engaged in friendly conversation by our district's very own anthropologist-
in-residence. It was actually their second residency in the area, a decade
after their first (Walker 1973). The place and space of an archipelago of
relations has emplaced my islandness 'on the ground' and 'in the mind',
including my community of practice of research.

    I have written in relation to islandness before. Not explicitly on
'islandness' but situated in ethnographic and relational terms of people
'doing identity' in the Hebrides and the wider *Gàidhealtachd* (which is certainly more than emplaced islandness). The relationships and articulations
of emplaced islandness (and identities) that emerged from that research
focussed on proximities and communities, and the relationality of 'home'
and 'away' or 'rootedness' and 'connectedness'. These can be understood as
variations of islandness 'on the ground' and 'in the mind'. In this analysis,
emplaced islandness emerges (or any situated identity), where

> locality is 'primarily relational and contextual rather than scalar or spatial' (Appadurai
> 1996: 178). But as Doreen Massey (2005) argues, in reclaiming space from a conflation
> with place-making and from being subject to 'time', space is the very product of such
> interrelations, including as identity, as not fixed and given, but moving, a sphere of
> 'multiplicity' and 'always under construction' (ibid.: 9). She writes, 'I would argue
> that identities/entities, the relations "between" them, and the spatiality which is part
> of them, are all co-constitutive' (ibid.: 10). (Oliver 2011: 13)

This is not to diminish in any way the relevance or value of place in
islandness. Instead, it is to make a distinction between a latent imper-
meable boundedness in place-making, and emplacement as an absorbent
space of potential for ethical relations, reflexive and progressive.

*

    Scotland's islands are marked with a multiplicity of stones. They are
elemental to the landscape and its social and cultural relations, including
in the names of many places. Largely a series of landscapes revealed by

seas, scored by ice and cleared of forest, stones have provided a long legacy of connecting people to place, and as an index of emplacement. The ancient standing stones, stone circles and brochs attest to thousands of years of dwelling and emplacement. Mixed in with the stone of the landscape are more recent remains of dwellings cleared, depopulated or disused resonant earlier emplacements with land that you can (more or less) easily encounter.

Stone Vernacular

In the island of Harris
she is renovating her home.
She lives in the old croft house
where her mother was born.
Her grandparents had lived there too
building it from stones on the land
and former dwellings
all surrounding.
Our common ancestors
on that side
had been shepherds
and moved around the islands
from one place then to another.
One place was in Lewis
on the other side
where there are only ruins now.
When the renovation is done
she will go to Lewis
she says
to get stones from that place
on the other side
she says
and she will place them
at the front of her home.
She tells me she remembers
another woman who had done the same
a few crofts along.

Her plan is to collect more stones
from other places.
The shepherds had moved
and were moved
often.
She tells me she remembers
the times my grandparents visited
and filled their car with stones
from the shore
on their way back to Skye.
I told her I remembered
the stones
at the front of their home.
I take my daughter to see my parents
and I want to tell them this story
but I forget
and now I'm leaving.
Those are from Harris
she says
and points to the stones
at the front of their home.

This is a family story I have translated from ethnographic material as antropoesía: 'Verse with an ethnographic sensibility' (Rosaldo 2014: 106); a creative non-fiction of emplaced islandness 'on the ground' and 'in the mind'. It draws attention to a particular configuration and negotiation of islandness – neither exceptional nor essential – but by extension reveals island relations. What I am emphasising here are the ongoing dynamics (and fusions) of islandness 'on the ground' and 'in the mind' within our social imaginary and experience: on open archipelago of more-than-island relations. As iterated throughout, these become emplaced encounters of ethical relations and futures: axiological and ontological. How to re-centre ethical relations between people, place and environment is the engaging and critical, more-than-just-human, challenge of our time.

*

Political theorist Chiara Bottici keenly observes that modernity and the neo-liberal ordering and division of the imagining of individuals from the social imaginary gives us 'a political world full of images but deprived of imagination' (Bottici 2011: 56). Scotland's islands as contemporary places (in all periods), and contending with wider political relations of modernity, have consistently been objectified and mapped, branded and commodified by this hierarchy of 'images' over 'imagination'. Islandness encompasses thinking with islands and with archipelago, as an appropriate decentring and reimagining of relations. Thinking *with* islandness then, not as separations, isolations or exclusivity, but as emplaced relationality, opens up imaginations and futures. This is a common theme in the chapters of this book, whether focussed on island economies, (is)land futures, or identities over time, or indeed as communities of work and practice.

This brings into focus the ethics of relationships. Islandness is necessarily complex: in its structuring (or how societies configure and relate to it); in its functioning (or how cultures articulate it); but most importantly in its emplacement (or how people embody it, experience it, are entangled in it). Again, we can see this is engaged with consistently in the chapters of this book. In articulating, acknowledging and respecting the relationality of everyday emplacements in islandness, the binary dichotomies that reproduce hegemony and conditions of social alienation, reduction and or oppression can be transcended. This opens up the space of ethical relations, a space of 'boundary' for negotiation, which is integral to ethics. Islandness conceived of as emplaced ethical relations, *is* political, social and cultural imagination in action. The range of enquiry in this volume engages our thinking with islandness: an emplaced relationality of 'on the ground' and 'in the mind' islandness becomes future-oriented and progressive. This will help to inform further our (ethical) relationship with land and place. Including for our islands.

Bibliography

Akama, Y. (forthcoming). 'Archipelagos of Designing and a ko-Ontological Encounter'. In Seppälä, T., Sarantou, M., and S. Miettinen (eds), *Decolonising Participatory Research through Arts-Based Method*. Routledge Advances in Art and Visual Studies. London: Routledge.

Anderson, B. (1991). *Imagined Communities*. Second Edition. London: Verso.

Appadurai, A. (1996). *Modernity at Large*. Minneapolis: University of Minnesota Press.

Bottici, C. (2011). 'Imaginal politics', *Thesis Eleven*, 106 (1), 56–72.

Gillis, J. R. (2004). *Islands in the Mind: How the Human Imagination Created the Atlantic World*. Basingstoke: Palgrave.

Hauʻofa, E. (1994). 'Our sea of islands', *The Contemporary Pacific*, 6 (1), 147–161.

Kohn, T. (2002). 'Becoming an Islander through Action in The Scottish Hebrides', *Journal of the Royal Anthropological Institute*, 8 (1), 143–158.

Lane, C. (2016). 'Mapping the Outer Hebrides in Sound: towards a sonic methodology', *Island Studies Journal*, 11 (2), 343–358.

Massey, D. (2005). *For Space*. London: Sage.

Nadarajah, Y., and Grydehøj, A. (2016). 'Island studies as a decolonial project', *Island Studies Journal*, 11 (2), 437–446.

Oliver, J. (2011). 'Articulating 'home' from 'away': 'cultural identities, belonging and citizenship', *Anthropology in Action*, 18 (2), 9–18.

Pahl, R. (2005). 'Are all communities communities of the mind', *The Sociological Review*, 53 (4), 621–640.

Pink, S. (2015). *Doing Sensory Ethnography*. Second Edition. London: Sage.

Pugh, J. (2013). 'Island movements: thinking with the archipelago', *Island Studies Journal*, 8 (1), 9–24.

Rosaldo, R. (2014). *The Day of Shelley's Death*. Durham: Duke University Press.

Stratford, E., Baldacchino, G., McMahon, E., Farbotko, C., and Harwood, A. (2011). 'Envisioning the archipelago', *Island Studies Journal*, 6 (2), 113–130.

Walker, M. (1973). *Social Constraints, Individuals, and Social Decisions in a Scottish Rural Community*. PhD Thesis. University of Illinois at Urbana-Champaign.

Wenger, E. (1998). *Communities of Practice*. Cambridge: Cambridge University Press.

Notes on Contributors

ROSIE ALEXANDER is a researcher, lecturer and careers adviser based in the islands of Orkney. She specialises in research relating to career development, education and guidance, with a particular focus on rural and island communities. Rosie currently holds a position as a senior lecturer (Research) at the University of the Highlands and Islands as well as running a small consultancy business.

KATHRYN A. BURNETT is a senior lecturer in the Division of Arts and Media, University of the West of Scotland teaching across interdisciplinary undergraduate and Masters programmes in Creative Arts Practice and Media. With a background in social anthropology, sociology and cultural studies, Kathryn's research interests include the mediatisation and representation of remote and island spaces; identity and place narratives of Scotland's rural communities; cultural work of islands; Scottish cultural heritage contexts for applied creative practice; and sustainability, enterprise and cultural policy in small island and remote contexts. Kathryn is co-director of the *Scottish Centre for Island Studies*.

RAY BURNETT is a writer and researcher based on Benbecula. With a focus on the transnational dimension of the cultural and social history of Scotland's islands, Ray has lectured on Scottish island studies at universities, graduate schools and summer schools across Scotland, Europe, Canada, and the Far East and served on the Executive Committee of the International Small Islands Studies Association. A commitment to knowledge transfer has extended to treatments and research for television documentaries on aspects of the social history of Scotland's islands and the initiation of various island community-based cultural and social history projects. Ray initiated and co-founded the *Scottish Centre for Island Studies*.

HUGH CHEAPE is professor of Highland history and culture and teaches a postgraduate programme through the medium of Scottish Gaelic at *Sabhal Mòr Ostaig*, the National Centre for Gaelic Language and Culture, at the University of the Highlands and Islands. The MSc *Cultar Dùthchasach agus Eachdraidh na Gàidhealtachd* ('Material Culture and Gaelic History') drew on a career in the National Museums Scotland (1974–2007). Hugh's expertise contributes to a range of key scholarly partnerships on the wider valuing of Highlands history and culture, with an associated range of publication and outputs on Scottish culture, language, ethnology and musicology.

NICOLA CROOK leads on the Delivery of the National Islands Plan within the Islands Team of Scottish Government. She is an affiliate of the Strathclyde Centre for Environmental Law and Governance (SCELG) at the University of Strathclyde, where she obtained both her LLB and LLM in Climate Change Law and Policy with distinction. Nicola previously worked as a Legal Researcher on projects for the European Parliament and European Commission, with a focus on the legal analysis of environmental law and policy. She co-wrote this chapter whilst collaborating with the Scottish Government on the implementation of the Islands (Scotland) Act 2018.

MIKE DANSON is an economist and Professor Emeritus of Enterprise Policy, Heriot-Watt University and Fellow of the Academy of Social Sciences. He has published widely on rural, regional and island economies, microbreweries, minority languages, and many other areas of Scottish economic policy and social development. Chair of Basic Income Network Scotland, Chair of the 2021 BIEN (Basic Income Earth Network) world congress, depute Convenor Jimmy Reid Foundation, Trustee of Nordic Horizons and Community Renewal, Mike is on the Scottish Government's Just Transition Commission and has advised, national and international organisations: OECD, WHO, EC, trades unions and community groups. Mike is co-director of the *Scottish Centre for Island Studies*.

LYNDA HARLING STALKER is an Associate Professor of Sociology at St Francis Xavier University in Nova Scotia, Canada. Lynda also holds research associate positions with the Institute for Island Studies at the University of Prince Edward Island and the *Scottish Centre for Island Studies* at the University of the West of Scotland. She researches cultural work, rurality and narratives particularly in the context of North Atlantic islands. Her latest article (co-authored with Patricia Cormack) explored controversy around the "Chase the Ace" phenomenon on Cape Breton, Nova Scotia.

ANDREW JENNINGS is a lecturer and researcher with the Institute for Northern Studies, University of the Highlands and Islands, and lives in Shetland. He has a particular interest in the history, culture, folklore and literature of Shetland, the impact of the Vikings on the Scottish islands and island communities across the globe. When not researching island onomastics or the impact of bridges on small island communities, he can be found walking his dog on the beach, taking his boat to isolated islands or axe throwing.

CALUM MACLEOD is Policy Director for Community Land Scotland and a freelance Sustainable Development Consultant, originally from the Isle of Harris in the Western Isles and now living in Glasgow. He led post-legislative scrutiny of the Land Reform (Scotland) Act 2003 on behalf of the Scottish Parliament in 2010 and has undertaken feasibility studies for numerous islands communities in relation to community-land purchases in the Inner and Outer Hebrides. Calum occasionally writes on land reform issues for the West Highland Free Press, the UK's first employee-owned newspaper.

JAMES OLIVER is a Hebridean Gàidheal and a transdisciplinary academic, educator and writer. He has over twenty years of professional practice across a range of disciplines (creative arts and design, social sciences, ethnography, arts development, community practice). This has nurtured a 'practice-as-research' career beyond traditional disciplinary boundaries,

particularly at the intersections of cultural relations and indigenous practice research.

FRANCESCO SINDICO is the Founder and Co-director of the Strathclyde
Centre for Environmental Law and Governance (SCELG) at the
University of Strathclyde. He leads the EILEAN initiative at SCELG,
an effort to better understand how island communities engage with legal
and political processes to promote resilience and sustainability. Francesco
has collaborated with the Scottish Government in the implementation of
the Islands (Scotland) Act 2018 by providing technical advice to the consultation leading to the National Islands Plan and working on guidance
related to island communities impact assessment.

Index

Studies in the History and Culture of Scotland

Valentina Bold, General Editor

This series presents a new reading of Scottish culture, establishing how Scots, and non-Scots, experience this devolved nation. Within the context of a rapidly changing United Kingdom and Europe, Scotland is engaged in an ongoing process of self-definition. The series will deal with this process as well as with cultural phenomena, from debates about the relative value of Gaelic-based, Scots and Anglicised culture, to period-specific definitions of Scottish identity. Orally transmitted culture – from traditional narratives to songs, customs, beliefs and material culture – will be a key consideration, along with the reconstruction of historical periods in cultural texts (visual and musical as well as historical). Taken as a whole, the series will go some way towards achieving a new understanding of a country with potential for development into parallel treatments of locally based cultural phenomena. The series welcomes monographs as well as collected papers.

Vol. 1   Valentina Bold.
James Hogg: A Bard of Nature's Making. 376 pages. 2007.
ISBN 978-3-03910-897-8

Vol. 2   James Porter (ed.).
Defining Strains: The Musical Life of Scots In the
Seventeenth Century. 386 pages. 2007.
ISBN 978-3-03910-948-7

Vol. 3   Aaron Kelly.
James Kelman: Politics and Aesthetics. 251 pages. 2013.
ISBN 978-3-03911-130-5

Vol. 4   Jonathan Murray.
Discomfort and Joy: The Cinema of Bill Forsyth. 270 pages. 2011.
ISBN 978-3-03911-391-0